Motions, Emotions and Commotions: Social Learning at Home and in the Classroom

J. RONALD GENTILE

State University of
New York at Buffalo

Drawings by:

Doug A. Gentile
Ed Kohrn
J. Ronald Gentile

**KENDALL/HUNT
PUBLISHING COMPANY**
Dubuque, Iowa

Copyright © 1984 by J. Ronald Gentile

Library of Congress Catalog Card Number: 83–83311

ISBN 0–8403–3262–9

Printed in the United States of America

A   403262   01

Contents

Preface

The first day of school every parent dresses up Johnny and Mary, gives them money for lunch, and sends them off to school with such warm wishes as, "School is going to be fun," "You're going to love your teacher," "There will be new games to play," and "You're also going to learn how to read." By the end of the first day (if not the first year,) Johnny and Mary know better: in school you must sit quietly until told you may move or talk, the bigger kids beat you up and take your lunch money, and you didn't learn to read. In fact, of the three reading groups, you didn't make the "bluebirds" or "redbirds"; rather, you were assigned to the "buzzards."

This is your child's first experience, in school at least, of *rapanoia*. What is rapanoia? You've heard of paranoia, of course—the irrational fear of imaginary or unreal threats. Well, *rapanoia is the nonfear of real threats that should indeed be feared*. As such it is much more serious than paranoia because there is a real threat, only you are not aware of it. To raise the consciousness of the public about this problem Gentile once wrote a song and two papers about the concept (Gentile, 1974; 1981; the song is reproduced in Appendix A), but to this day awareness is still too limited to protect the public.

But we digress. Rapanoia can be thought of as the opposite of paranoia, from which the word was derived: rapanoia is paranoia is spelled sideways, or sort of. It also emphasizes that you are taking a rap.

Children in schools are constantly suffering from rapanoia, which is why we brought it up. So are teachers, principals, and at times the whole of the public. But for now we want to emphasize what happens to children. From the age of five or six until sixteen they are legally required to attend school. While there, the students have certain requirements to meet or courses to take. The schedule, including when they eat and often when they go to the toilet, is by and large determined by others. These facts of school life are obvious and most citizens are cognizant of them. The significance of these facts, however, is not easily recognized unless they are placed in a larger perspective.

Philip W. Jackson attempted to provide such a perspective in his book *Life in Classrooms* (1968). He estimated, for example, that in most states a student spends about 1000 hours per year in school, so that if he has attended kindergarten and has been reasonably regular in attendance, he may have logged up to 7000 hours in class by the time he enters junior high school. Jackson goes on to say (p. 5):

> The magnitude of 7000 hours spread over six or seven years of a child's life is difficult to comprehend. On the one hand, when placed beside the total number of hours the child has lived during those years it is not very great—slightly more than one-tenth of his life during the time in question, about one-third of

his hours of sleep during that period. On the other hand, aside from sleeping, and perhaps playing, there is no other activity that occupies as much of the child's time as that involved in attending school. Apart from the bedroom (where he has his eyes closed most of the time) there is no single enclosure in which he spends a longer time than he does in the classroom. *From the age of six onward he is a more familiar sight to his teacher than to his father, and possibly even to his mother.* (emphasis added)

Viewed in this perspective, the schools are in a remarkable—and in some ways frightening—position. No matter that some say the home or genetic factors have more influence than schools. Schools still have a significant amount of control over the lives of students, if only because of the time students spend there. Moreover, this control occurs during significant developmental years— years in which work habits are established, attitudes toward learning and authority figures are formed, self-concepts and interests are acquired, and patterns of functioning with peers are learned. In short, the schools in general and teachers in particular have an immense responsibility—one which is difficult to overestimate by whatever evaluative standard is used.

Precisely because of this responsibility it is extremely important for teachers and school administrators to understand the child in *interaction* with the teacher and the rest of the school environment. Interaction has been emphasized because teachers not only do to children, but are changed by them. And all aspects of the classroom—objectives, discipline rules, seating arrangements, rewards and punishments, tests and grading procedures, etc.—need to be understood.

This book is written to provide an understanding of the events that occur in classrooms and their effects on the people in those classrooms. It also provides some suggestions for structuring events in such a way as to be maximally effective in reaching educational goals while at the same time developing a strong concept of self in student and teacher alike. This, it seems to us, is (or should be) the purpose of educational psychology as a discipline; it is certainly the raison d'etre of this book.

One cannot understand how to educate people from a behaviorist point of view, nor from a humanist point of view. Neither can one understand people from an affective vs. cognitive dichotomy. As the saying goes (Barth's distinction; see Bloch, 1980, p. 78), "There are two types of people; those who divide the world into two types and those who don't." People are not rational or emotional; people are rational *and* emotional. People don't respond to stimuli or create; people respond to stimuli *and* create. People aren't controlled by heredity or environment; they are controlled by heredity *and* environment.

The approach to be taken in this book aims at deemphasizing dichotomies. At the same time it is not just eclectic, because it does not present all points of view as though they are equally viable as alternatives. We have a point of view on most of the topics covered and we will state it as clearly as possible and label it as such. And, to the extent possible, issues and beliefs will be treated seriously, but not humorlessly.

THE PLAN AND STYLE OF THIS BOOK

This book deals with the interdependence of the emotions, motivations, and cognitions within and between individuals. After an overview in the Introduction, chapter 2 shows how emotional development occurs, primarily through classical conditioning, and then deals with such topics as stress, learned helplessness, competence, biofeedback, and relaxation and counterconditioning as ways of dealing with the emotions. Chapter 3 goes into purposeful behavior and motivation, introducing the topics of operant conditioning, including surprising effects of negative reinforcement (escape learning) and punishment. Chapter 4 describes modeling, social learning and other group effects including aggressive behavior, self-control, norms and interpersonal relations. Chapter 5 treats the question of discipline as the crucible for testing the previous ideas, analyzing discipline problems, providing a cross-cultural perspective, and suggesting specific techniques for handling discipline problems. Throughout the emphasis is on applying social learning theory to practical situations.

The book assumes no prior background in psychology, although those with such a background should find the applications interesting and important. It is appropriate for pre-service teacher education courses, or for graduate courses in learning and instruction, behavior modification or human development courses for teachers.

The book is written in the "editorial we" style, though in this case the "we" will eventually be true. The present chapters (2–5) are planned to be one section of a general textbook on educational psychology that I am writing with Dr. John R. Dilendik of Moravian College, Bethlehem, PA. Other sections of the book will be concerned with human development, cognition (including retention, thinking and problem solving) and educational and evaluation practices (including retention, thinking and problem solving) and educational and evaluation practices (including grading, individualization and "the little red electronic schoolhouse").

Though this book is a section of a larger book, it does stand on its own: an understanding of social and behavioral processes is critical to what has come to be known in education as the "affective domain," which is integrally related to the development of self-concepts, motivation and discipline. On the other hand, since these chapters will soon be revised for incorporation into the larger volume, I am especially interested in hearing reader reactions. Please write with your specific comments and suggestions to me at the following address:

Department of Counseling and Educational Psychology
409 Christopher Baldy Hall
State University of New York at Buffalo
Buffalo, New York 14260

STUDY AIDS

Appendix B provides a list of *Study Questions* for each chapter in the book. These may be taken as the author's list of instructional objectives. If you can adequately answer these questions you have understood the major points in the book.

There is also a *Glossary* of important terms provided after the references to help you easily find definitions of terms. Throughout the chapters are also recommended readings, the complete citations for which are in the *References*. *Footnotes* occur at the end of each chapter.

ACKNOWLEDGEMENTS

In addition to Jack Dilendik, I wish to thank the following individuals for their reactions to various chapters of the book: Nanci Monaco, Vicki Rachlin, Pat Simoneau, Jim Donnelly, and Anne Himmel. Thanks also to Dian Jensen for typing the manuscript.

Much appreciation is also expressed to Ed Kohrn and my son, Doug Gentile, whose artistic skills transformed my jokes and one-liners into cartoons.

Finally, I wish to thank my wife, Kay Johnson-Gentile, who provided many real-life examples to which the principles of the book apply, and who also provided constructive criticism and continual encouragement throughout the preparation of this book.

J. R. G.

CHAPTER I
A Psychology of Behavior

INTRODUCTION

Every time I go to the dentist an interesting thing happens to me. As I begin to get out of the car in the parking lot, I feel a bit uneasy. By the time I enter the office I laugh a nervous laugh when checking in with the receptionist. And even as I whistle (a happy tune?) to the background music and tap my toe to the beat, it is clear to me that it is more a release of tension than it is demonstration of innate or acquired rhythm. By the time I am reclining in the chair with the dentist about to put his instruments and hands in my mouth, I have a death grip on the chair that is worthy of a sumo wrestler. The amazing thing about this is that I haven't experienced any real pain at the dentist for as long as I can remember.[1]

How do these things happen? Although it may be impossible to know for sure, it is possible to make some educated guesses. Consider what happens, for example, to many infants on their first trip to the pediatrician for shots. The child is being held closely and comfortably by the parent, feeling warm and relaxed—a case of rapanoia—when suddenly some cold alcohol is felt, followed by a needle to the posterior. The needle is painful of course and produces an immediate reaction of screaming, thrashing, and other indices of discomfort. Infants don't read, but many parents report that on the occasion of the next visit to the doctor, the child hardly gets in the door and past the sign before he or she reacts with the same screaming and thrashing as before.

Many people have had the same one-trial learning experience in taking their pet to the veterinarian. After the first painful experience with the vet, try to drag your dog through the door. It doesn't matter that the physician or veterinarian is being kind[2] or saving the organism's life; something about him or his office (the odors, colors, etc.) have become associated with sufficient pain to produce this very common kind of fear.

We are not born with a fear of dentists, doctors, vets (either veterinarians or veterans), teachers, or math for that matter. But we are physiologically wired for fear reactions to painful events. Painful needles or shocks elicit a pot pourri of physiological reactions, among which are the following: increased blood pressure, heart rate, respiration rate, and muscle tension; sweaty palms; stomach contractions; dilation of the pupils of the eyes; and a release of various chemical substances, including adrenalin, to prepare the body for "flight or fight."

THE CASE OF THE DENTA-PHOBIC PSYCHOLOGIST[1]

Once upon a time there was a clinical psychologist who had a fear of dentists. Now this man was used to helping others cope with their fears through various relaxation and biofeedback techniques so he decided to apply his expertise to himself. The strategy was to monitor his own anxiety and then actively try to relax whenever he began to feel anxious. Already he had been practicing the relaxation technique (via production of alpha waves in the brain), so it remained only to apply the technique to his fear.

To monitor his anxiety, he hooked up a portable GSR (galvanic skin response) instrument to his palm. Like a lie detector, this instrument records the changes in the electrical conductivity of the skin due to perspiration, and was connected to a buzzer. So whenever he began to get anxious, his palms would sweat and the GSR would produce a buzz. He also had an earphone so that it could buzz without anyone else hearing it.

So prepared, he drove off to his appointment with the dentist. As he was driving into the parking lot, there was a soft buzzing in his ear, so he concentrated on relaxing and, indeed, the buzzing stopped. As he was called to the chair the buzzing started again and once more he was able to relax. The incidences continued while the dentist examined him.

Soon it became clear to the dentist that this man with the earphone and electrodes attached to the hand was either dancing to a different drummer or was just plain weird. When he asked, the psychologist told him what he was doing. So the dentist said, "Well, don't keep it a secret; play it out loud."

The psychologist removed the earphone and the rest of the session went something like this. The dentist said, "This isn't going to hurt."

B U Z Z Z Z Z Z!

The moral of the story is, whenever someone tells you something is not going to hurt, it is a case of rapanoia: that is exactly when it is going to hurt. And whether you are consciously aware or not, your body is.

1. With thanks to Dr. Gene Brockopp who may be held responsible for the true story, but not necessarily for my embellishments of it.

This natural physiological reaction to pain is a built-in reflex which probably has evolutionary significance in protecting organisms from harm: you must pull back quickly from painful shocks, heat, or threatening objects to stay alive very long. In other words, this fear response is unlearned, being a reflex of the following form:

(1)   Painful Stimulus $\longrightarrow$ Physiological Fear Response

The painful stimulus and fear response are called *unconditioned stimulus (US)* and *unconditioned response (UR)*, respectively, to emphasize the fact that no learning had to occur in order to obtain the reaction. It is an unlearned or unconditioned reflex of the same form as the patellar reflex (leg kick that occurs when the knee is struck just below the knee cap), and eye blink to a puff of air. Thus in more general terms we can diagram the above reflex as follows:

(2) Unconditioned Stimulus $\rightarrow$ Unconditioned Response

or more simply, as

(3) US $\rightarrow$ UR.

THE HUMAN ORGANISM

Humans are born with a number of such reflexes, along with other behaviors that are probably not reflexive. With age, their bodily structures and functions mature and their behavior changes correspondingly. They not only get larger and grow hair and teeth, but they learn to chew in addition to sucking, they reach for objects, they vocalize, they crawl, etc. Many of the structures and behaviors of the young child are common to most living organisms: for example, a digestive system and the behavior of eating, a respiratory system and breathing. An increasing number of behaviors that emerge are distinctly specific to the human species: for instance, the characteristic human crawl and subsequent upright walk, the human vocalization and subsequent language.

The structures and behaviors which characterize the developing child as human are evidence of a genetic endowment and maturational plan which sets some boundary conditions on us. We are not adept at swinging from tree limbs for long periods, or swimming under water for long periods, or for scratching our own backs. But while our genes may impose some limits on our maturation rate and the behaviors associated with them, those limits cannot begin to compare to the limits which human cultures impose through the process we have come to call socialization. Child (1954, p. 655) defined socializaton as follows:

. . . the whole process by which an individual, born with behavioral
potentialities of enormously wide range, is led to develop actual behavior which
is confined within a much narrower range—the range of what is customary and
acceptable for him according to the standards of the group.

What we come to eat, to fear, to feel comfortable with, to study, and to do with our free time—to mention just a few topics—is much more a function of our prior experiences and the presses from significant others than it is from our genetic endowment.

This is not to say that there are not tremendous variations in humans' shapes, sizes and abilities, much of which is traceable in large measure to genetic predispositions. Undoubtedly such individual differences exist and they may help describe the variations among humans. They do not, however, define the limits of structural, physiological or intellectual growth. Such limits may,

3

in principle, be unknowable because hereditary mechanisms always interact with the environment to produce organisms' structures and their behaviors, and who can ever be sure that a different environment (a better food or better teaching procedure) could not be devised to produce a stronger athlete or more intelligent student?

We present the above argument not to take sides on the nature-nurture question, but to sidestep it. From our point of view what is important is that developing humans have (1) genetic endowments and maturational patterns that provide for structural and behavioral characteristics that are at once common to the human species (and a few characteristics common to other species) and unique to the individual; and (2) learning histories and patterns that build on (1) and that emerge from continual interaction with an environment which at once changes, and is changed by, the individual. In more simplified terms, learning occurs on top of development and that, of course, affects future development.[3]

As we pursue the various aspects of human psychology and its application to teaching, this interactionist perspective will provide a common theme. The remainder of this chapter describes three fairly distinct kinds of human behavior, shows how they interact with each other, and then how they interact with another person's behavior. We begin with reflexes—the most easily identifiable species-specific behaviors—and show how they develop in interaction with the environment.

ONE LEVEL OF BEHAVIOR: RESPONDENT CONDITIONING AND EMOTIONS

Fear of dentists and the like is more than an unconditioned reflex. It requires a reflex, but adds another stimulus to it—a neutral stimulus which, when paired with the US, can come to elicit the same UR. This process is called *conditioning,* or to be more precise, it is variously called *classical conditioning, Pavlovian conditioning* (after Pavlov), or *respondent conditioning.* The latter term, attributed to Skinner (1938), is the most descriptive since it emphasizes the fact that the behavior occurs in response to an eliciting stimulus—that is, a stimulus that forces a response in an involuntary manner.

The previously neutral stimulus—e.g., a dentist—can come to elicit the fear response if associated with pain, as follows:

(4)   Dentist—Pain → Fear
(5)   Neutral Stimulus—US → UR

This should be read as indicating that the dentist, a neutral stimulus to begin with comes to be associated with the US by occurring in temporal *contiguity* with it. In other words, the dentist is present when the pain occurs—note that he does not have to cause the pain. Since the pain itself (the US) elicits the physiological fear reaction (the UR), the neutral dentist is present when the unconditioned reflex is set in motion. And usually in only a few pairings of dentist and pain (or in only one trial if the pain is sufficiently severe) the dentist comes to elicit the same kind of reflex response, now called a *conditioned response (CR)*. The previously neutral stimulus is now called a *conditioned stimulus (CS)*. The entire procedure can be diagramed as follows:[4]

(6)   CS   ------- [US   →   UR]
        (dentist)   [(pain)   (fear)]
                                    CR
                                  (fear)

If we speak of the fear (in either the unconditioned or conditioned variety) as a *respondent,* then we can think of this conditioning process as a procedure that can be used to bring the respondent under the control of a previously neutral stimulus. Learning has occurred.

While in the process of studying basic digestive processes which won him a Nobel prize, Pavlov (1927) first demonstrated classical conditioning in much the way we have described it. Pavlov sounded a tuning fork immediately before placing meat powder in a dog's mouth. The meat powder (the US) elicited a salivation response (the respondent or UR). After a number of presentations of meat powder preceded by the tuning fork, the sound of the tuning fork acquired the capability of eliciting salivation from the dog. The previously neutral tone had become a CS and elicited salivation even though meat powder (the US) was no longer presented.

Since Pavlov's first demonstration there have been repeated investigations of the effects of his basic procedure for producing conditioned respondents on many species of animals, including humans, and for many different types of reflex responses. One of the most famous of these studies (Watson and Rayner, 1920) demonstrated that conditioned emotional reactions could be produced by pairing a neutral stimulus with an aversive US. In this study a white rat was placed before an infant named Albert who was at first attracted to the animal. Then on successive trials, introduction of the rat into the room was immediately followed by a loud noise. Parents will attest to the fact that a sudden loud noise causes a startle reflex and fear responses in an infant, and that was the effect the loud noise had on Albert. In only a few more pairings of the rat, followed by a loud noise which elicited the fear response, the previously attractive white rat had become a negative and unattractive stimulus which caused a fear response. That is, the white rat had become a CS for a fear response.

The Watson-Rayner study demonstrates a point alluded to earlier—namely, that respondent conditioning can occur by chance. The white rat in Albert's case was only incidentally related to the loud noise; it certainly did not produce the noise and thus, objectively, Albert had no reason to fear it. But such is the nature of classical conditioning. *There need be no causal relationship between the CS and US; all that is necessary is that the CS precede, or occur simultaneously with, the US so that they are perceived as related, and conditioning will occur.*[5] The rate at which conditioned fears are formed and their final strength depends upon the magnitude or severity of the aversive stimulus used. What is important to realize at this point is the apparent ease with which these conditioned fear respondents are formed in situations which involve aversive stimuli—such as those which include punishment or threats of punishment. Moreover, the effects of these conditioned fears are not confined to the conditioned stimulus alone, but often *generalize* to other similar stimuli (as will be described in more detail in a later chapter). Thus Albert not only learned to fear the white rat, but his fear generalized to other furry objects such as a rabbit and a fur coat as well.

All of this is to say that respondent or classical conditioning is a very important aspect of behavior. In fact, we shall go so far as to call it one of three levels of behavior—*the level of emotions and involuntary behavior.* Emotions such as fear, anxiety, comfort, love, embarrassment, and perhaps all emotions are conditioned to people and objects in this way. This is not to say that love and fear can be reduced to nothing but classical conditioning; rather it is to say that such emotions have large respondent components and we can understand a lot of behavior by analyzing how these respondents become conditioned to people, things and environmental events. Neither is there a claim being made that love and fear cannot be voluntary actions; rather, the bodily feelings that are conditioned to people we love or things we hate are elicited by the stimuli present (see cartoon). They can be controlled voluntarily—bio-

When Harry and I were courting, we used to sit in the parlour and talk. But Daddy was always upstairs directly above us—and whenever we stopped talking he would stamp his foot on the floor.

Yeh, and to this day I get hot and bothered whenever I hear tap dancing.

KOHRN/GENTILE

feedback techniques have been developed for this purpose—but they are not typically within our awareness in such a way as to be under our conscious or voluntary control. Hence, the term involuntary is often applied to respondent conditioning.

A SECOND LEVEL OF BEHAVIOR: OPERANT CONDITIONING AND MOTIONS

Most of our experiences in everyday life are much more noticeable or available to our consciousness than the reflex responses we called respondents. We seldom feel as though we are puppets on a string, reacting reflexively to environmental pushes and pulls. To the contrary, except in extraordinary circumstances, we feel very much in control of our lives: we turn on the television in order to see a program, we turn the spigot to get water, we run after a ball to catch it, we work to receive pay, and so forth. *These are voluntary behaviors performed with purpose,* which defines the second level of behavior.

Such behaviors were called operant behaviors, or *operants,* by B. F. Skinner (1938) to emphasize that they operate on the environment in order to produce some desired consequence. Other authors have called them *instrumental responses,* in recognition of E. L. Thorndike's (1911) early research showing how these behaviors are instrumental in obtaining rewards or avoiding punishments. Walking, talking, swimming, drawing, eating, drinking—in fact, almost any behavior you can think of—are all instances of operants.

When he defined their characteristics and named them operants, Skinner was contrasting them with respondents. Behaviors that were reflex reactions to unconditioned stimuli were respondents; behaviors that were not, which were all the rest, were operants. This distinction is still widely acknowledged, but it is clear that the boundaries are fuzzier than originally believed. It is possible, for example, to bring respondents under voluntary control (the procedures for doing so provide the basis for a later chapter) as current research in biofeedback demonstrates nicely. Nevertheless, the distinction holds under normal conditions and it is convenient for didactic purposes to talk of respondent and operant conditioning as two separate but interactive levels of behavior.

If operant behavior is voluntary or purposeful, how then is it conditioned? The simple answer is by the consequences of the behavior. If you touch a hot stove, the touching behavior has the consequence of a painful burn. The behavior is punished and you learn not to touch hot stoves. If, on the other hand, you find that you can have anything you want as long as you say, "please", you learn to say it with much higher frequency than other words. ("Please" is not called the magic word for nothing!) Both of these examples—the former built on negative, punishing consequences, the other on positive, rewarding consequences—are instances of operant conditioning.

7

There are a number of ways in which operant behaviors are controlled, of which positive reinforcement and punishment are just two, but they will be presented in detail in a later chapter. For now, the important point is that operant behaviors are controlled by their consequences. A diagram for the punishment example follows:[6]

(7)   Touching Hot Stove → Painful Burn
(8) $R \rightarrow S^{AV}$

The reinforcement (reward) example can be diagramed thus:

(9)   Saying "Please" → Toy
(10) $R \rightarrow S^{RF}$

Operant conditioning is sometimes called instrumental conditioning (because the behavior is instrumental in obtaining the consequence), sometimes Skinnerian conditioning, (after Skinner) and sometimes it is referred to as S-R (Stimulus-Response) learning. The latter is mostly a misnomer as we have seen because, although there may be a stimulus in the presence of which behavior occurs, the important stimulus event is the consequent one. For example, while you may need a spigot or feeling of thirst (antecedent stimuli) to turn (the behavior), the stimulus which determines whether you engage in this behavior frequently or not at all is whether you get water (reinforcing or consequent stimulus). Thus instead of being called S-R learning, operant conditioning should be called *R-S learning*. This also has the effect of emphasizing the *active* role of the organism at this operant level of behavior in contrast to the reactive role at the respondent level.

Because of the emphasis on the active organism in operant conditioning, it is not too far-fetched to think of the *motions* of the organism (the physical motions of walking or of the vocal cords in talking, for example) in recalling this level of behavior. Then another mnemonic device for distinguishing between operant and respondent behaviors is in terms of *motions and emotions,* respectively, which is the reason for the title of this book.

A THIRD LEVEL OF BEHAVIOR: COGNITION

If you ask a teacher what he or she teaches, the answer will hardly ever be motions and emotions, willingness to participate, or even fear or love for a subject. The most likely answer is, "reading", "mathematics", "educational psychology", "chemistry", "French", etc. Teachers are hired to teach because of their expertise in subject matters. They know the facts, concepts, principles and methods of their discipline and can presumably impart them to others.

Teachers do indeed teach the facts and principles of their fields, but they never do so without at the same time affecting their students'—as well as their own—motions and emotions. This is recognized in part by teachers who respond to the "what you teach" question by answering, "children" or "students." The recognition is that there is a whole child who is an emotional as well as a rational being. But in so saying it is easy to overlook the profound extent to which we have been and are continuing to be operantly and respondently conditioned, and thus to a gloss over many important details which may help to explain why we feel the ways we do.

Having emphasized the impossibility of dealing with the substance of education—facts, concepts, methods—in the absence of the other two levels, the converse is also true. Living organisms know facts, form concepts, have expectations and make predictions, create new behaviors, and invent new methods to solve old problems. And much of what these organisms perceive and think about concerns emotions and consequences of their motions. Thus motions and emotions do not occur without at the same time affecting cognitions.

We are describing three levels of behavior which exist in a totally interdependent state. And we used the term living organism above to emphasize that this is not only true for humans, but also for many other species of animals.

The third level of behavior, then, is here defined as *cognition* and it includes all aspects of the behavior of organisms that cannot be easily explained by respondents and operants, including thinking, creating, remembering and transfering. This is the stuff of education, about which educational objectives have been developed in the so-called cognitive domain (e.g., Bloom, 1956). But it turns out it is also the vast majority, if not all, of the behaviors in the so-called affective domain (e.g., Krathwohl et al., 1964), at least as typicallly assessed by interviews, survey methods, questionnaires, and projective techniques (e.g., Bloom et al.,1971). The reason these objectives are considered cognitions instead of emotions is because they are so indirectly assessed. We don't measure how people feel when rock music is being played; we ask instead whether they would go to a rock concert or a concert of classical music (and then it is only hypothetical—we don't actually see to which they go).

As defined, then, the level of behavior we are calling cognitions is quite broad, including the following types of behaviors from the cognitive and affective domains:

knowledge	receiving
comprehension	responding (attending)
application	valuing
analysis	organizing
synthesis	characterizing (by a value complex)
evaluation	

THE INTERDEPENDENCE OF MOTIONS, EMOTIONS AND COGNITIONS

One of the beliefs that hinders progress in education, according to Combs (1979), is "the myth of the affective domain." He states (p. 162)

> The argument about whether education should be affective is a waste of time. The fact is, unless education is affective there will be no learning at all!
>
> How students feel about subject matter, teachers, fellow students, school, and the world in general cannot be ignored. Emotion is part of the process of learning and is an indication of the degree to which real learning is occurring.

Well, we don't know exactly what Combs means by real learning (as opposed to unreal learning?), but he has made an important point which we would rephrase as follows: unless education is affective there will be no learning at all, because the student is dead.

No matter what is being taught, an emotion is being conditioned to it. The emotion may be fear, liking, discomfort, comfort, or indifference or boredom, but some affect is being associated with the subject, teacher, or learning environment.

Likewise, instrumental behaviors are being associated with whatever is being taught—a tendency to approach or leave; a willingness to attempt a solution to a problem or to say, "I don't know," and hope the teacher will stop asking questions; or a behavior of falling asleep in class. These operants provide direct measures of attending, valuing, etc.

A hypothetical example of the interdependence among these levels is given in Table 1. A first-grader is not paying attention well enough to suit the teacher, so he does not learn that $2 + 2 = 4$. And, after a frustrating day the teacher punishes the child by yelling at him (and some teachers have a tone of voice that can make a marine drill sergeant cringe!) for not paying attention. On the cognitive level the teacher, of course, wants the student to learn the number facts, along with the principles and procedures for discovering and proving

TABLE I
The Interdependence of the Three Levels of Behavior

Level of Behavior	Teacher's Question	Student's Answer	Teacher's Response	Probable Effect
Cognition	"How Much is $2 + 2$?"	"I don't know" or "5"	Yelling	May learn or may not
Operant	S^D ------------R ----------→ S^{AV}			Student will
	Discriminative Stimulus or Cue "$2 + 2 = $?"	Trying, says "5" or "I don't know"	Yelling (punishment)	try to avoid teacher or math
Respondent	CS --------------------------- US---------→ UR			
	Neutral Stimulus		loud noise	tension, fear

them. It is not clear what effect yelling has on this. People often learn well when threatened (probably to avoid punishment in the future), but then there are cases in which they do not. The science of cognitive development is not far enough along to predict what will happen on this level.

On the other levels, however, it is relatively straightforward. If the operant behavior of trying to answer is punished, the child will suppress his behavior for a while. If the punishment is severe or continual and there is no way to avoid it, he may learn to say "I don't know" to extinguish the teacher from asking questions, or he will stop trying altogether. If he can avoid the teacher or class, he will. On the respondent level an emotional reflex will have been set in motion. Yelling, and the actual pain with which it may have been associated in the past, actually elicits muscular tension and the general fear reflex described earlier.

No teacher has the goal of making a child unwilling to come to class or feel tense while there. The interaction of teacher and student may nevertheless have that effect if punishment is routinely used. But the extreme hypothetical example is not meant to imply that motions and emotions are involved only when punishment occurs. If reading, for example, is associated with gentleness and warmth through snuggling, then one would expect the student to be willing to read (operant level), to feel relaxed and comfortable while reading (respondent level), and to learn to read better and better (cognitive level), though the cognitive effect is expected on the basis of time spent reading rather than because of a direct connection between snuggling and comprehension.

A THEORY OF BEHAVIOR: SOCIAL LEARNING THEORY

If it is clear that there is an interdependence among motions, emotions and cognitions within a person, it is equally clear that no one exists in a vacuum. There is an old joke about a rat in a Skinner box who says to his mate, "Boy, do I have this experimenter conditioned: every time I press the bar, he gives me a pellet of food."

Presumably the reason that joke is funny is that people expect the experimenter to be in control, while the lowly rat is being conditioned. But conditioning is never a situation of controller-controllee. It is more accurately described as control-countercontrol (e.g., Skinner, 1971), in which the experimenter controls the rat's bar pressing by giving food contingent upon that behavior and the rat controls the experimenter's food-giving by pressing the bar contingent upon receiving food. Perhaps the best way of describing it is as a mutually beneficial interaction or, to paraphrase the song "Mutual Admiration Society," a mutual reinforcement contingency.

Any account of behavior must include both the organism and its environment, including other organisms, in a mutually interacting way if it is to be reasonably comprehensive. An account which does this is Bandura's (1977) Social Learning Theory, which will serve to complete this overview of a psychology of behavior.

Bandura's theory grew out of his prolific research on the topics of imitation or modeling, self-control or self-reinforcement processes, aggression, and behavior modification (e.g., Bandura 1969; 1971; Bandura and Walters, 1963). His findings convinced him that behavior and environment are so mutually interdependent that it is impossible to find the cause for a particular behavior. In his words (1977, p. 203):

> Environments have causes as do behaviors. It is true that behavior is regulated by its contingencies, but the contingencies are partly of a person's own making. By their actions, people play an active role in producing the reinforcing contingencies that impinge upon them. As was previously shown, behavior partly creates the environment, and the environment influences the behavior in a reciprocal fashion. To the oft-repeated dictum, 'change contingencies and you change behaviors,' should be added the reciprocal side, 'change behavior and you change the contingencies.' In the regress of prior causes, for every chicken discovered by a unidirectional environmentalist, a social learning theorist can identify a prior egg.

Bandura refers to this environment-behavior interaction as a case of *reciprocal determinism* and he provides as an exemplar a classic study in avoidance learning. Organisms are individually placed in an experimental apparatus in which a shock is delivered through the grid floor every minute. However, if an organism presses a bar protruding from the wall, the shock is postponed for 30 seconds. Organisms which learn to press the bar find that they can create an environment free of shocks. Those which do not learn to press the bar find themselves in a shocking state of affairs (pun intended).

Bandura's interpretation of this type of experiment follows (1977, p. 196):

> Though the *potential environment* is identical for all animals, the *actual environment* depends upon their behavior. . . .the organism appears either as an object or an agent of control, depending upon which side of the reciprocal process one chooses to examine. When the rate of self-protective responses is

measured, the environmental contingencies appear to be the controller of behavior. If, instead, one measures the amount of punishment brought about by each animal, then it is the environment that is controlled and modified by behavior.

Teachers constantly find they react differently to each student in a classroom because of the student's behavior toward them. This is despite their efforts to establish a classroom milieu and rules which are fair to all and treat all as equals. Of course, the teachers' differential responses to the student then further affect each student's behavior, and so on. How can we get to the bottom of this to decide who started it? We cannot because there is no bottom: first causes sink into a murky abyss.

The situation is already quite complicated when trying to explain the relatively simple experimental situations of rats in Skinner boxes receiving rewards or shocks. In those we do not usually have to attribute many cognitive capabilities to the animals—though it is now well established that they have many—in order to explain the results. In humans, whom we know use such capabilities through a rich language to reinforce or punish themselves, to explain events and infer causes, to predict future effects of current behaviors, and so forth, cognitions serve to guarantee that behavior and environment are reciprocally determined. The person will never just react to the environment emotionally; he or she will operate on the environment in an operant sense and be analyzing the effects of the interaction all the while. And just as behavior and environment are reciprocally determined, so are motions, emotions and cognitions. Each component can be analyzed separately and can sometimes occur without engaging the other parts (e.g., a reflex can occur without cognition), but rarely do any of the components occur in isolation. Over time the events and behaviors have to interact in a reciprocal determination process.

NOTES

1. This first-person account is a true confession of the author. He is now overcoming his fear of dentists through "transcend-dental" meditation.
2. Most physicians and veterinarians are indeed kind. In fact, one toddler was so impressed with a veterinarian's kindness toward his dog that he asked his parents if they were going to send the vet a card on Veteran's Day. (Yes, Doug, you said it, but we published first!)
3. To see another argument on the nature-nurture issue, turn to Appendix C for a reinterpretation of John B. Watson's infamous argument.
4. Note that an arrow → implies "produces" or "elicits" (e.g., pain produces fear) while a dash — implies "occurs in the presence of" (e.g., dentist is present when pain occurs).
5. As we shall see in Chapter 2, however, this statement will have to be qualified slightly to take into account species-specific behaviors.
6. Note that we're using R = Response which is the traditional symbol for Operant Behavior and S = Stimulus, sometimes with superscripts (e.g., S^{RF} = Reinforcing Stimulus or S^{AV} = Aversive Stimulus) to indicate operant conditioning, while CS, US, CR and UR were used as symbols in respondent conditioning. This distinction of symbols for the two levels of behavior will be maintained throughout the book.

CHAPTER II
Respondent Behavior: Emotions

INTRODUCTION

As part of his treatment for leukemia, a six-year old boy was receiving chemotherapy intravenously while in a cancer research hospital. While having obvious benefits in alleviating the disease, the drug treatments also have some common negative side effects, including inducing nausea, the loss of hair, and general weakness. Often he was awake and receiving intravenous drip treatments early in the morning with little to do but watch television. And so it came to pass that he spent many mornings with his treatment inducing vomiting with the Captain Kangaroo show in the background.

The treatment was awful enough, but as you have probably already anticipated, another side effect of this daily routine emerged when the child, no longer on drugs, was recuperating at home. When he turned on Captain Kangaroo, he became suddenly nauseous.[1]

Many critics have been arguing for years that television programs can make a person nauseous, but it is unlikely that this six-year-old was simply giving literal expression to such a sentiment. More likely, Captain Kangaroo and he were unwitting victims of respondent conditioning: the drug (the US) inducing the reflexive vomiting (UR) in the presence of a previously neutral stimulus, the Captain, who now becomes a CS capable of eliciting the nausea. As already demonstrated in Chapter I, this process can be diagramed as follows:

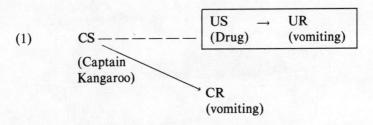

Captain Kangaroo, of course, did not cause this behavior; he and his show just became associated with a respondent behavior and the rest just happened. Respondent conditioning sometimes happens in this unplanned way. It can also be planned, as we shall see in some treatments to help people overcome a desire, say, for cigarettes. The process was vividly portrayed in *A Clockwork Orange* by Anthony Burgess (1963) in which a drug was used to induce nausea to any kind of violence in a sociopath named Alex. Alex was to be cured of violent tendencies by the (ethically questionable) procedure of being forced to watch violent films after having been injected with a drug that induced nausea. After two weeks of such treatment, Alex gives the following first-person account of the queer interchange he had with the discharging officer (p. 110):

> "Would you," he giggled, "like to punch me in the face before I go?" I frowned at that, very puzzled, and said:
> "Why?"
> "Oh," he said, "just to see how you're getting on." And he brought his litso [face] real near, a fat grin all over his rot [mouth]. So I fisted up and went smack at this litso, but he pulled himself away. . . . And then, my brothers, I felt real sick again, just like in the afternoon. . . .

As these real and fictitious examples show, respondent conditioning is already familiar to us in many ways. In this chapter, we shall explore the principles by which respondent conditioning occurs, and can be controlled or eliminated, and explore many other related topics concerned with feelings.

"My friends, our children are hooked on TV. To get them off, join the *U*nion of *P*arents for *C*hildhood *H*ealing through *U*nprogramming by *C*onditioning *K*ids *T*o *V*omit, which we call simply Project UPCHUCK TV."

RESPONDENT CONDITIONING AND EXTINCTION

PSYCHIC SECRETIONS AND CONDITIONED REFLEXES

Respondent or classical conditioning was first systematically explored, as we have seen, by the Russian physiologist Ivan P. Pavlov who was studying reflexes of the digestive system. By an ingenious minor surgical procedure on the duct of a dog's parotid gland saliva was diverted from the inside of the mouth to an opening of the cheek. There the saliva was collected and could be accurately measured. Pavlov was studying a wide variety of conditions related to the amount of saliva which flowed, under very controlled conditions. As food (the US) reached the dog's mouth, saliva (the UR) flowed freely: This was the basic salivary reflex.

There was a certain "psychic secretion," however, which was especially troublesome for a complete physiological account of this digestive reflex. When a tuning fork was regularly sounded a few seconds before the food was presented, the dog was salivating in anticipation of the food. The procedure, diagramed before with different reflexes, is worth diagraming once more:

$$(2) \qquad CS_{tone} --- US_{food} \rightarrow UR_{salivation}$$
$$\downarrow$$
$$CR_{salivation}$$

What was occurring was a *stimulus substitution,* in that the previously neutral stimulus, the tone, was able to substitute for the stimulus to which the salivation reflex was natively "wired," the food, to elicit salivation. Pavlov termed this anticipatory salivation a *conditioned reflex.*

Pavlov's genius lay not in "discovering" the conditioned reflex. The reflex was probably known to millions of people who went before him, if only in such common experiences as "thinking of slicing a lemon." If you think about that now, you can probably produce salivation as a psychic secretion. Pavlov's contribution, rather, was in separating the psychological from the purely physiological components, and in systematically researching the conditions under which conditioned reflexes could be produced, maintained and eliminated.

EXTINCTION

As Pavlov began to understand the experimental conditions under which the CR could be reliably induced, he began to explore how the reflex could be inhibited and eliminated. Several procedures were found that could interrupt the CR, including (1) the presentation of a distracting stimulus, (2) the presentation of a stimulus associated with a contrasting behavior, and (3) the discontinuation of the US. This latter procedure Pavlov called experimental extinction or, simply, *extinction.*

DR. PAVLOV, DO YOU KNOW HOW TO KEEP YOUR DOG FROM DROOLING?

NO, HOW?

TEACH HIM TO SPIT.

Extinction, to be precise, is the procedure of presenting the CS without following it by the US. In the context of the previous conditioning, the CS will elicit the CR. However, since the US does not follow, the CR has been evoked in vain: why salivate if there is no food coming? The organism learned during conditioning that the CS reliably predicts the US. During extinction trials, on the other hand, it learns that the CS reliably predicts *no* US. Thus it becomes counterproductive to salivate to a tone when it is reliably followed by nothing. The procedure for extinction can be diagramed as follows:

(3) Previous Conditioning Trials: CS_{tone} — — — — $US_{food} \rightarrow UR_{salivation}$

$$CR_{salivation}$$

Current Extinction Trial: CS_{tone} — — — — — — — — No $US_{No\ food}$

$$CR_{Salivation}$$

In the conditioned reflex, the key word is *reflex*. Since the extinction trials do not activate the actual physiological reflex, the salivation that occurs in the CR is not being reinforced by the native response tendency. In other words, the psychic secretion is adaptive to the organism only so long as it anticipates, or is reinforced by, the appropriate physiological state.

By the way, extinction eventually eliminates the CR, at least as far as any measurable response can be detected, but not forever. After a break of some minutes or days in which neither the CS nor US were presented, presentation of the CS will elicit the CR. This is called *spontaneous recovery,* but we'll delay further discussion to Chapter III.

RESPONDENT CONDITIONING OF EMOTIONS

Psychic secretions of saliva, however important they were to the history of conditioning, are mainly interesting today as an analogue for understanding emotions. Watson and Rayner's (1920) creation of conditioned fear in Albert (described in Chapter I) was the most influential, if not the first, experimental demonstration that neutral stimuli could come to elicit conditioned reactions from other physiological systems of the body. Indeed, Watson (1913; 1919) made the identification of natural reflexes and their ability to be conditioned a central feature of his behaviorism. Subsequent studies identified many procedures which could induce conditioned emotional reactions (e.g., H. E. Jones, 1930; 1931; and Jones and Jones, 1930), some which could not (e.g. Bregman, 1934; English, 1929), and procedures which might be used to eliminate such fears (e.g., M. C. Jones, 1924).

In one early case study, for example, a mother offered a 28-week-old child a black stuffed cat to play with. She had already cuddled with it in the past. On this occasion, however, her older sister, whose toy it was, was present. Just as mother offered the toy to the baby, the older child ". . . set up an indignant howl of protest at the invasion of her property" (English, 1929, p. 221) causing an emotional outburst similar to Albert's. The same response was elicited when the cat came into view hours later.

Lest you think that it is only humans that learn to fear cats, consider how humans might affect cats (Gebhart, 1979, p. 313):

> Cats may develop fears analogous to human phobias. They have few innate fears, but rapidly learn stimuli associated with unpleasant experiences. One of our cats was boarded with a family with noisy children. Following this experience she would run behind the sofa and vomit at the sound of children.

Just as a cat can become a CS for fear in children, so can children become a CS for fear in cats. Indeed, in principle, any neutral stimulus can become attached to a reflex (i.e., a US→UR combination) and then elicit similar bodily feelings and reactions. It is for this reason that respondent conditioning is so intimately tied to feelings and emotions which, in turn, are intimately connected to the various organs and glands of the body. It is not surprising, therefore, that in the several decades since Pavlov's and Watson's pioneering work, researchers have produced a large number of conditioned respondents from a wide variety of bodily organs in many species (e.g., Kimble, 1961). Bower and Hilgard (1981, p. 58) summarized the current state of affairs as follows:

> For example, a physiological stressor can be applied to a dog (as a US), producing hypertension as an unconditioned reflex, and this hypertensive

response can be conditioned to any of a variety of either external or internal stimuli. Similarly, by use of drugs or special implanted electrodes, enhancements in normal activity can be reliably elicited from and conditioned in such organs as the pancreas (insulin release), the liver (glycogen uptake), the kidneys (urinary extraction), the bladder (urination), the heart, the stomach (flow of secretions), and the gall bladder, as well as in various and sundry endocrine glands (e.g., adrenals and salivary). It would seem that almost anything that moves, squirts, or wiggles could be conditioned if a response from it can be reliably and repeatedly evoked by a controllable unconditioned stimulus.

FACTORS AFFECTING CONDITIONING

A number of factors affect how quickly or strongly a CR is established. Some of the more important of these will be discussed in this section.

NUMBER OF CS-US PAIRINGS

Reliable conditioning of such a wide variety of bodily respondents does not necessarily occur in only one or two trials, although there are some cases, notably phobias (to be discussed later), in which that is sufficient. Most conditioning, however, occurs upon *repeated pairing of the CS and US in temporal contiguity or proximity.* In general, the more pairings of CS with US, the greater the magnitude of the CR and the faster it occurs following the CS (e.g., Hovland, 1937). If we think of the US, since it always elicits the UR, as reinforcing the CS, then this principle can be restated as follows: the more reinforcements of the CS with the US, the greater (or faster) the CR will occur.

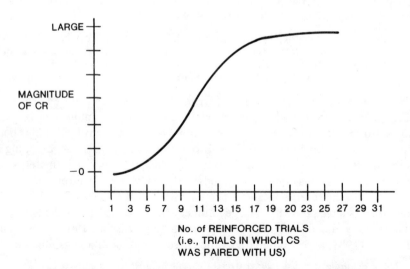

Figure 1. Typical learning curve relating number of reinforcements (CS-US pairings) to magnitude of conditioned response.

The first pairings may not produce too much reaction, while subsequent trials will add substantially to the strength or latency of the conditioned response. After many trials, say 30 or 40, the increments will not be as great; thus the learning curve may be somewhat s-shaped as shown in Figure 1.

INTERVAL BETWEEN CS AND US

In Chapter 1 we promised to qualify our definition of respondent conditioning somewhat. We said that all that was necessary for conditioning to occur was that the CS precede the US or that they occur *contiguously*—that is, simultaneously. Although this is commonly the way the respondent conditioning law is stated, it is an oversimplification due to the fact that Pavlov considered any interval from zero to five seconds preceding the US to be contiguous. In empirical fact, it has been all but impossible to produce a CR when the CS occurs simultaneously with the US (e.g., Gormezano and Moore, 1969). Likewise, if the CS occurs, then disappears for, say, 10-seconds before the US is presented, conditioning is difficult. Exactly what the optimal interval might be has been an elusive search that is beyond the scope of this treatment.[2] Suffice it to say that it depends on the species and the latency of response of the reflex involved, but it is probably in the 1-sec. to 5-sec. range (but see the section below entitled "Belongingness").

For most normal human situations, this fine of a distinction does not matter because (1) the CS precedes the presentation of the US and (2) remains at least until the US occurs. This procedure satisfies the optimal conditions. For instance, it was some time after Albert saw the white rat that the loud noise occurred, but the rat was still present. Had the rat been taken away some seconds before the noise occurred, it is unlikely that Albert would have associated rat and noise—something else in the room would likely have drawn his attention and become associated with the noise. Likewise, if the noise (US) preceded the rat (CS) conditioning would probably not occur, since the US would elicit the UR before the CS occurred, rendering the CS irrelevant as a predictor of the US.[3]

INTENSITY OF THE US

Common sense tells us that a strong US (e.g., a strong shock) will elicit a more extreme reaction (e.g., a conditioned fear) than a weak one. The empirical evidence supports this conception (e.g., Gormezano and Moore, 1969).

"BELONGINGNESS" BETWEEN CS AND US

There is now a growing body of evidence that some stimuli seem to "belong" with each other better than others, and to the extent that belonging stimuli are paired for conditioning, conditioning is easier. For example, suppose an organism were fed a certain food which was tainted with a substance that induced nausea. The food (US) induced vomiting as the UR. If the neutral stimulus (CS) to be associated with this food were a distinctive odor or taste, conditioning would be much faster than if it were, say, a sound or a light.

21

Odors and food, taste and illness, seem to belong together, while lights or sounds and food are not as related in nature.

Studies similar to the one just described have been done (e.g., Garcia and Koelling, 1966; see Rescorla and Holland's 1982 review, with the results described above). Moreover, when CS and US belong together, at least for such conditioned aversions as in tastes and illness, there can be long delays of up to hours between CS (taste) and US (induced nausea). This result goes contrary to the evidence on the optimal CS-US interval presented above, but is probably true for only especially "prepared" behaviors of a given species. This particular result, however, may explain why many young children are reluctant to try any new food. The children have learned that old foods' tastes and odors are safe—they have been conditioned to feel comfortable and secure with them. New foods, on the other hand, may be guilty until proven innocent in this regard: on a past occasion with a new, distinctive taste, the child may have felt sick and associated the new food with that feeling. Though this is a somewhat hypothetical explanation for children's taste preferences, it is not implausible based on the research evidence. Moreover, one can also imagine the species survival value of such a mechanism.

Turning to more general matters of belongingness, a neutral stimulus is seldom truly neutral. It probably elicits certain bodily reactions on its own, which may or may not be easily conditionable to other bodily reflexes. The sudden appearance of a light (CS) to be associated with food (US) may produce a frozen, passive waiting near the food dispenser, much as an animal freezes his position when caught in a spotlight in the dark. A sudden auditory stimulus, on the other hand evokes an exaggerated startle and other bodily movements (e.g., Rescorla, 1980). We are tempted to speculate on the relation of such animal research findings to humans, particularly with reference to certain colors or sounds (musical beats?) and hyperactive behaviors. Perhaps one of you readers will pursue research in this area.

To conclude this section, we would just like to alert you that we shall see two other examples of belongingness in subsequent sections: (1) the part-whole question under higher-order conditioning; and (2) the "preparedness" question under Phobias, to which we now turn.

PHOBIAS

If emotional reactions can be conditioned to any neutral stimulus as described above, then extreme emotional reactions—fears of falling, of snakes, etc.—should be simply conditioned via more intense USs, right? Not exactly. As we shall have occasion to discover throughout this book, the laws of psychology are not yet at the stage where they can be simply stated. Extreme fears, usually called phobias, provide an interesting case of the complexity of respondent conditioning.

Some of the first evidence that conditioning emotions was not as straightforward as Watson and Rayner's (1920) exerience with Albert would lead us to believe ocurred as early as 1929, when English was unable to condition a fear to a wooden duck using the loud noise as a US. Bregman (1934) was also unable to condition fear to wooden objects that were described as "without intrinsic biological interest or significance." These studies were not without flaws in their design or methods, but they drew attention to some distinctions that needed to be made. Recent research has provided a plausible explanation (e.g., Seligman, 1971).

To put it as succinctly as possible, phobias and conditioned fears may be quite different.[4] Phobias, first of all, seem to be limited to objects or events for which we are *biologically prepared,* for species-specific defense and adaptation. Common phobic reactions occur to specific animals, insects, heights, darkness, etc. As Seligman (1971, p. 312) put it

> . . .only rarely, if ever, do we have pajama phobias, grass phobias, electric-outlet phobias, hammer phobias, even though these things are likely to be associated with trauma in our world.

This leads to a second way in which phobias and conditioned fears may be different. Phobias usually occur in only one or two trials, whereas conditioned fears usually take between three and six repetitions to occur.

A third difference between them is their ability to be extinguished. For most conditioned fears, the normal extinction procedure of presenting the CS without following it with the US gradually reduces the fear to the CS. The person is learning—cognitively as well as emotionally—that the CS no longer predicts the frightful US. Eventually, though it will take a while, the CR will be reduced to zero for all practical purposes. For phobias, however, this extinction procedure, however rational, rarely works. A much more active procedure, such as counter-conditioning along with desensitization procedures (to be described later), must be used to eliminate phobias.

According to this view, then, we are natively prepared to fear certain objects, presumably because there is a survival value in avoiding those objects without having to go through an extended period of learning. Presumably furry creatures that are, or look, alive can activate this preparedness so that, if a loud noise occurs when a furry creature is present, a fear will easily develop. The same US may not be sufficient to induce fear to an inanimate, non-furry neutral stimulus like a wooden duck, however.

It is uncertain, of course, whether this explanation is sufficient in and of itself to account for the intricate differences that occur in the development of fears. With so many different sorts of objects and so many possible traumas to which they can become associated in the histories of individuals, we may never fully account for the development of fears. Nevertheless, this explanation accounts for many of the differences we see between "normal" conditioned fears and phobias. It is also consistent with a growing literature on other species-specific defensive reactions in the realm of operant behavior (see, for example, Punishment and Its Amazing Effects in Chapter III). Finally, it is also consistent with the qualitative relationship of belongingness between CS and US mentioned in an earlier section.

GENERALIZATION AND DISCRIMINATION

When little Albert was "traumatized" into fearing the white rat by pairing it with the loud noise, his fear generalized to other stimuli as well, particularly to a white rabbit and other furry objects (Watson and Rayner, 1920). Most of us can relate to that through some personal traumatic experience. An anxiety-laden first piano recital made many people fearful not only of performing in public, but also of getting up in front of an audience for any reason. Or a child's fear of a doctor, from the pain associated with a shot, may also be transferred to other people or settings in which white coats or medicinal smells may be present, such as a barbershop. This process of the CR being elicited not only by the original CS, but by other CSs similar to it, is called *generalization* (or more correctly, *stimulus generalization*).

Fortunately, it is a rare case indeed in which a conditioned emotion is so undifferentiated as to be associated with very many settings. More typically, emotions generalize only to stimuli which are very similar to the original CS assuming, of course, that there are no other presentations of the US. The curve that can be drawn to show that "the more similar a new stimulus is to the original CS, the more likely the CR will occur" is called the *generalization gradient* (e.g., Hovland, 1937; Kalish, 1969).

As we go through life, we learn more and more to *discriminate* between stimulus situations, which is to say we respond differently to each situation. Thus our emotions become associated to specific stimuli: we fear only dentists, not barbers; or we feel relaxed and interested in one teacher's class, but not all teachers' classes. The more training or experience we have differentiating situations, the more discriminating we become. As we shall see, this process is similar for operant behavior as well, so we shall defer further treatment of it until the next chapter (see also Figure 3).

HIGHER-ORDER CONDITIONING

Many people have particular emotional reactions to certain musical melodies. That a melody can induce a feeling directly should no longer be too surprising, assuming it is directly associated with a US for an emotional reaction. If lovers make love with "Bolero" in the background (as was done in the movie "10"), then Bolero should evoke romantic feelings on some future occasion. The song has become a CS for the feelings elicited by the actual love-making reflexes. This immediate association of CS and US can be thought of as direct or first-order conditioning.

But songs can be emotional CSs even when they have not been directly associated with a US as, for example, when a melody has been associated with the restaurant dinner you had with your lover before you first made love. The actual sexual stimulation was the US for the amorous reflexes. The person becomes a CS for those feelings: all he or she has to do is come into view or call you on the phone and you can begin to feel sexually excited. The song, then, is associated with that person. This is a case of second-order or, more generally, higher-order conditioning since a neutral stimulus can come to elicit an emotional reaction by being paired with a CS.

The first studies of higher-order conditioning were conducted by (whom else but?) Pavlov (1927), but he concluded that the resulting conditioned reflexes were unstable. More recent studies (e.g., Davenport, 1966; Rescorla, 1980) have demonstrated such second-order conditioning to be quite stable. An actual procedure for demonstrating higher-order conditioning is worth exploring for a moment because of its importance in understanding emotions. In the first stage a light (CS_1) is reliably followed by a shock (US) which, in turn, elicits the physiological stress reaction we commonly call fear.[5] When the light regularly elicits the fear reaction, Stage 2 begins. Now a tone (CS_2) precedes the light (CS_1), which is no longer followed by the shock (US). What happens is that the tone acquires the capability of eliciting fear, too, solely on the basis of being paired with the light.

Several surprising results emerged from studies like the one just described, as well as some using food as the US. First, after only a few conditioning trials (in one study 8 trials pairing CS_1 and US and 6 pairing CS_2 and CS_1), extinction of the CR commonly took many trials more than to condition it in the first place. Rescorla (1980, p. 10) commented that ". . . this eventual demise of responding to S_2 [CS_2] is frequently very slow indeed, often requiring hundreds of trials." This finding that it often takes much longer to extinguish a CR than to condition it, it should be noted, is something that also occurs in first-order conditioning.

A second surprising finding from Rescorla's studies was that, in many cases the CR elicited by CS_2 was of greater magnitude than that elicited by CS_1. In fact, it sometimes appeared that a CR had not been acquired to the CS_1 (there was little or no observable reaction to the light) until it was found capable of transfering a reaction to CS_2 (the tone).

Third, when the CR (emotional reaction) was extinguished to the CS_1 (the light) by being unpaired with the US, the conditioned emotion remained to CS_2 (the tone). Despite the fact that the CS_1 was necessary for the conditioned emotion to be attached to the CS_2, once the $CS_2 \rightarrow CR$ connection was made, it had a life of its own. The second-order conditioned emotional reaction was independent of what happened to the earlier conditioned reactions through which it was learned. Returning to our music example, this finding supports common experiences people have. Our favorite melody (CS_2) may remain capable of eliciting warm feelings even when the person (CS_1) from whom those feelings were transferred no longer elicits such feelings.

The basic procedure used for producing the above findings is shown in Figure 2. An additional point worth making relates to "belongingness" which we described earlier in this chapter. Another finding of Rescorla's (1980) was that if the CS_2 were a part of a whole, represented by CS_1, conditioning was

Stage 1	CS$_1$ — — — Light $\searrow$ CR Fear	US $\longrightarrow$ UR shock fear	First-Order Conditioning
Stage 2	CS$_2$— — Tone $\searrow$ CR fear	CS$_1$ $\longrightarrow$ CR Light fear	Second-Order Conditioning
Stage 3		CS$_1$— — — No US Light No Shock CR fear	Extinction to CS$_1$
Stage 4	CS$_2$— — — $\searrow$?	No CS$_1$ . . . . No US No Light No Shock	Test for reaction to CS$_2$

Figure 2. A procedure for demonstrating second-order conditioning.

accelerated over conditions in which CS$_1$ and CS$_2$ were unrelated. In this study with pigeons the CS$_2$ was the black outline of a triangle, while CS$_1$ was the whole of a red triangle. The two CSs belong together and can thus more easily substitute for one another in eliciting the emotional reaction.

While many more empirical findings might be reported here on the belongingness of stimuli (e.g., blocking or overshadowing effects) or on second- or higher-level conditioning in general, we shall leave you to seek them out elsewhere.[6] It remains for us to provide more plausible examples of how this affects humans.

As a final example from our proverbial lovers, the voice of the loved one on the phone can easily come to elicit amorous feelings once it has been associated with the "object of our affection." The voice (CS$_2$) is a part of the whole person (CS$_1$) who has been conditioned to evoke the loving feelings through direct contact.

Analogous situations may occur in school settings where a teacher's tone of voice or angry scowl can come to elicit a fearful response as CS$_1$ by being paired with actual punishment administered by that teacher. Then other neutral stimuli in the environment, such as math problems, books, or music appreciation classes (as CS$_2$) can come to elicit those same feelings by being paired with the teacher's tone of voice or scowl. Actual punishment need not occur.

Physical deformities caused by accident, disease or birth defect can cause a natural revulsion as an unconditioned reflex. If we now attach words like "sinful," "cancer," or "handicapped" to those feelings, we can come to feel revulsion at the sound of the words. When we then say that "Mary has cancer" or "George is handicapped" we are engaging in second-order conditioning, attaching a person's name (CS_2) to a word (CS_1) which has been attached to an actual US for a fear or revulsion reaction.

It should be becoming clearer that this is likely one of the mechanisms involved in stereotyping ethnic groups—that is, by calling them "lazy and dirty"—since these words have been associated with actual emotional experiences. In an experimental study on exactly this problem, Staats and Staats (1958) were able to change attitudes either positively or negatively about two European groups by pairing them with such positive words as gift, sacred, and happy or such negative words as bitter, ugly and failure. They were able to do the same with names of people, like Tom and Bill.[7]

Keeping names from hurting, as the cartoon shows, is no easy task given the above. If Mowrer (1954) was even partly correct that a sentence is primarily a conditioning device, then much of our communication is conditioning higher-order emotions to the subject of the sentence by what feelings are elicited by the predicate. The statement "Bill is hyper" is perhaps more effective as a conditioner of feelings about Bill by the listeners than it is as a descriptor of Bill's actual behavior or a prescriptor of what to do about it. Given all of this, one must wonder what damage we are doing with such labels as "retarded," "dyslexic," "learning disabled," and so forth.

STRESS AND HELPLESSNESS

In 1958 a soon-to-become famous experiment was conducted in which one member each of several pairs of rhesus monkeys was given shocks that could be avoided (postponed) by pressing a bar within a certain time. The second member of the pair was "yoked" to it, so that every time the first monkey was shocked, the second also received a shock of equal intensity and duration. The only difference between what happened to the two monkeys in the pair, therefore, was that the former was in control of its own destiny, while the latter had no control over whether shocks would be received. Because the former monkeys were making the decisions, they came to be known as the "executive monkeys." After repeated "decision-making trials" in which both members of the pair successfully avoided or received shocks on the basis of the decisions of the "executive", the animals were examined for gastroduodenal ulcers, among other things.

With no additional information, and before reading further, answer the following multiple-choice question to see how "obvious" or "common-sensible" psychological findings appear to you.

> *Item:* Which of the following monkeys in the pair should be expected to have a greater number of and/or more severe ulcers?
> A. The "executive" monkeys whose decisions controlled whether they received shocks, or
> B. The "yoked" monkeys who had no control over whether they received shocks.

If you chose A, then you have predicted (or remembered) the results of the original study (e.g., Brady, 1958; Brady et al., 1958; Porter et al, 1958). You can also find a great deal of popular support for your choice in the common-sense belief that ulcers are the price that one pays for an executive lifestyle.

If you chose B, however, you are most probably correct. Despite these earlier findings and the popular consensus of opinion, it is not the stress of decision-making that causes ulcers, or other psychogenic disturbances; rather, it is the *lack of predictability and control over the outcome* that causes such problems.[8] With lack of predictability and loss of control come fear, often helplessness and depression, and sometimes even death.

LEARNED HELPLESSNESS

Stress, produced by environmental changes or demands on an organism, has many psychological and physiological effects. But exactly what the effects of stress are depend, in turn, on whether the organisms have control over—or perceive they have control over—the outcome. Some of the earliest research to suggest that the availability of successful coping behavior could reduce stress and helplessness was done by Mowrer and Viek in 1948. They were able to demonstrate that hungry rats who could control the amount of shock they received by jumping did not allow the anticipated shock to disrupt their eating when food was made available. Rats who were equated with them in the amount of shock received, but whose jumping or other behavior had no effect on the shock, had their normal eating behavior severely disrupted. These rats, who had no control over the shock, were characterized by Mowrer and Viek as showing "fear of fear."

Perhaps the point about helplessness and its devastating effects was made most vividly by Seligman (1975). He and his co-workers were studying various aspects of fear conditioning by subjecting dogs to shocks that were unavoidable, producing respondent conditioning as described earlier in this chapter. Following a number of such unavoidable shocks, each dog was placed in a shuttle-box in which escape from shock could easily be achieved by jumping over a barrier from one side of the box to the other. Seligman describes the results as follows (1975, p. 22):

> What we saw was bizarre, and can best be appreciated if I first describe the behavior of a typical dog that has not been given uncontrollable shock.

> When placed in a shuttle box, an experimentally naive dog, at the onset of the first electric shock, runs frantically about until it accidentally scrambles over the barrier and escapes the shock. On the next trial, the dog, running frantically, crosses the barrier more quickly than on the preceding trial; within a few trials it becomes very efficient at escaping, and soon learns to avoid shock altogether. After about fifty trials, the dog becomes nonchalant and stands in front of the barrier; at the onset of the signal for shock it leaps gracefully across and never gets shocked again.

> A dog that had first been given inescapable shock showed a strikingly different pattern. This dog's first reactions to shock in the shuttle box were much the same as those of a naive dog; it ran around frantically for about thirty seconds. But then it stopped moving; to our surprise, it lay down and quietly whined. After one minute of this we turned the shock off; the dog had failed to cross the barrier and had not escaped from shock. On the next trial, the dog did it again; at first it struggled a bit, and then, after a few seconds, it seemed to give up and to accept the shock passively. On all succeeding trials, the dog failed to escape.

This phenomenon has come to be known as *learned helplessness*. It apparently arises from encountering a situation in which you are at first incapable of controlling what happens to you; you learn you are incompetent or helpless. When you are subsequently exposed to a similar situation that is within your control, your previous experience renders you unable or unwilling to learn new adaptable behaviors.

More specifically, organisms who are exposed to these learned helplessness conditions show deficits in all three areas of behavior of interest to this book—namely, the emotional (respondent), the motivational (operant), and the cognitive. The emotional effect occurs as a heightened state of fear which, with prolonged exposure to uncontrollable events, can turn into apathy or depression. The motivational effect is evidenced by a diminished tendency to initiate any motions or actions which might serve as trial-and-error. There is

29

little willingness to try anything new since everything that was tried before didn't work. The cognitive deficit shows up in the organism's not learning what controls the environment or in not perceiving what events predict what outcomes. Their previous experience has adversely affected their thinking about the current situation (a form of negative transfer called proactive interference).

The basic findings described above have now been replicated on many species, including humans. Hiroto (1974) exposed college students to inescapable loud noise. Then when they were given a situation in which they could turn off the loud noise by a simple movement, their escape was much impaired, as compared to control groups of college students whose prior experience was either training to escape loud noise or no exposure at all to the noise. Hiroto's study is interesting because it also explored the effects of instructions on escape. Fewer students learned to escape if they were *told* that escape was determined by chance rather than by their skill.

Finally—and this is quite relevant to developing personalities—Hiroto studied the factor of locus of control (Rotter, 1966). Half of his students had identified themselves on a personality inventory as believing that their successes and failures primarily result from their own effort and skill. Such persons are said to have an *internal locus of control.* The other half of the students subscribed to an *external locus of control,* in that they were more likely to attribute their own successes and failures to luck or the ease or difficulty of the situation. Hiroto found that external students became much more helpless in his experiment than internals.

At this point, we could easily introduce what has come to be known as *attribution theory,* because it integrates the above locus of control concerns into a broader conception of people and to what they attribute their successes and failures. We shall resist that temptation, however, because it would lead us too far afield and, instead, draw some conclusions and applications of direct relevance to this book.[9]

While there do indeed seem to be personality types who are more susceptible to learned helplessness, none of us is immune to becoming helpless in some type of situation, e.g., in math or in a cancer hospital. Similarly, to return to such psychosomatic reactions to stress as ulcers, there are apparently personality types which are more or less vulnerable. But we must also ask the question how they developed the kind of personality that made them vulnerable. Even if such traits are inherited, they must interact with the environment, as we saw in Chapter I.

Developmentally, learning to cope with various stresses begins quite early in life and, of course, never ends. The sudden infant death syndrome, or crib death, in which there is no discernable sign of pathology in the deceased babies, is perhaps a case in point. Lipsitt (1978), for example, points out that a peak period of occurrence of crib deaths is in the age range of 2–4 months. This is a critical time of transition for infants when they are progressing from their inborn reflexes to becoming more intentional, mastering voluntary behaviors. If this transition does not progress smoothly, as Lipsitt put it, potentially hazardous conditions might develop. Certain responses like the grasp reflex, which are strong at birth, may begin to weaken and indeed be all but gone at 5 months. The infant may not be able to defend himself adequately when threats to respiration, for instance, occur. Although Lipsitt does not implicate learned helplessness as the cause, there do seem to be striking parallels between his description of crib deaths and Seligman's conception of helplessness.

Most persons experience at least one case of unexplained death in their lifetimes: someone who has weathered a successful operation, but who just seems to give up hope and die; someone who has lost a loved one and then seems to die from grief; or someone who goes off to a nursing home and soon afterward dies. Autopsies generally reveal no known causes for these deaths, though there may be other ailments from which the deceased was suffering. Is it possible that these deaths, "unexpected" from a medical perspective, are very much expected from a learned-helplessness point of view? Seligman (1975) offers impressive anecdotal and experimental evidence for such a view. These persons may have learned that whatever they do does not change things, they do not understand what is happening to them very well and cannot control their treatment, and they lapse into severe depressions and, finally, hopelessness and despair.

In less lethal cases, learned helplessness may be a promising explanation for many of the learning deficiencies and lack of confidence we see in large numbers of school children. So-called "math anxiety" is a persistent theme in this regard. A few particularly traumatic experiences with math can, as we have seen, condition emotional experiences that can last a long time even if the student is successful in math. If such experiences are coupled with repeated failures in math, we have the conditions for the development of learned helplessness. The student becomes anxious, does not grasp the cognitive requirements of the new task (because the prerequisites were not learned adequately), and soon stops trying. The student has learned to be helpless in math.

Dweck and Licht (1980, p. 21) give a very convincing argument for why mathematics is particularly ripe for learned helplessness and, incidentally, why from an attribution theory standpoint girls are more prone to it than boys. They point out that people are more likely to encounter difficulties in mathematics than in verbal areas of study, because of some fundamental differences in these pursuits. Verbal skills like speaking and reading tend to be acquired and improved upon in small increments. In addition, they are similar to the skills used in daily life outside of the classroom. In stark contrast to that, however, are typical math courses in which each new unit may involve very different concepts or procedures. The relevance of past learnings and the applicability to experience outside of class may not be easily appreciated. Each new unit may, as Dweck and Licht (1980, p. 21) put it, ". . . entail large, sudden qualitative changes as, for example, when one goes from arithmetic to algebra to geometry to calculus and so on." Under conditions like these, if the teacher does not take great pains to prevent it, confusion may be rampant with the introduction of each new math unit. Such confusion, particularly with girls in our society, can lead students to doubt considerably their abilities in math which may carry over through subsequent mastery of the material. It is as if the students say to themselves, "I got through this time, but I was lucky."

Similar phenomena may occur in other school subjects as well. Butkowski and Willows (1980), for example, provide evidence that many of the behaviors of poor readers resemble the learned helplessness syndrome. They studied fifth-grade boys and found that, in contrast to good readers, poor readers (1) had lower expectancies of success on reading task and a puzzle-solving task (which was deliberately made to appear not related to reading); (2) did not persist as long at the task at hand; and (3) were more likely to explain their failures as resulting from internal, stable causes such as poor ability, rather than to external, variable causes such as a difficult task. Poor readers also took less credit for successful outcomes, ascribing the responsibility to an easy task, for example.

PREVENTION AND CURE: COMPETENCE

If learned helplessness implies that there is a loss of control over one's life, it may be useful to conceptualize its opposite as mastery over the situation or, in a word, *competence*. When people are subjected to a traumatic event, their bodily reaction is the stress response, with the dominant emotion being fear. This state remains until they learn to control the trauma—they learn a competent behavior—at which time the fear and general stress response dissipates and, as Seligman puts it (1975, p. 54), ". . . gives way to an efficient and nonchalant response." If the traumatic situation is truly uncontrollable, the fear and stress response will also dissipate, giving way to depression and eventually perhaps hopelessness and death. The motivation for competence (White, 1959) has been thwarted.

Cures for any emotional disturbance are always much more difficult and time-consuming than the original learning. Learned helplessness also impairs the operant and cognitive levels of behavior, as we have seen, so the cure will have to at least do the following: (1) produce new behavior that is adaptive to the situation, (2) produce information that is relevant to understanding the situation or predicting the consequences of behavior in that situation, and (3) allow extinction of the fear in the situation.

To cure his dogs of helplessness in the shuttle box, Seligman (1975) had to drag the dogs from one compartment to the next so they could learn there was no shock to fear in the other compartment, and that there was an adaptive behavior that could escape the shock and reduce their fear or depression. The therapy was effective, but in the beginning the whole weight of the dog had to be pulled by the leash. In later trials less and less force was needed, until toward the end a nudge was sufficient and finally, the dog went by itself and never again failed to escape. That's the good news. The bad news is that it took from 25 to 200 draggings.

Prevention or immunization was easier. When Seligman's dogs were first given a series of trials in which they first successfully learned to escape shock, then were exposed to the unescapable shocks, their performance in a subsequent controllable situation was not impaired. The critical factor was that the *first experience was successful*. The competence that was established there could then withstand a period in which the organism had no control. Learned helplessness was prevented.

Many questions arise in applying this idea to humans, not the least of which are some basic problems about how many competence experiences are needed to withstand ten (or twenty or fifty) experiences of uncontrollable outcomes. Future research will surely aid our understanding in this regard. But we do not feel that it is too far-fetched to suggest that Seligman's prevention technique could be profitably adopted by teachers at all levels with no conceivable harm and possibly with great benefit.

Every teacher has encountered students who, as soon as a problem is presented, show signs of confusion, anxiety—often total bewilderment. They seem unable to understand that anything they do or think about can control the situation, analyze the problem, or answer it. They are, as Holt (1964) described them, "answer-grabbers." He goes on to describe some of them (1964, p. 73).

> Monica wants the right answer, yes; but what she wants, first of all, is an answer, any old answer, and she will do almost anything to get some kind of answer. Once she gets it, a large part of the pressure is off.
>
> . . . The strategies of most of these kids have been consistently self-centered, self-protective, aimed above all else at avoiding trouble, embarrassment, punishment, disapproval, or loss of status. This is particularly true of the ones who have had a tough time in school.

Such students have not developed competence and, as a result, have no confidence in their ability to solve a problem. With repeated experiences like this, they may give up trying.

But answer-grabbing and giving up are not the only difficulties helpless students have. Because they see the problem as out of their control, either because it is beyond their ability or the situation militates against them, they take little or no responsibility for whether or not they successfully complete a task (e.g., Dweck and Repucci, 1973). Dweck (1975) capitalized on this idea and provided a long-term training procedure to twelve boys and girls aged 8 to 13, who were identified as showing severe signs of learned helplessness. Her procedure taught half of these students, randomly selected, to take responsibility for their failures and, moreover, to attribute their failure to their own lack of effort. Of course, the tasks and the criteria for success were known to be within the capabilities of the students. When these students were compared to the other half who received 100% success experiences only (i.e., they had no experience with failure or attribution of failure to their own effort), the attribution retraining group coped with subsequent failure experiences much better.

As we shall see in the next chapter, it is important to learn frustration tolerance by not being reinforced for every effort one makes, whether correct or not. Neither should one be exposed to a situation in which every attempt appears to be totally incompetent, particularly in the early stages of a new task. Dweck's (1975) study does not prove superiority of her method over other methods; it does show one way of beginning to convince students that they must develop competence in each new task and assume responsibility for the effort. On the other hand, behavior does not occur in a vacuum. The task difficulty must be appropriate to the current capabilities (entering behavior) of the students so that they can truly develop some competence, if only some small approximation to what will be required later.

If each new lesson in, say, math were approached with the plan of helping each student attain competence, then the cognitive, motivational and emotional components of learning math would be within each student's control. Granted, this is not easy to do and, given some students' past histories, may be impossible. But the emphasis on developing early competence and thereby avoiding the conditions that can lead to learned helplessness may be well worth the effort.

We believe this same approach would be useful in hospitals and nursing homes. Patients should early on be given information about, and as much control as possible over, their treatment. Even if they do not want to know, they should be educated about how to control their own symptoms, what to do under certain circumstances, etc. If this is considered frivolous or too time-consuming by the medical personnel in charge, it may be why we have sayings like, "the operation was a success, but the patient died."

THE INTERACTION OF MOTIONS, EMOTIONS AND COGNITIONS

Learned helplessness provided many examples of the continual interplay among operants (actions and motivations), respondents (emotions) and thoughts (cognitions) about the situations people find themselves in. There is a continual debate in psychology about which comes first—the thought, the emotion, or the action?

To bring clarity to the issue, consider the following common experience. You are walking home at night with a friend when, suddenly as you pass a dark alley, your friend bolts ahead of you running as fast as he can. You, naturally, begin to run too, and later when you are catching your breath together, he asks you why you ran so hard? He ran just as a joke. If you don't hit him on the spot, you may laugh at yourself as the butt of the joke. But why *did* you run? Did you run (operant) because you perceived something (cognition) that made you afraid (respondent)? Did you run (operant), and did the running make your heart pound (respondent) which you then judged to be fear (cognition)? Did you think before you ran?

An early account of the relation among these different levels of behavior came to be known as the James-Lange theory, which in part stated that when we feel afraid, it is because we run away—not conversely. William James (1904) stated that although such an account was probably exaggerated (but not very much), he was certain that the main core of the idea was true. However, he did take a more moderate stance with regard to causality in one of his Talks To Teachers, called "The Gospel of Relaxation" (1904, p. 133):

> Action seems to follow feeling, but really action and feeling go together; and by regulating the action, which is under the more direct control of the will, we can indirectly regulate the feeling which is not.

As in so many other areas, James set the agenda for much research and theorizing to follow decades later. The last part of his statement can be interpreted as a belief that involuntary behaviors such as emotions can be brought under voluntary control—a topic we shall discuss in the next sections. The first phrase of the statement does not need to be changed much to provide the consensus view in the same debate, now removed to the 1980's where the major interest is the relation of thoughts and feelings, with less emphasis on actions. Two of the major figures on somewhat different sides of the debate are R. B. Zajonc and R. S. Lazarus. Despite the evidence and arguments they amass to make their points, they nevertheless agree on the following:[10]

> The full experience of emotion . . . normally includes three fused components: thoughts, action impulses, and somatic disturbances. (Lazarus, 1982, p. 1019)

> In nearly all cases, however, feeling is not free of thought, nor is thought free of feelings. (Zajonc, 1980, p. 154).

We believe that at this stage of our understanding of the relationships among thought, action and feeling—which after all has not changed that much in a century—this consensus position is not only the safest position to take, but also has some surprisingly practical implications. One of these we shall touch on only briefly here, defering fuller discussion until chapter V—namely, the question of attitude change. It is a common complaint of teachers that "there's nothing you can do with that kid because he has a bad attitude." The prescription seems to be: first you change the attitude, then appropriate behavior can follow. First of all, the empirical evidence favors the opposite conclusion: attitude change is best accomplished by changing behavior so that the person has proper experiences (e.g., Bem, 1970). More importantly, if motions, emotions and cognitions are conceptualized as always interacting in an interdependent way, then none of them is primary and all are important. Then a student can be reached via any or all of these modalities or levels of behavior.

Another practical implication has already been mentioned, but deserves repeating. The labels we give to people—primarily cognitive behavior—can never be seen as unrelated to a person's emotions or behaviors. They may arise from the behavior (i.e., Johnny is overly active so we call him hyperactive), but they also can become determiners of behavior in a self-fulfilling prophecy. When we call someone a "victim" of cancer (instead of, say, a client), the person stands a great chance of assuming the emotionally depressed and helpless state of a victim. A similar problem has been identified by Rounds and Hendel (1980) in the diagnostic use of the term "math anxiety." The term often confuses many issues—e.g., the fear of mathematics per se vs. test anxiety vs. the fear of the setting—and when indiscriminately applied to students can condition the students to become anxious in the ways we've described above. These interacting labels and feelings have operant components as well, as when we learn to be hyperactive to get attention, to be math anxious to avoid taking a statistics course, or to be the poor cancer victim to avoid certain responsibilities.[11]

A final implication concerns the bidirectionality of all kinds of learning. Logan (1972, p. 1060) gave the following example.

> Suppose a person is for some reason feeling depressed, guilty, or just sorry for himself. Suppose further that that person then engages in some form of self-reinforcement—perhaps sexual relief, perhaps alcohol, perhaps any way to get a "kick." Regardless, there are two clear messages. The first is that since reinforcement increases the probability of any behavior, the person is more likely to feel depressed, guilty, or sorry for himself in the future. At the same time, the person is equally likely to resurrect those feelings when he engages in

such behaviors. A person who daydreams when feeling lonely will learn to feel lonely when daydreaming. A person who drinks when mad at the world will learn to be mad at the world when drinking. A person who engages in sex when feeling sorry for himself will tend to feel sorry for himself when indulging in sex.

Nothing we do on one level of behavior is separated from other aspects of our behavior. The physiological explanation in the cartoon may be wrong, but the behavioral, emotional and cognitive patterns that arise will tend to repeat. Perhaps we can do no better than in concluding this section, to repeat the advice William James gave to teachers in his talk "The Laws of Habit" (1904, p. 58):

> . . . the great thing in all education is *to make our nervous system our ally instead of our enemy. . . . For this we must make automatic and habitual, as early as possible, as many useful actions as we can,* and as carefully guard against the growing into ways that are likely to be disadvantageous. [Italics in original]

TO KNOW THYSELF: EXPLAINING EMOTIONS

The body's homeostatic reactions, as the last cartoon satirizes, are subject to various interpretations. Many emotional states show a general pattern that is characteristic of excitation of the sympathetic nervous system. However, there are apparently few physiological cues which we humans have come to associate uniquely with particular emotions so that we can reliably discriminate among them. Thus increased heart rate can accompany fear, joy, anger, or sexual excitement. Similar statements can be made about such other physiological measures as blood pressure, stomach contractions, breathing rate or shortness of breath, and perspiration. Polygraph measures of the electrical conductivity of the skin, prominently known in "lie detection," cannot easily discriminate among states of euphoria, anger, or fear. What the polygraph apparently can do—and then anything but perfectly—is detect physiological changes that are likely to be accompanied by emotions. The "lie detector," as Skinner (1953, p. 161) put it, ". . . detects, not dishonesty, but the emotional responses generated when the individual engages in behavior for which he has previously been punished."

Since the polygraph is such an important and popular tool in American society—a television show, "Lie Detector," starring criminal lawyer F. Lee Bailey was even introduced to exploit its popularity—it is worth considering what psychophysiologist and polygraph expert David Lykken had to say about it. In a 1978 paper, he pointed out that (p. 173)

> . . . the same physiological response can have very different meanings, can be associated when different psychological responses, in different individuals. Thus, for example, if two subjects both give the same large GSR [galvanic skin response] in response to a certain question, it may be that one of them is lying—and fearful of being found out—while the other is telling the truth—and fearful or even indignant about being wrongly accused.

Lykken gives a reasoned argument about the uses and abuses to which the polygraph can be put, pointing out, among other things, how its use as a screening device for employees is biased against honest, truthful people. This well-written well-reasoned paper should perhaps be required reading for all people concerned with civil rights. In particular, it is difficult to ignore his concluding comment (p. 190):

> I once believed that the single application in which the lie detector might do more good than harm would be in official criminal investigation. I now withdraw that opinion. In every arena in which the lie test is used, it is apparently abused. It is time for the lie detector to be retired to those same museums where we keep examples of the rack and the Iron Maiden.

Such are the complexities of "getting in touch with our feelings." How *do* we get in touch with emotions? Suppose you were a subject who volunteered for an experiment on the effects of vitamins on vision, and found the following situation. An experimenter meets you at the laboratory and explains that, if you agree to allow it, a vitamin compound, "Suproxin," wil be injected into you. Since he explains that the injection itself is harmless, you agree to participate. He then tells you about some side effects of the Suproxin that you will begin to feel anywhere from 3–5 minutes after the injection. Unknown to you, he either tells you the correct side effects—that is, effects that are known to be caused by the drug—or incorrect ones. Then he leaves the room.

A few minutes later, a physician enters, takes your pulse and gives you the injection. Again, unknown to you at this point, the injection is either a saline-solution placebo, or epinephrine (adrenaline) which is associated in the body's normal state with the flight or fight response. The saline-solution has no physiological effects whatsoever, but epinephrine has the following major effects (of which, at this point, you are either correctly or incorrectly informed): increases in systolic blood pressure, respiration rate, heart rate, muscle and cerebral blood flow, blood sugar and lactic acid.

Finally, the experimenter returns with another person whom he says is another subject in the experiment who, like you, just received an injection of Suproxin. He asks that you wait together for 20-minutes to allow the vitamin to go through the blood stream, following which you'll both have your vision tested. Once more you are being duped, because the other subject is a stooge of the experimenter who now acts out one of two roles. He either becomes euphoric, bouncing around the room, shooting baskets with crumpled paper, etc.; or else he becomes angry, objecting to everything that he's been asked to do, culminating with an early and stormy departure.

The question is, what are you feeling? You received an injection, were told the side effects, are either feeling some real physiological changes or are not (depending on whether you received the drug or the placebo), and then you've just witnessed another person act either euphorically or angrily after taking the drug. Do you simply tune in to your body and feel the effects, or no effects, of the drug?

The answer, like the experiment,[12] is somewhat complicated. Schachter and Singer (1962), who conducted the experiment, found that in situations like these, people are very much affected by cognitive factors in interpreting their emotions. Their theory suggests that an emotional state is a result, first of all, of a physiological arousal. If you have no physiological changes from the drug (e.g., the placebo), you are unlikely to conclude that you are in any particular emotional state. Likewise, if you are in a physiological aroused state and have an adequate explanation for it (e.g., your physician accurately described the symptoms that you now feel), you have no need to consider that you are in any particular emotional state.

However, if you find yourself in a physiological arousal state but have no immediate explanation (e.g., you received a drug, but you were not informed, or were misinformed, about its effects), then you are likely to describe your feelings according to the environmental information you have available to you. Other people's reactions to the drug can provide some of that information and, therefore, you will be likely to interpret your feelings as being like them. If they are acting angrily, you may "feel" angry; if they are acting euphoric, you may "feel" euphoric. As Schachter and Singer described it (1962, p. 380),

> . . . an emotional state may be considered a function of a state of physiological arousal and of a cognition appropriate to this state of arousal. The cognition, in a sense, exerts a steering function. Cognitions arising from the immediate situation as interpreted by past experience provide the framework within which one understands and labels his feelings. It is the cognition which determines whether the state of physiological arousal will be labeled as "anger," "joy," "fear," or whatever.

Similar arguments have been made of our self-perceptions of the effects of alcohol, marijuana, and other drugs (e.g., Bem, 1970). The drug may be having an effect, but whether the experience is labeled a "good trip" or a bad one, is more a function of the social situation than of the drug itself. To take another example, the voluntary production of alpha waves in the brain—the so-called "alpha experience" of yoga and other relaxed meditative states—was considered to be a physiologically naturally pleasant state. But recent research has found that whether the alpha rhythms of the brain are interpreted as pleasant, neutral, or unpleasant is more a function of instructions and situational expectations than of the physiology itself (e.g., Katkin, Fitzgerald and Shapiro, 1978).

Schachter and his colleagues did a number of related studies in order to validate their theory. One of them concerned tolerance to pain (Nisbett and Schachter, 1966). Subjects were administered a pill named—you guessed it—Suproxin, which was said to have some effects on skin sensitivity. In this study all subjects received the same pill, a placebo, but half were told the pill produced side effects of hand tremors, palpitations, increased breathing, and butterflies in the stomach. These effects were actually effects they would later feel, but caused by shocks to the hand. The other subjects were misinformed

about the pill's side effects (i.e., the effects were not likely to be perceived). Following this all subjects received shocks.

Again, the study was more complex than described here, with parallel results to the previous study. Subjects who attributed the symptoms they experienced to the pill tolerated more shock and reported experiencing less pain than those who attributed those same symptoms to the shock itself.

What, then, does it take to "get in touch with one's feelings"? Certainly more than just talking about them to a friend or therapist, though that may not hurt. Certainly, more than meditating or focusing your attention on a particular organ or system of the body, though that may be a start. Most of all, it takes understanding what the environmental situation is and how it is reinforcing or punishing you, and what cognitive information you are receiving from it. Knowing ourselves, from an emotional standpoint, means knowing our history and our current situation, as well as our physiological arousal state.

VOLUNTARY CONTROL OVER INVOLUNTARY BEHAVIORS

Can you wiggle your ears without raising your brow? Can you wiggle one ear at a time? Can you contract just the muscle directly behind the ear? Most people cannot. Furthermore, if asked to will themselves to do so, they still cannot. Because of the complete inability of most persons to contract the muscles around the ear, particularly the retrahens muscle behind the ear, a remarkable experiment was reported in 1901 by J. H. Bair, an experiment that Yates (1980) describes as one of the important precursors of the field that has come to be known as biofeedback.

Bair found that, although no subjects could contract this retrahens muscle on their own, all of them could learn to control the muscle by the following procedure. An ingenious helmet was contrived which connected to the three muscles around the ear, through which an electrical current could pass to stimulate a reflexive contraction of the muscle, and by which the flexion of the muscle could be recorded on paper. First, the retrahens muscle was contracted by the current once per second for ten to thirty times, while the subject remained passive. In the second phase, the subject was asked to help the current contract the muscle. Next, subjects were to attempt to prevent the current from contracting the muscle. Finally, subjects tried to contract the muscle voluntarily without any assistance or counter-assistance from the current. Bair described his results systematically, from the beginning stages of total lack of ability to contract the muscle and general confusion about how to accomplish it, to the final stages of maximum contractions of the muscle without using any other muscle to mediate the behavior.

But who cares about wiggling the ears except rabbits and comedians? We do, because as Bair (1901) argued, there is no reason to believe that the physiological processes involved in learning to control the movements of the ear are not the same as learning to control any other movement—e.g., that of the hand or of an internal organ.

Bair was clearly ahead of his time[13] in choosing to study the voluntary control over a muscle that was, at least for most persons, never used voluntarily. His methodology was also unique in using an electrical stimulation to call attention to the muscle through its involuntary, reflexive reaction to the electrical current. Thus, his subjects did indeed seem to be bringing an involuntary reaction under voluntary control.

Yet, sixty years later Kimble (1961) concluded that Bair's study, and others like it had *not* conclusively demonstrated that involuntary reactions could be brought under voluntary control. His influential conclusion (Blanchard and Epstein, 1978, called it a "principal impetus" to the development of the field) was based on a strict interpretation of direct operant conditioning of the respondent behavior in question (without any intermediary effects). Examples of such confounding mediating effects were increasing your breathing rate to control the heart rate, relaxing muscles to decrease blood pressure or, as we mentioned earlier, tensing your brow to twitch your ears. If these involuntary behaviors were controlled by such indirect means, Kimble argued, it could not be concluded that they had been conditioned. Controlled, yes; conditioned, no. In Kimble's words (1961, p. 102).

> Many responses, as we have already seen, are producible in two or more physiological ways, one of which is involuntary, the other voluntary. Descriptions of the Yoga procedures which provide the most impressive

41

examples of voluntary control over involuntary responses suggest that the method makes use of this fact, and that the involuntary responses are controlled indirectly through skeletal mechanisms.

We mention this issue because it is still being debated today, with an important difference. In the years that followed, the field of biofeedback was born and concern became more directed to the practical issues and less to issues of theoretical purity. Thus it is safe to say that today most researchers and practitioners would say that the important thing is to help people learn to *control* their involuntary behaviors, however they can learn to do it. It doesn't matter if their method is "pure, direct conditioning" of the involuntary behaviors or by impure, indirect, skeletal muscles controlled by cognitive means (e.g., Katkin, and Murray, 1968; Katkin et al., 1969). Our concern is practical, of course, so we turn now to biofeedback—its methods and its uses.[14]

BIOFEEDBACK

DESCRIPTION

Biofeedback is probably best defined as a process whereby physiological functions not ordinarily under voluntary control or in our awareness—or perhaps usually in control but regulation has been disrupted—are mirrored back to us, usually by instrumentation, to allow those functions to be brought under voluntary control (e.g., Blanchard and Epstein, 1978; Fuller, 1977).

The physiological functions of interest usually fall into four categories: (1) muscle tension, as might occur in tension headaches; (2) arousal or anxieties, as might occur in phobias, stuttering or asthmatic attacks; (3) brain wave patterns, as might be of interest in solving disorders of attention or insomnia; and (4) blood flow, which might be of concern to people with high blood pressure, migraine headaches, and some sexual disorders.

The instrumentation of biofeedback can be as simple as a common thermometer for measuring temperature, or as complex as electro-encephalographs (EEGs), electromyographs (EMGs), or polygraphs for measuring brain waves, muscle tension, or changes in skin perspiration, respectively. Because people are not normally aware of their muscle tension, brain waves or peristaltic actions in their stomachs, for example, instruments can monitor what is happening in these systems. Then when properly amplified and played back, the individual can see or hear his bodily functions. Thus organs and muscles of which individuals were previously unaware, come into their awareness and can then be brought under control. Or, in Lang's (1970) turn of the phrase, the individual learns "to play the internal organs."

It should be noted that instrumentation is not specifically necessary to learn control over bodily functions. Bladder and sphincter control are cases in point. Most of us learn to control these reflexive functions as toddlers without instrumentation and usually with no awareness of *how* we learned. We do not know the process by which we control our urination any more than the processes by which we can sing on pitch or throw a ball at a target, all processes which require feedback from our biological systems in order to allow voluntary control. What makes biofeedback different, then, is only that it provides systematic approaches to dealing with disorders of our psychophysiology, bringing involuntary or unconscious processes to our attention so that we can control them for our therapeutic or preventive benefit. Some examples of this follow.

A CASE OF PHANTOM LIMB PAIN

Angela, a press operator and union president, lost two fingers of her right hand in an industrial accident. Despite attempts to save her hand, surgeons had to amputate it and subsequently, due to medical complications, amputated her forearm as well. Two years later, because of intense pain, she had a sympathectomy operation, but the chronic pain in her stump continued and interfered with her being fitted for a prosthesis. After five years of seemingly trying everything, she was seen by DeRoo (1982) complaining of a perception of pain in the missing limb, as well as heaviness, coldness, cramping, and episodes of burning or shooting pains and periods of numbness.

The twice-weekly treatment sessions combined two types of biofeedback instrumentation and relaxation training. The first biofeedback sessions concentrated on the muscle tension in both upper arms and shoulders, attaching electrodes to those sites connected to the electromyograph (EMG). Using feedback from the EMG, Angela was able to reduce her muscle tension to an acceptably relaxed level. Next, thermal biofeedback was used to allow her to increase the temperature and, consequently, the circulation in her stump.

Concomitantly, Angela was given relaxation training, breathing and imagery practice, and exercises which she could do at home along with a cassette tape. She also regularly recorded on a chart the intensity of her pain and the occasions on which she took medication and did her "homework."

DeRoo (1982) reported that after 22 biofeedback and additional "homework" sessions, Angela reported being pain free for as long as eight hours at a time, reducing her medication to "virtually nothing during the day and only two tablets (Tylenol and codeine) at night." The pain reduction was sufficient to allow her to be fitted for and become facile with a prosthetic claw. At the time of the report, she was looking forward to being fitted with a more aesthetic prosthesis with a longer-range prospect of returning to her job.

A CASE OF MIGRAINE HEADACHE

Werder (1978) described four similar cases of childhood migraine headaches and treatment by use of temperature regulation. The oldest of the children, a seventeen year-old identified as J, had been having migraine headaches since age 6. These headaches occurred about once a week and lasted up to 8 hours. Her treatment was 1–2 Darvocet–N 100 medications.

43

A temperature sensor was taped to the right index finger and a visual display of the hand temperature was provided as biofeedback. Treatment consisted of learning to increase the temperature in her hand—a standard migraine treatment which dilates the blood vessels of the hand.[15]

J was also taught relaxation through body awareness and breathing exercises and so-called autogenic phrases (self-instructions to relax). She was seen on five successive days for 90-minute treatments and was also permitted to take the temperature trainer home for five days to practice.

By the fourth day of 90-minute intensive training J was able to raise her hand temperature from 2 to 5° within three minutes and she was able to report the increase. She also had a successful encounter with a headache, aborting it by using the relaxation-temperature control technique. A follow-up two-years later revealed that "only one severe migraine" had occurred during this period. She had continued to practice the procedures learned during treatment.

A CASE OF HYPERACTIVITY

Steven was 6–1/2 years old when referred to a Learning Disability Center for treatment of "extreme hyperactivity" (Braud, Lupin and Braud, 1975). He had not been taking any drugs. After receiving the standard battery of tests given at the session, split up over three days because of his hyperactive, distractible behaviors, including emotional outbursts and crying, it was decided to try EMG biofeedback training.

Steven came to the Center twice a week for three weeks and then once weekly for five additional weeks. While there, the activity of his frontalis muscle (the forehead) was monitored, amplified and fed back to him. When the muscle was too tense—indicating a high level of general physical or mental activity—a tone sounded. When the muscle was relaxed to a pre-determined relaxation level, there was no tone. Steven was instructed to "keep the tone off" by becoming as still and relaxed as possible. During these training sessions, he was also observed and rated on a 10-point scale for muscular activity, for tension, and for emotionality. Following the eighth treatment session, Steven's teacher and mother were asked to assure that he practice this technique at home and school, particularly if he became upset or overactive.

Braud et al. (1975) report dramatic decreases in Steven's frontalis tension both within training sessions (i.e., the difference between the tension in his muscle when he came to the clinic and after treatment) and between sessions (i.e., from week to week). Ratings of activity, tension and emotionality decreased over treatment sessions, and were maintained in a follow-up session seven months later. His teacher and parents also reported marked improvement in his behavior and his standardized test scores even improved (interpreted by the authors as indicating that his previous scores had been depressed by his poor attention and hyperactivity).

44

Steven also showed a "dramatic change in confidence and self-concept" along with corresponding decreases in emotionality and frustration. Characteristic comments from Steven in the early sessions were, "I can't sit still; I try but I can't." These changed to, "I think I can do this; I am doing good" over the middle sessions. By the eleventh session he said, "I can do this and I don't need any help." Braud et al. (1975, p. 424) point out that this is a welcome side effect of this training, since drugs (which are the usual treatment for hyperactive children) may improve attention span and reduce overactivity, but do not usually affect these other emotional levels of behavior.

A CASE OF CEREBRAL PALSY

Harry[16] was a typical athetoid cerebral-palsied child, ten-years old, whose movements were grossly uncoordinated, exaggerated, jerky and seemingly random and purposeless. His parents and he believed that his condition was a result of damage to the motor areas of the brain which did not allow messages from the cerebral cortex to arrive at the appropriate muscles in the normal manner required for coordinated movement. He was seen by Harris, Spelman and Hymer (1974) because they had developed a procedure that might change all that.

Based on a new theory of cerebral palsy (Harris, 1971), Harry was treated as though his athetoid movements were a result of a faulty monitoring system in knowing where the muscles are at any time. This faulty proprioceptive feedback (roughly like a faulty thermostat in monitoring heat in the house) makes it difficult to move the muscles smoothly (to continue the heating analogy, so that the house is either too hot or too cold). Harris et al. (1974) developed, therefore, a sensory monitoring system to provide the feedback that was naturally lacking.

Harry was first connected to the head control device, which is a helmet with electronic connections to an auditory display monitor. Thus any time the head is tilted, front to back or side to side, a series of clicks is heard. The further it tilts, the more clicks. The child was told to keep the clicking from occurring. Thirty minutes of therapy per day was given on this device three times weekly for several months.

In the early baseline stages of the study, graphs of Harry's movements showed continual large movements. After two months, however, he had gained considerable head stability. His ability to hold a fixed posture of the head increased from a few seconds to over five minutes. And this was accompanied by a strengthening of the neck muscles.

Similar results were then obtained using a limb position monitor. The initial jerking movements gave way to more uniform, smooth movements. After two months of treatment, Harry was able ". . .to make either large- or small-scale movements with a minimum of tremor, could hold any position assumed, and could make repetitive movements of almost identical amplitude and time course" (Harris et al., 1974).

These results have generalized in part beyond the clinical laboratory. Thus Harry was able to hold a cane steady enough to touch the clinician's nose with it repeatedly. Most importantly, he has progressed far enough to begin walking by crutches instead of with a rolling walker.

BENEFITS OF BIOFEEDBACK

As this wide variety of cases show, there are good therapeutic reasons for being optimistic about biofeedback and its effects on difficult, but common human problems. Several advantages accrue from biofeedback types of approaches to such problems. First, we learn something about our bodies—how our motions, emotions and cognitions interact and interdepend. This is something that can indeed be taught to normal people in schools, with both students and teachers learning something (e.g. Englehart, 1978). Children seem to learn these techniques easily, probably more easily than adults (e.g., Kater and Spires, 1975; Loughry-Machado and Suter, 1979), possibly because they have not yet rigidified their thinking about mind vs. body and possibly because they view the machinery as a challenge instead of a threat.

A second advantage of biofeedback is that it may contribute to reconceptualizing various disorders from being primarily "medical problems" to a more holistic approach. It is important to realize that, just as it is natural for bodily structures and functions to get old and wear out from use and abuse, it is also natural for the body to repair itself, or at least to bring itself to some homeostatic balance. As we saw in the case study of cerebral palsy, a reconceptualization of the problem and its solution is possible once we realize that such individuals are capable of controlling their muscles if proper feedback can be given. Moreover, as we learn more about voluntary control of single motor units,[17] there may be reason for much optimism that many handicapping conditions can be overcome. Similar comments may be made about controlling pain (e.g., Liebenskind and Paul, 1977).

Third, and most important from our standpoint, biofeedback provides the advantage of allowing individuals to gain competence (and confidence) in controlling their own psychophysiology. As was noted in the hyperactive child, personal control over behavior has positive emotional and other effects that cannot accrue from drug control, even if the drug had equivalent effects on the overactivity. When children are on drugs, the effects are attributed to the drug and a psychological dependency is established. More will be said on drug effects in later chapters (for example, psychological dependency due to negative reinforcement effects in Chapter III); meanwhile, we have already discovered the importance of control in avoiding helplessness and, generally, in the human need for competence. The panic is taken out of stressful or painful situations when we know there is something we personally can do to control it.

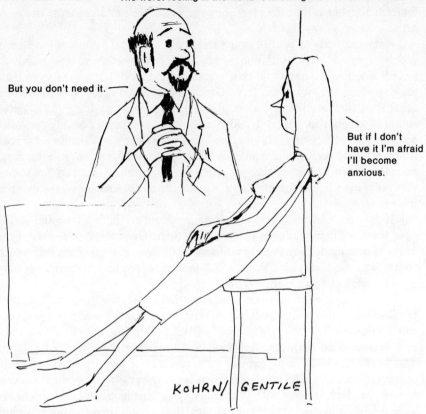

Perhaps a nine-year-old hyperactive boy who was undergoing biofeedback training summarized the point best (in Ross and Ross, 1982, p. 275):

> What I would like most of everthing is millions of days just like yesterday. . . . I could tell I'd be extra good all through church, not like last Sunday, and I was. Everytime I started to wriggle I just said, "Now, relax, so the train goes slow,[18] you dummy" and when it got to people going up for communion when I usually start getting in trouble, I just kept having train-talks to myself and after church my mom gave me a special smile and said, "I was *really* proud of you today, Stu," and my dad said, "That goes for me too, son," and I had this real good feeling. I never had that good a day before in my whole life.

LIMITATIONS OF BIOFEEDBACK

With all of the above going for it, why do authors write of biofeedback's "promise as yet unfulfilled" (e.g., Blanchard and Young, 1973; Yates, 1980) or warn "Don't hold the party yet" (Melzack, 1975)? There seem to us two main issues left unresolved: (1) too much is claimed for biofeedback and similar voluntary control processes, much of it unverifiable at present; and (2) the

47

active therapeutic ingredient in the training may, in many cases, not be the biofeedback, but rather the relaxation response. Let's address these issues in turn.

Amazing feats of control over various physiological functions have been widely reported. Yoga practitioners account for many of these reports, which include stopping the heart and producing temperature differences of more than ten degrees in the two hands (e.g., Green and Green, 1977, give an extended account of their studies of Swami Rama). An account by Lang (1970) presumes to account for Harry Houdini's ability to escape by opening padlocks when he had no key. In fact, Houdini had a key safely concealed in his throat which he could regurgitate when not being observed. To accomplish this feat, he had to learn to control the gag reflex which naturally occurs when something is caught in the throat. This trick may be as remarkable as the escapes themselves.

If only one-tenth of these extraordinary feats are in fact true and verifiable, there is still much for us to learn from them. One must be quite skeptical of the claims made, however, because many of them are not replicable under controlled conditions (e.g., Yates, 1980) or may indeed be magic tricks or outright fraudulent (e.g., Hall, 1975).[19]

Turning to the second issue—namely, what causes the gains made in biofeedback—we find a complicated picture. Consider the complex syndrome called migraine headache. Migraine headache often (though not always) begins with a period of intense constriction of the external arteries of the head. This later changes to an extreme dilation of the same arteries which, because of the pressure this puts on the surrounding pain-sensitive tissue, causes this terrible headache (along with such other symptoms as nausea). If the headache is caused by swelling of the arteries, then appropriate treatment would seem to be constriction of these arteries. But the Werder (1978) and Sargent et al. (1973) procedures act by warming the hands, which dilates the blood vessels in the hands. If that procedure is to work, dilation of the arteries in the hand must somehow work to constrict the arteries in the head. If that is what happens, the mechanism for it is unknown (Blanchard and Epstein, 1978).

But why not simply learn to constrict the external arteries of the head by biofeedback? Friar and Beatty (1976) taught migraine sufferers to do just that in a comparison of biofeedback control of both external cranial arteries and those of the finger. When the cranial arteries were constricted by biofeedback control, subjects reported fewer headache symptoms—in addition, their finger arteries were constricted. This result is contrary to the practice and results we have seen, but makes more theoretical sense in view of what is known about the vascular system.

The above description is quite brief and necessarily oversimplifies the research and arguments based on it. The interested reader should begin with the original research reports cited, as well as Blanchard and Epstein (1978) and Yates (1980). For our purposes, the problems are sufficient to conclude that all is not yet well in understanding how the biofeedback works. That suggests that placebo effects or other factors may be operating.

These contradictory findings are reminiscent of a problem with studies of drugs on hyperactive children. It seems that for some children, depressant drugs work to reduce their hyperactivity; however, for others, stimulants serve the same function (e.g., Juliano and Gentile, 1974). This should alert us to a problem of diagnosis—there may be at least two types of hyperactive children—or problems of reliability and validity of treatment procedures. These same difficulties remain in biofeedback studies of hyperactive children. Perhaps this is the reason that, despite the very promising results of Braud et al. (1975), reviewers are cautiously optimistic at best (e.g., Barkley, 1982; Cobb and Evans, 1981; Ray, Raczynski, Rogers, and Kimball, 1979; and Ross and Ross, 1982).

All of the above reviewers, as well as Blanchard and Epstein (1978), Miller (1978) and Yates (1980), have concluded that the main feature in the positive biofeedback results may well be relaxation. In 1978 Braud himself reported a comparison study of a relaxation technique with biofeedback (control via the EMG of the forehead muscle) with hyperactive children, and concluded that except for reduction of tension in the forehead muscle, the EMG group was no better than the relaxation group in ratings of behavior. Both the biofeedback and relaxation groups were significantly improved over a control group. Braud (1978, p. 86) argued further that this is an important finding since ". . .in the long run, progressive relaxation training is easier, less expensive, and more practical."

Indeed it is since it needs no equipment. This is not to say that biofeedback techniques and equipment cannot be helpful in learning to relax, or to learn to attend to and later to control certain muscle groups or bodily functions. There seems to be no doubt that they can. But as Katkin et al. (1978, p. 286) concluded, the research issues are many and varied:

> Biofeedback may provide future generations with important new weapons against disease. The current state of evidence neither supports nor denies that hope. There are many tough questions yet to be asked and no shortcuts to meaningful answers.

Meanwhile, it is interesting—is it not?—that relaxation training of one form or another was a major ingredient in three of the four case studies we described (the exception being cerebral palsy). There is an old joke about the chemist who mixed gin and tonic and got drunk; then he mixed scotch and tonic and got drunk; finally he tried bourbon and tonic and got drunk. Since the common ingredient was tonic, he concluded that tonic makes you drunk. We'll try not to draw the same conclusion just yet with regard to relaxation as the common ingredient in successful biofeedback cases, but it nevertheless deserves to be considered in its own right.

RELAXATION AND COUNTERCONDITIONING

MEDITATIVELY

Help me find the rest I need when I am feeling low.

In this hec-tic life we lead we ought to move more slow.

some-time ev-'ry day------we ought to hes - i -tate,

slow-ing down our pace------to let us med - i - tate

Help me find the rest I need when I am feel-ing Low.

Give me time to rest and think and give me time to grow.

RELAXATION TECHNIQUES

If your purpose in reading this book is to better understand psychological principles, then you are probably not feeling very tense at this point. If your purpose is to learn enough to pass a test that your instructor has scheduled for you, then a little relaxation right now may be useful. Set aside some extra time, say 10–15 minutes, and actually go through the following exercises with us.

First, find a quiet place, relatively free of distractions. Music can be playing, but it must be quiet, gentle music without heavy rhythm.

Second, get in a comfortable position (Note: stay out of positions like the lotus position unless you are well-practiced at it; otherwise it will provide more instead of less tension).

Third, clench your right fist, tighter and tighter so that you can feel the tension. Become aware of each muscle that becomes tense. Now let go. Repeat this tension-relaxation sequence several times.

Fourth, do the same with your left fist, tensing and relaxing in sequence. Then with both hands at the same time.

Fifth, bend your elbows and tense your biceps and follow the same procedure. Then repeat the previous.

Sixth, tense your forehead and relax it in sequence. Move on to the rest of the head muscles one at a time: your eyes, your jaw, your lips, your tongue.

Seventh, press your head back as far as possible, observing the tension in your neck. Roll your head right and left. Then let go. Press it forward to your chest and then let go. Repeat these sequences several times.

Eighth, pull your shoulders up and repeat the tension-relaxation sequence.

Ninth, breathe in deeply and hold it noticing which muscles become tense. Then breathe out and force the air all the way out and hold it. Then let go and repeat several times.

Tenth, tighten the stomach and let go, repeating the same procedure as above.

Next, follow the same procedures of tensing and letting go with the following muscle groups:

11. your back (arch it, focusing attention on the lower back);
12. your buttocks;
13. your thighs;
14. your knees and calves;
15. your feet and toes.

Finally, repeat the procedure with the following muscles as groups:

16. hands and arms;
17. head, face and shoulders;
18. chest, stomach and back;
19. buttocks, legs and feet;
20. deep breathing.

How do you feel? If you actually performed the motions and your experience is like most people, you feel as if much tension has been drained from you, similar to having had a massage. The procedure is adapted from Jacobsen's *Progressive Relaxation* (1938), which is now a widely used system of teaching people to relax.

It may seem strange to need to *teach* people to relax, since it is often taken for granted that we know how. Even in the otherwise helpful manual entitled

The Relaxation and Stress Reduction Workbook, the authors (Davis, Eshelman and McKay, 1980) slip and give step one of progressive relaxation as "Get in a comfortable position and relax" (p. 24). If you could relax, you wouldn't need the exercise. In fact, few people are able to relax very completely without extended practice. Often this is because, as we saw earlier, a state of rapanoia exists when someone says, "relax," and our bodies react to this. Surprisingly to many, it is even possible to sleep tensely; thus relaxation exercises such as the above can help people drain tension from their muscles and get a more restful sleep.

Other relaxation procedures use imagery. One widely used procedure in biofeedback (e.g., Green and Green's, 1977, procedure) is autogenic training (e.g., Luthe, 1969). This procedure uses a series of verbal suggestions or images to produce a relaxed state. For example, you might say to yourself, or listen to a tape in which the speaker says, slowly, with repetitions and with long pauses between sentences, the following:

My right arm is heavy. . . . My left arm is heavy . . .
Both arms are heavy. . . . My right leg is heavy . . .
etc.

If a sensation of relaxation and "heaviness" is not achieved, imagery could be added: you might imagine yourself with weights attached to your arms, or think of your arms made of concrete slowly sinking into a bog.

The differences between the states of relaxation that can be achieved by the progressive relaxation and autogenic training procedures are apparently not very great, though the latter uses a more cognitive approach. The former may therefore be more appropriate for people who are not as aware of their bodies, or are beginners or younger children (e.g., Fuller, 1977).

There also appear to be few differences in the states of relaxation achieved through these methods and such other methods as self-hypnosis or meditation (e.g., Davis et al., 1980), though the means to achieving the relaxed state may differ. Meditation and self-hypnosis use methods to focus attention, to narrow the range of experiences in your awareness through repetitious movements like pendulums, mantras, affirmations or decrees, and so forth. The similarity between these approaches and those described above is most striking (see also Mikulas, 1981, for some other interesting similarities). Of course, as our daily experiences and the introductory song (Gentile, 1977) suggest, music can also provide a means for achieving relaxed states.

SYSTEMATIC DESENSITIZATION AND COUNTERCONDITIONING

It is a small step from learning how to relax to using your relaxation skill as a therapeutic aid to reduce anxieties. Joseph Wolpe (e.g., 1969) did just that in a procedure he called systematic desensitization. He assumed, first of all, that not all aspects of an anxiety-producing situation are equally threatening, but that there is a hierarchy of stimuli involved in the anxiety response and they have to be identified. Treatment then consists of ". . . the breaking down of neurotic anxiety-response habits in piecemeal fashion" (p. 91). To do that, he first makes a list of all the aspects of the target situation and ranks them in their order of anxiety-production, from most to least. Then he uses progressive relaxation or another relaxation technique to reduce the anxiety to each stimulus situation in turn, beginning with the least anxiety-producing stimulus and working over days or weeks to the most feared object or situation.

Take test anxiety.[20] Wolpe reports the case of C, a 24-year-old art student who reported being anxious when she had to take tests. When she was asked to rate which of several situations made her most anxious, the following list occurred from most-to-least-anxiety-producing (summarized and abridged from Wolpe, 1969, pp. 117–118):

1. Going to the university the day of the test;
2. Answering the questions on the test;
3. Waiting outside the test room;
4. Waiting as the exam papers were being distributed;
5. The night before the test;
6. The day before;
7. Two days before;
   •
   •
   •
14. A month before the test.

Once the hierarchy has been established, the anxiety is counteracted by relaxation. Clients are helped into a relaxed state. While in it, they are told to raise only their right index finger if they feel any anxiety. Then the therapist describes scenes and asks the clients to place themselves in them and monitor how they are feeling. The scene might begin with,

It's a beautiful fall day. . . . The sun is shining . . . You are sitting on the steps of the library at the university. . . . Many people are passing by. . . . You have a book open on your lap. . . . It is one month before your English exam. . . .

If at this point C raised her finger, the therapist would go back to describing relaxing things and reintroduce the "one month again" later. When they were able to get beyond the month, they would move up to the next point, always stopping and retracing imaginal steps whenever the client felt anxious. In this way, the relaxation counteracts the anxiety: the client is being systematically desensitized to the feared object or situation.

Eventually you reach the point in the hierarchy that is the most anxiety-producing and deal with it in the same way. Finally the real-life situation is encountered and the client uses the relaxation skills to counter the anxiety. Wolpe reports that C's test anxiety (along with some other anxieties not described here) were eliminated in 17 desensitization sessions with generalization occurring to the real situations, and her examinations were passed four months later without anxiety.

Wolpe argued that the efficacy of this procedure depended in large measure on the fact that the anxiety-producing events were presented in weak form. Thus the anxiety was never allowed to occur in its full-blown state. The relaxation state was therefore able to be *counter-conditioned* to the same stimuli. In other words, where the test used to be a CS for anxiety, it was now being counter-conditioned by being paired with a relaxation response to be a CS for feeling relaxed and all right.

There is, in fact, some evidence that counter-conditioning is the mechanism by which such anxieties are reduced or eliminated by systematic desensitization (e.g., Bandura, 1969; Davison, 1968; Krasner, 1971), though relaxation is not the only way of achieving this. M. C. Jones (1924) was probably the first researcher to demonstrate counter-conditioning of fears. She associated the feared object with what she called a "craving-object" by introducing the feared CS while a child was eating candy. This was one of only two methods for removing fear responses that met with "unqualified success" in her study (the other was the "method of social imitation").

One of the advantages of the relaxation/desensitization techniques are their adaptability to settings other than clinics and psychotherapists' offices. For example, a 6-1/2 year-old-boy was treated for being too anxious to speak or read aloud in front of his special education classmates by working through a systematic desensitization hierarchy (Kravetz and Forness, 1971). A five-year-five-month old girl was treated in her Head Start classroom for fear of going to the toilet alone (McNamara, 1968).

Another advantage of the relaxation/desensitization approach is its adaptability to group settings, particularly classrooms. For groups a standard hierarchy must be developed out of the situations feared by most of the members of the group. The rankings then come out to be a composite of the anxieties, and no two persons in the group are likely to fear the items in the list in the same rank order. Nevertheless successful results have been reported in reducing test anxiety by Kondas (1967) and Barabasz (1973), among others (Morris and Kratochwill, 1983, provide other evidence). By no means are all of the results in on such techniques. The studies in some cases have less than clear-cut results, have tested usually small numbers of children, and often have viable alternative interpretations of the results. The procedures are interesting, nevertheless, and suggestive of ways that teachers can deal with the "affective domain" in their own classrooms. We shall return to this point at the end of the chapter.

OTHER COUNTER-CONDITIONING TECHNIQUES

Continual Presentation of the CS

Some therapeutic techniques might best fall under the general heading "Making Things Better By Making Them Worse" to quote the title of a popular psychotherapy book (Fay, 1978).

A method called *flooding* is similar to the bronco-busting technique: the CS is presented for a long enough period that the organism eventually becomes weary of continued escape attempts, and learns that there is no longer anything to fear. An experimental study (Polin, 1959) showing the efficacy of the procedure trained animals to fear a buzzer by avoidance conditioning; that is, they had to jump a hurdle within a certain time to avoid shock. Then an extinction period was begun in which shock would not follow the buzzer. One third of the subjects had a barrier placed so they could not jump while the buzzer sounded. Another third, the flooding group, could do anything they wished but the buzzer stayed on for 100-sec. continuously. The final third of the subjects, in contrast, just rested. The flooding group extinguished their fear to the buzzer CS the fastest and it lasted the longest.

In therapeutic applications of flooding, people are surrounded by the feared object. For example, little Albert might be totally surrounded by his feared furry objects. A child who is afraid of water might be held in a swimming pool until he stops struggling. The point is that fearful behavior uses up a tremendous amount of energy and eventually it will become fatigued and the tension will be gone. If it is fatigued in the presence of the CS, the fear will be replaced by relaxation.

Some imaginal versions of this idea have also been used in therapy in which the clients are asked to imagine being inundated by the feared object. If you fear rats, for instance, you are asked to imagine two or three of them climbing all over you and nothing you do can shake them off. In an extreme version of this idea called *implosion* (Stampfl and Levis, 1967), the clients are given massive exposure to quite extreme visual images, and asked to lose themselves in the role they are playing. The reasoning behind this (based on a paper by Solomon, Kamin and Wynne, 1953) is that extinction of an emotional response is best accomplished by arranging that an extremely intense emotional response occurs in the presence of the CS, thereby reinstating the conditions that presumably existed when the CS was paired with the US in real life. The non-occurrence of the US will cause a large decrement in the emotional response by extinction.[21]

Persons who fear blood, for example, might be presented in therapy with the image of coming upon a massacre in which everywhere they look are mangled bodies, bloody stumps, and so forth. And the blood gets on their own hands and clothes and won't come off. Such scenes are presented over and over with embellishments until emotional reactions cease, on the logic that if you've lived in a septic tank, you'll no longer fear the dirt in a wastebasket (e.g., Bandura, 1969).

As some reviewers have pointed out, however, the flooding therapies—and particularly the extreme imageries of implosive therapy—must be used with caution, if they are to be used at all (e.g., Bandura, 1969; Morris and Kratochwill, 1983). There is a very considerable distinction that should be drawn, as Bandura pointed out (p. 404),

Why does Dad keep yelling and yelling at Mom? She just ignores him anyway.

I think it's a kind of psychotherapy called flooding or implosion.

KOHRN/GENTILE

. . . between exposing people repeatedly to a fearsome collection of rodents without any adverse effects and depicting them eating human flesh. Some of the portrayed consequences may never have occurred to phobic subjects and could establish, at least temporarily, a new basis of fearful self-arousal.

With that caveat, there are obvious benefits of *in vivo* presentations of feared CSs that may initially overwhelm us, but through continuous exposure, we learn to get past them. Many people have revulsions to disabled people, cancer patients, or old people in nursing homes. Perhaps the simplest and most effective way to counter-condition these fears and attitudes is through direct and continuous exposure. By doing volunteer work in a nursing home or cancer hospital, working directly with the patients and getting to know them, fear will be replaced by empathy or love. Mainstreaming disabled children can do the same for the average children—that is, those whose disabilities are not physical, but emotional (if a disabled person is a CS for their own anxiety).

Massed Performance of Unwanted Behavior

Flooding and implosion are based on the continual presentation of the CS. The counterpart approach to that is to elicit the unwanted response in a continual fashion. To stop smoking, for example, one might smoke a whole pack at a time. If one cigarette is pleasant, a whole pack of cigarettes one after another is anything but pleasant.

A child we knew well, to take a different example, was sneaking matches out of the house when he was three or four years old. Fascinated by them, he would light them and throw them so he wouldn't get burned. One day his father caught him at it and told him that it was all right if he struck matches, but he would have to strike all of them. He then brought him several packs of matches and would not allow him to stop until he had struck every one. Of course, long before he reached the end he was tired of this behavior, and the emotional attraction matches had for him had turned instead to being, at best, boring.

Other therapeutic uses on which this idea has been used are to eliminate involuntary tics and speech mannerisms. Head-jerking or eye-blink tics might be treated by having the client voluntarily repeat the movement over and over in front of a mirror for five or ten minutes at a time, several times a day. Some speech impediments or annoying mannerisms, such as saying "aah" or "you know," can sometimes be profitably treated this way.

As with other therapies, these techniques do not always work and when they work, it is often not clear why. Positive results may be due to reaction fatigue, relaxation, increased self-control, or some combination of the above.

Self-Control Approaches

A very common and yet severe problem for many families is children's fear of the dark. Severe fears of the dark are often quite disruptive of the home, with exasperated parents sometimes telling the children, "relax, there is nothing to fear," and sometimes resorting to warning them to stay in the room or suffer dire consequences. Night lights may avoid the problem, but do not extinguish the fear.

A direct counter-conditioning technique to reduce fear of the dark is based on *self-control training,* in which both the family and fearful children are included. The children are taught to counteract their anxiety by a three-pronged approach that includes relaxation, imagining a pleasant scene, and saying such special words as, "I am brave. I can take care of myself alone and in the dark" (e.g., Graziano and Mooney, 1980; Kanfer, Karoly and Newman, 1975). The children are told that the main difference between those who are afraid of the dark and those who aren't, is that the latter know how to *make* themselves unafraid by saying such special words. Practice with the technique is begun with a therapist, but is then taken over by the parents and children each night at home. The authors reported very positive results for these procedures in controlled research studies.

A similar notion, which Suinn and Richardson (1971) called *anxiety managment training,* involves the client's learning to use feelings of anxiety to evoke relaxation responses and feelings of success. The authors reported success in treating mathematics anxiety in university students in this way.

More will be said on other self-control approaches in later chapters, where we shall also have occasion to explore the impact of modeling and other social variables on emotions as well as on operant behaviors. For those who want additional practical preparation on some of the procedures mentioned in this chapter, the following sources are recommended: Davis et al. (1980), Fuller (1977), Sulzer-Azaroff and Reese (1982); Wolpe (1969).

A TENTATIVE CONCLUSION

Most students—not to mention their teachers—have school-related anxieties from time to time. Some are like Charlie Brown's sister Sally's fear of her first day in school. She told Lucy she was afraid of going to school because she heard that they ask a lot of questions there. Lucy confirmed this, but asked why that concerned her. Sally replied, "There are certain things I'd just rather not have brought up."

One of the things students would rather not have brought up is their incompetence which, ironically, schools were invented to stamp out. The dilemma is how to eliminate incompetence without focusing on it and developing *feelings* of incompetence, fears of math, and so forth. Researchers who have studied extreme cases of school-related fears, so-called school phobias, usually conclude that at least the following are necessary (e.g., Kelly, 1973): early intervention, recognition of the first signs (resistance to attend school, somatic complaints, clinging to the home), firmness in keeping the child in school and dealing with the problem there as much as possible, and direct intervention to allay the anxieties (e.g., counterconditioning procedures and, as Kelly put it, "patient gentleness to allay his anxieties").

We have seen in this chapter how emotions and other involuntary behaviors become conditioned to neutral objects and situations. We have seen how conditioned emotions can become severe enough to be debilitating. We have also seen, however, how voluntary control can be obtained over these respondents by biofeedback, systematic desensitization, relaxation, and various counter-conditioning techniques. When such control is managed by the clients themselves, a sense of mastery—of competence—can be acquired that will serve the person well.

As we noted in the first chapter of this book, no subject is ever taught only in a cognitive sense. Teachers are not "book-learning" people. Students learn not only how to think in math or chemistry or English, but also how to feel and whether to approach or avoid what they are supposedly thinking about. Much lip-service is rendered to the "affective domain" of feelings, attitudes and values. From our perspective, the really important issues involved in the affective domain are those presented in this chapter: the tensions, emotions, bodily reflexes that are set in motion in the presence of a teacher or a school subject.

NOTES

1. This true story was related by Kay Johnson-Gentile, who worked with children and their parents while she was Director of a Music Therapy Project at Roswell Park Memorial Hospital in Buffalo, NY from 1977–1979.
2. But see Gormezano and Moore, 1969, if you wish to follow the history of the search.
3. This case of the US preceding the CS is technically called backward conditioning. For the reasons described, conditioning cannot easily be attained by this procedure, if at all. In fact, there is *now* evidence (e.g., Hulse et al., 1980) that organisms actively learn to suppress making an association between US and CS when presented in this order. This is because the CS signals the end of a trial, and thus a long wait until the beginning of the next trial when the US will be presented.
4. Differential definitions of fears and phobias have not been conclusively stated to the agreement of all in the field. However, it is generally agreed that ". . . *fear* is a normal response to threatening stimuli, whereas phobia is an unreasonable response, often to usually benign or ill-defined stimuli" (Graziano et al., 1979, p. 805). Furthermore, it is common to regard phobias as fears which (1) are out of proportion to the situation, (2) cannot be reduced by reasoning, (3) are beyond voluntary control, and (4) lead to avoiding the feared object or setting (e.g., Marks, 1969; Morris and Kratochwill, 1983).
5. The reader interested in the measures taken and the control groups established by Rescorla and his colleagues is encouraged to consult Rescorla's very readable monograph entitled, *Pavlovian Second-Order Conditioning* (1980).
6. Excellent places to start are Bower and Hilgard (1981); Hulse, Egeth and Deese (1980), and Rescorla (1980).
7. See also Early (1968) and Roden and Hapkiewicz (1973).
8. There was a serious design problem that inadvertently led Brady and his collaborators to the wrong conclusion. More carefully controlled research was done by Weiss (1968; 1970; 1971) who, in studies on rats, isolated the operative factors to be predictability and control—or rather, their absence—in producing ulcers and emotionality. An excellent discussion of the "executive monkey" and related research is found in Seligman's book *Helplessness* (1975, particularly pp. 116–121), which provided the impetus for this section in the book.
9. The reader interested in attribution theory and its relevance to learned helplessness is encouraged to pursue the following sources as a beginning: Abramson, Seligman and Teasdale (1978); Diener and Dweck (1978); Dweck (1975); Dweck and Repucci (1973); Garber and Seligman (1980); Hiroto (1974); Heusmann (1978); Miller and Norman (1979).
10. The interested reader is encouraged to consider their arguments by going directly to the sources. You may also wish to consult Schachter and Singer, (1962).
11. Some of these kinds of problems may be what Sidman (1960) had in mind when he spoke of "Normal Sources of Pathological Behavior"—that is, abnormal behaviors which arise from lawful, normal interactions between organism and environment.
12. The Schachter-Singer (1962) experiment is even slightly more complicated than described here; the interested reader will find going to the source quite informative.
13. It is interesting to note that other researchers were studying the voluntary control of muscles around that time (e.g., Woodworth's 1901 study in the same issue of the Psychological Review), but these were studies of muscles already known to be under voluntary control. These researchers were trying to understand how people learned to control them.
14. The reader interested in exploring the continuing saga of this debate is encouraged to begin with Skinner (1938) and Kimble (1961), then turn to Katkin and Murray's (1968) review of the evidence up to 1968. They drew some methodological and substantive conclusions that led to a "reply" by Crider et al. (1969) and a rejoinder by Katkin et al. (1969). A more recent summary, as well as an excellent history, is provided by Yates (1980).

    A point worth emphasizing in passing is that various theoretical camps (e.g., behaviorists and humanists) have claimed the "discovery" of biofeedback. In part, this is because "the behaviorist" position was considered to be that voluntary control over involuntary behaviors was impossible (e.g., Brown, 1974). This was not the case, we have now seen. Nevertheless, Green and Green (1977) who, in *Beyond Biofeedback,* equate behavioristic with "antihumanistic" (p. 14), went on to thank Barbara Brown for "discovering" Bair's (1901) research (p. 43). That would presumably make Bair's study, with which we opened this section, part of their camp's evidence. Of course, Kimble (1961) had previously reviewed Bair's research, so it could be claimed to be part of the behavioristic camp's evidence.

While it is often true that opposing theoretical camps are not aware of the research that the others are doing, we prefer the view that the zeitgeist—the spirit of the times—sets the agenda for what research occurs and is considered acceptable (what Kuhn, 1962, called "normal science"). In the case of biofeedback, a fascinating and varied history, technological breakthroughs in instruments to measure bodily functions, and researchers from all kinds of backgrounds converged to give rise to this new field. The history included a variety of antecedents of biofeedback from "evoked potentials" of brain waves (e.g., Brown, 1974) to Bair's (1901) research to Alexander Graham Bell's research on "visible speech" (Yates, 1980) to studies of relaxation training and meditation in yoga masters (e.g., Green and Green, 1977; Yates, 1980). It also included operant control of heart rate in humans by avoidance conditioning (Frazier, 1966), and the incredible "breakthroughs" in operant conditioning of a wide range of autonomic functions in curarized animals (where their musculature was totally paralyzed) by Neal Miller and his associates (Miller, 1969). Despite the fact that the Miller studies could not be replicated (e.g., Miller, 1978; Miller and Dworkin, 1974), they stimulated a large amount of interest in research in this field.

All of this encouraged such a variety of approaches to the field that biofeedback may be the best example of a truly eclectic discipline.

15. This treatment is similar to a procedure first reported by Sargent, Green and Walters (1973). How dilating the vessels of the hand operates to eliminate the vascular problems of the head is a topic we'll discuss shortly.

16. Harry, whose name we made up, is actually a composite of some of the children described by Harris, Spelman and Hymer (1974). Since they did not describe the children case by case, we are taking the liberty of explaining their results by his hypothetical composite case study.

17. See Blanchard and Epstein (1978) and Yates (1980) for excellent reviews of the research on control of single motor units.

18. An ingenious biofeedback display device described by Brown (1974): the more electrical activity generated by the muscles or brain waves, the faster a train moves.

19. Miller (1978, p. 377) for example, describes how learned, often unconscious, mechanical effects may mediate visceral processes and account for some of the Yogis who claim to be able to stop their hearts. They ". . . perform an exaggerated Valsalva maneuver that builds up sufficient pressure in the thoracic cavity to shut off the return of blood via the veins to the heart. . . . It stops the pulse and, since heart sounds are produced by the action of the blood on the valves, stops them as heard by stethoscope, but an ECG [electrocardiagram] proves the heart is beating faster than normal."

20. If you are a Henny Youngman fan, you may want to rephrase that as "Take my test anxiety—please."

21. As Davison (1968) noted, however, it is not necessary that a direct one-to-one correspondence exist between the procedure by which an emotion was associated with a situation and the therapy which seeks to reverse that learning. In more practical terms, a counter-conditioning therapy might usefully extinguish a fear that was learned in some way other than by the specific CS-US pairing assumed in respondent conditioning. Likewise, it is possible that other, non-behavior-therapeutic approaches (e.g., psychodynamic approaches) could alleviate fears that were indeed learned by respondent conditioning.

CHAPTER III
Operant Behavior: Motions

INTRODUCTION

Cries from new-born babies are likely to be reactions to internal or external stimulation, for example, like pangs of hunger, wetness, or other discomfort. As children mature such crying continues as reactions to physical or emotional pain or frustrations. But with children's growing awareness of their surroundings also comes another kind of crying which parents unfortunately come to know too well: crying for attention.

Caring parents, especially inexperienced ones, naturally come running when their baby starts to cry. They are quick to discover the source of the problem, if any obvious external source exists, and they pick up the child to provide food and comfort. In so doing, parents are teaching their children their first lesson in controlling the environment—namely, that crying gets results. This must be an amazing discovery to a child. If at this developmental stage children's nervous systems and linguistic abilities were sufficiently developed to permit it, they would probably say, "Wow, only a few weeks old and already I have my parents conditioned: everytime I cry, they give me attention and food." Crying as an operant behavior has emerged.

As children mature, they attempt to control more and more of their environment and, in so doing, develop an increasing array of skills. From touching an overhead mobile and showing delight at making it move, to building a tower of blocks, to hitting tennis balls with topspin, to programming a computer to perform complex tasks—yes, even to teaching a friend how to treat you—children learn the skills which allow them to deal with the objects and people in their environment. They learn these skills for the most part by actively "doing unto others" and then seeing the consequence of what "others do unto them." Sometimes they learn by the school of hard knocks: they touch something hot or ride a bicycle too fast and fall. In dealing with people, they may learn to "do as you would be done by!" or, in dealing with some people, to "do unto others before they do unto you." In any case, it is their active behaviors, or motions, which produce the consequences, and this interaction of behavior with consequences is what allows children to master (or cope with) their world.

Because the consequences, and not the antecedents, are the most important events controlling these behaviors, it is clear that we are describing a class of behaviors most people would call voluntary or purposeful (e.g., Tolman, 1932; 1959; called such behavior "purposive" and spoke of the organisms' "expectancies" of obtaining desired ends by various behavioral means). Even

61

Skinner, who is known to avoid such "mentalistic" terms as purpose, called these behaviors *operants* to call attention to their active nature in operating on the environment. He describes it as follows (Skinner, 1974):

> . . . operant behavior is the very field of purpose and intention. By its nature, it is directed toward the future: a person acts *in order that* something will happen, and the order is temporal. (p. 55)

> Operant behavior is essentially the exercise of power: it has an effect on the environment. (pp. 139–140)

> We often overlook the fact that human behavior is also a form of control. That an organism should act to control the world around it is as characteristic of life as breathing or reproduction. A person acts upon the environment, and what he achieves is essential to his survival and the survival of the species. (p. 189).

TYPES OF OPERANT CONDITIONING

Having defined an operant as a purposeful behavior does not mean that it is free from control by external forces. On the contrary, most of our voluntary behavior is under varying amounts of control by external forces, such as significant others, specific stimuli, natural consequences and contrived consequences, such as rules or laws. For example, foreign visitors to the U.S.A. are often amazed that native drivers will stop at red traffic lights and wait until the light turns green to go, despite the fact that there may be no other traffic as far as the eye can see. There is no natural reflex to stop on red and go on green, as can be seen from the fact that (1) in other cultures such signals may have other meanings (e.g., red means stop, then go if the coast is clear), and (2) that when you are taking a loved one to a hospital, you may hardly even slow down at the red light. Clearly, the red light does not *make* you stop and wait; rather it is the consequence or threat of consequence (such as paying a fine or losing your driving license) which controls such behavior.

Similarly, the act of driving itself consists of voluntary motions, but these are not free from control. You drive on the right side of the road (on the left in Britain and Japan), except to overtake another vehicle. You drive at various speeds according to traffic conditions, turn when the road turns, and leave the road only when there is another road to turn on to, because the consequences of not behaving in these ways would be disastrous. Few of us are aware that our driving behaviors are so conditioned, but they are.

Less trivial instances of operant conditioning concern taking valium or drinking martinis to relieve tension, raising your hand in class to get your teacher's attention, and teaching in order to receive a paycheck. How such voluntary acts come to be controlled or conditioned is the subject of this section. There are four basic classes of operant conditioning,—namely, positive reinforcement, negative reinforcement, extinction and punishment, with several variations on these. Before considering these in some detail, we will be well-served to adopt the technical meaning of the word "reinforcement."

REINFORCEMENT

When we say that a response has been reinforced, we mean that its probability has been increased or maintained at a high level (under certain conditions). In this sense, reinforcement serves as a *regulation* of the behavior (e.g., Bandura, 1977), affecting the frequency with which the behavior occurs (and under what conditions). Reinforcement does not "strengthen" the behavior itself, as exercise strengthens a muscle or as additional troops strengthen an army. Rather, it alters the likelihood of the behavior's occurrence.

Usually a behavior will be reinforced in the above sense if it terminates in a desirable consequence, of which there are two basic types: (1) obtaining something you want or need and (2) escaping or avoiding something noxious or harmful. Either of these consequences, and usually no other, has the effect of increasing the probability of that behavior under similar circumstances. If so, we say that the behavior has been reinforced.[2]

When reinforcement occurs by achievement of something positive (satisfying a want or need), we call it *positive reinforcement*. When it occurs through escaping something negative (an aversive situation), we call it *negative reinforcement*. In both cases, the behavior is regulated to occur more frequently, or to be maintained if it is already occurring at a high rate.

POSITIVE REINFORCEMENT

The procedure for positive reinforcement is much like the common notion of it: a person behaves in such a way as to earn a reward, paycheck, recognition, praise, etc. Defined in this informal way, positive reinforcement can be said to be similar to reward training. The child eats his vegetables, or joins the "clean plate club" in order to receive his "just desserts" as a reward. In technical language we say that the operant response of eating vegetables was followed by a reinforcing stimulus, dessert.

$$(1) \qquad R_{\text{Eating Vegetables}} \rightarrow S^{RF}_{\text{Dessert}}$$

Continuing in a technical sense, it is important to note that a stimulus cannot be labeled a reinforcer in the absence of data on its behavioral effect. *In other words, a stimulus can be said to be reinforcing only if it increases or maintains the rate of responding.*

Here is one place where the everyday use of "rewards" and positive reinforcement part company. As many parents can attest, dessert offered as a reward for eating vegetables often does not work, in which case we cannot conclude that dessert is a reinforcer for eating vegetables (at least for this child under these conditions).

Another place in which reward differs from positive reinforcement is in the usual conception of controller-controllee. We see the parent trying to control the child by offering a reward for "good behavior." Behavior modification experts are often portrayed as sinister puppetteers, pulling the strings of their

63

unwitting victims through their knowledge of advanced behavioral technology. Or perhaps they are portrayed as clowns trying to manipulate kids with M & Ms. The prototype of this is, of course, the rat pressing a bar (or the pigeon pecking a key) for a food reward in a "Skinner box." As pointed out earlier, even the subjects in these examples (pigeons or persons) are engaged in behaviors which are controlling the significant others in their environment (experimenters, parents, teachers and friends). It is therefore only in special cases where one person has such control over another that he can significantly manipulate another's behavior against his will by use of rewards. This issue will be addressed more fully under the topic of Self-Control.

A third difference between the everyday conception of reward and positive reinforcement lies in what constitute effective rewards. Food, water, oxygen, sex, and money to buy those things can often serve as effective reinforcers, in the defining sense that people will behave in certain ways in order to earn them as consequences. Such items are conspicuous in their effect, especially those that satisfy biological needs, but that is not all that controls our behavior. Once our biological and safety needs are satisfied (e.g., Maslow, 1954), then social reinforcers such as praise or attention from others become important reinforcers, if only because they affect our self-esteem needs (in Maslow's terminology). Attention from another person would seldom be called a reward, especially if the attention is a reprimand. But such attention is often the most powerful reinforcer in an environment operating to maintain behavior.

Consider the beginning of each 47-minute high school class in English in which the teacher introduced class with a "search-and-deposit" mission: "Wrap that gum up in paper. Don't throw it naked into the basket."[3] The teacher was searching for gum chewers who, in addition to having to deposit their gum in the wastebasket in front of their peers, were fined 5 cents (the money was used to buy get-well cards for students or facial tissues for the students to use; perhaps the moral of the story is, "Clean mouths lead to Kleen-necks"). What was alarming to the observer and evidently overlooked by the teacher was that the students enjoyed this game and used it to avoid beginning their studies: class was delayed an average of 15 minutes per class when the topic was grammar and 5 minutes per class when it was literature. Among other things going on, it is clear that the teacher's and peer group's attention for chewing gum was a much more powerful reinforcer than the lesson, and completely overrode the presumed punishing effects of the fine or losing the chewing gum. The teacher was reinforcing, through her attention to it, the very behavior she sought to eliminate.

Americans, in particular, are extremely prone to reinforce unwanted behavior by their very attention to that behavior. How many adults have not had the experience of trying to carry on a conversation with another adult when, as soon as a child comes into the room, the adult interrupts the conversation to fulfill a request of the child? The adult's attention serves as a very powerful positive reinforcer to the child who learns a valuable lesson: interrupting other's conversations is not only all right, but will get me what I want immediately.[4]

Positive reinforcement, in sum, must be defined by its effect on behavior which, in turn, can usually be assessed only over some extended period of time. When that is done for most humans—at least those whose basic needs are already being satisfied—the most powerful reinforcer turns out to be attention from significant others. But attention does not have to be praise and adulation in order to reinforce behavior; disagreements, arguments, reprimands and even yelling and fighting, can serve to increase the probability of a behavior that has those consequences. In extreme cases it is perhaps as though the person is saying, "Say anything to me, just so long as you do not ignore me." Our attention, wittingly or unwittingly, does much to affect others' behaviors and teach them how to behave toward us.

NEGATIVE REINFORCEMENT

As already defined, *negative reinforcement is the escape or avoidance of an aversive state (or stimulus) as a consequence of some behavior.* The prototypical experiment for the study of such behavior is the shuttle box, in which an animal is placed in one side of an experimental space with a barrier in the middle separating it from the other side (e.g., Sidman, 1953). If the floor, which is electrically wired, delivers a continuous shock, the animal begins to scurry around until eventually it leaps the barrier and discovers the other side of the compartment to be free of shock. If the animal is now placed back in the aversive, shocking side of the box, it will again leap the barrier, only this time much faster. Repeat this procedure ten times and the animal's latency of jumping the barrier will become faster and faster. The probability of the animal's response of *escaping* the aversive situation is increasing. Diagrammed, the situation looks like this:

$$(2) \qquad S^{AV}_{Shock} \text{--------} R_{jumps\ barrier} \longrightarrow NoS^{AV}_{No\ Shock}$$

If we now turned on a yellow light which preceded the onset of the shock by 10 seconds, it would not take very many trials before the animal would use this predictive cue to jump the barrier before the shock came on. The anticipation of this aversive stimulus and acting to prevent it is called *avoidance* behavior and can be diagrammed as follows:

(3a) *early trials*

$$S^{D5}_{yellow\ light} \text{-----------} S^{AV}_{Shock} \text{-----} R_{jumps\ barrier} \longrightarrow NoS^{AV}_{No\ Shock}$$

(3b) *later trials*

$$S^{D}_{yellow\ light} \text{-----------} R_{jumps\ barrier} \longrightarrow NoS^{AV}_{No\ Shock}$$

65

Avoidance, in other words, is a more complex form of escape behavior, and both are based on negative reinforcement.

Note that, as in positive reinforcement (defined as the presentation of an attractive stimulus as a consequence of a behavior), the frequency of the escape behavior must be increased or maintained in order to conclude that negative reinforcement did in fact occur. Note also that, contrary to popular opinion, *negative reinforcement is not synonymous with punishment.* Whereas negative reinforcement occurs when an aversive stimulus is terminated contingent upon a behavior, punishment occurs when an aversive stimulus (e.g., a slap or shock) is the consequence of the behavior (e.g., talking back to your parent). The procedure of punishment is, therefore, the behavioral opposite of that for negative reinforcement. And so is the intended effect. Through punishment the behavior is expected to decrease, while in negative reinforcement, where the key word is reinforcement, the behavior will increase. Punishment will be discussed in more detail shortly, but perhaps the following difference will serve as a mnemonic: punishment is batting your head against the wall for a mistake you made; negative reinforcement is batting your head against the wall because it feels so good when you stop.

More serious examples of negative reinforcement are the following common to human experience.

Drug-Taking

Although not widely recognized, a number of typically human behaviors become habits mainly through the mechanism of negative reinforcement. In our pharmaceutically oriented society, for example, it is natural to take aspirin or cold tablets to relieve mild but annoying pains and cold symptoms. (In other societies, or in some circles in this society, it is more common to meditate, to learn relaxation techniques, or do biofeedback exercises to relieve such symptoms and return to a centered, healthy state). Because these remedies work, at least somewhat, they provide the defining features of negative reinforcement: an aversive state is reduced or eliminated as a consequence of taking a drug (or, for that matter, meditating or relaxing). Thus the patient learns to behave that way again when a similar aversive state exists, and we can see the formation of an "aspirin-taking habit." Note, by the way, that if aspirin didn't work to relieve the pain, our aspirin-taking behavior would be extinguished (extinction is the topic of the next section) and we would not develop the aspirin-taking habit. Our beginning dependency on aspirin begins because it does indeed work to escape a painful state.

Many other drug-taking excesses, drinking problems, and smoking habits are also maintained by the escape or avoidance paradigms. Valium, taken to relieve tension, has almost become the "opiate of the masses," taken by millions of people (mostly women) to relieve daily tensions. Because it works, these people become dependent on it, not because it is addictive—though it may also be addictive—but because it is psychologically habit-forming through

66

the mechanism of negative reinforcement. Needing an alcoholic drink or a joint to unwind from the daily tensions or to relax sufficiently to face someone or something difficult is, similarly, developing a behavior pattern based on escape or avoidance. That these substances can enhance other experiences or may be pleasurable in and of themselves, simply reinforces the potential strength of the habit.

Negative side effects aside—and many of these drugs have known damaging side effects—dependence on a substance to relieve tension means that you are not learning other ways to cope with stressful situations. By other ways is meant behavior patterns that may make the environment less stressful by, for example, learning noncombative ways to be assertive, taking a different job, learning new skills, etc. If these are not possible, other ways might include learning non-drug-related methods for reducing stress such as relaxation or biofeedback techniques (see Chapter II).

Peer Pressure

Adolescents in particular, but all of us in general, are tremendously influenced by our peers. Often the influence is direct and open, as when peers reward or punish behaviors. More often it is quite subtle with pressure being applied to people until they pass some rites-of-passage test to prove their bravery, loyalty, or with-it-ness. Smoking, drinking, and drug-taking are often first undertaken because peers dare that person not to: what are you, chicken? Acts of vandalism are often undertaken to create a macho image, which is another

way of saying that the so-called macho behaviors reduced the stress of not conforming to their peers. In the late 1970's and early 1980's peer pressure was so great that it was a tremendous act of courage to remain a virgin, and harder to admit to it. (This pressure spawned a counterculture, however, in which some adolescents started wearing buttons expressing their intent to sit out the sexual revolution, and thereby provide each other with reinforcement for this behavioral pattern). In that same period, ridicule was heaped on kids who did not listen to the proper music or wear the proper jeans or sports shoes. A decade earlier young teachers thought they were expressing their individuality and countering authorities by wearing jeans and shirts instead of coats and ties to teach. What they did not see was that in so doing, they were conforming to the pressures of their own group to wear jeans.

These and many other examples of growing-up behavior are based on negative reinforcement: the adolescent escapes or avoids ridicule by behaving in ways which conform to the behaviors of the peers. In so doing the "me" generation becomes the "me, too" generation.

Illness

In one edition of the syndicated Momma cartoon, Momma and two friends were discussing their techniques of relating with people. One said she found people like you better if you're not very smart. Another said they're much nicer to you if you have less money than they do. Finally, Momma said something to the effect that, "Those may work well for you, but what works best for me is to be sick."

Few people set out to escape from difficult, painful, or stressful occasions by becoming ill, but as we have seen, operant conditioning does not require conscious planning in order to occur. But when a person becomes ill, absent friends may show up or call and family members may be nicer to you than usual, positively reinforcing your ill behavior by this attention. In addition, people may take over your chores or excuse you from doing certain of them forever. This combination of positive and negative reinforcement is a very powerful force operating to produce a hypochondriac.

Well-intentioned people often go out of their way to help disabled persons, constantly doing things for them that their disability does not prohibit, or excusing them from trying. The most celebrated case of that was, of course, Helen Keller whose parents excused her unruly behavior, poor eating habits, and screaming because of her blindness and deafness. It took Anne Sullivan, a disabled person herself, to withhold food and attention from Helen until she behaved appropriately. No longer able to escape learning to care for herself, Helen not only learned appropriate manners, but learned to read, write, speak and became one of the world's great humanitarians (e.g., Keller, 1954; the film "The Miracle Worker" based on Gibson, 1960 shows this process vividly). People must do for themselves, must go through the motions, in order to learn to care for themselves. Loved ones, however well-intentioned, do the disabled a disservice if they let them avoid learning these skills and do them for them.

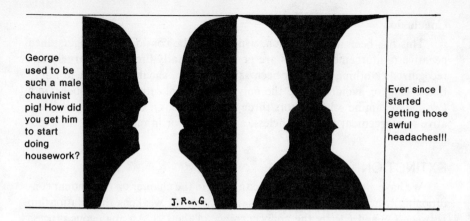

George used to be such a male chauvinist pig! How did you get him to start doing housework?

Ever since I started getting those awful headaches!!!

J. Ron G.

Often, as parents of very young children know well, it is easier to do things for them than to practice patience and let the child or disabled adult learn new skills through their own errors.

A school-related example of negative reinforcement is the child who has a stomach ache on the day there is a math test. If allowed to skip school on such days, the child is being allowed to escape a difficult or aversive situation through illness, real or feigned. The child learns avoidance of math, or school in general, instead of learning the skills and concepts required to do math fearlessly.

Playing Dumb and Being Obnoxious

A different and more common solution to the last problem is feigning stupidity. If whenever teachers call on you, you say "I dunno," teachers begin to expect less and less of you, to the point where they stop trying to teach you. When they reach that point, you are off the hook and need do very little any more. A number of factors often conspire to allow this, including the following: a grading policy which does not require attainment at a high level in order to pass the course, a peer group which punishes academic achievement and considers it macho to avoid assigned work, and the fact that teachers need reinforcement too. Thus teachers pay attention to students who reinforce them by paying attention and learning, while avoiding students who are not learning.

Faced with obvious rebellion from a student, the teacher will often throw students out of class or have them expelled. From both the students' and teacher's vantage point, this is escape behavior. Students escape a class, teacher, or subject by becoming a discipline problem (not to mention the positive reinforcement supplied by the macho friends!) And teachers escape the noise and annoyance of obnoxious students by dismissing them from class. More will be said on these kind of situations in the Chapter on discipline.

Conclusion

This has been a long section, which could be considerably longer, since negative reinforcement effects are pervasive in daily life, yet go largely unrecognized. Nothing that has been said, however, should be taken to imply that escape or avoidance are the only factors implicated in these behaviors (we shall examine other factors throughout the book). Conditioning via negative reinforcement is, nevertheless, a major factor in maintaining these behaviors.

EXTINCTION

We have already encountered extinction in the chapter on respondent conditioning, where it was described as a process that weakens the relationship between CS and CR by the nonoccurrence of the US. An analogous process operates in regard to operants when the behavior does not achieve the desired consequence—a previously reinforced behavior is no longer reinforced. A common example of that is having a coin swallowed by a machine without delivering your soft drink. The appropriate behavior did not lead to the reinforcing stimulus, and we can therefore say that the behavior is being extinguished. Diagrammed, an extinction trial for a previously positively reinforced response looks like this:

(4)　Previous Trials:　　$R_{deposit\ coin} \longrightarrow S^{RF}_{soft\ drink}$

　　　Current Trial:　　$R_{deposit\ coin} \longrightarrow NoS^{RF}_{No\ Soft\ drink}$

Extinction of a negatively reinforced behavior is similar in that the behavior does not achieve the desired consequence. But in this case, the desired consequence is escape or avoidance, so the extinction process would be a case in which the behavior did not bring about escape. An example of this is asking people at a party not to smoke, assuming smoke is aversive to you, but they do not comply. Your behavior of asking is being extinguished since it does no good. Extinction in a negative reinforcement situation, then, can be diagrammed as follows:

(5)　Previous Trials:　　$S^{AV}_{Smoke} \longrightarrow R_{asking} \longrightarrow NoS^{AV}_{No\ smoking}$

　　　Current Trial:　　$S^{AV}_{Smoke} \longrightarrow R_{asking} \longrightarrow S^{AV}_{Still\ smoking}$

As used above, the word extinction refers to the procedure of nonreinforcement and not to the effect of reducing the frequency of the behavior to zero, as when we say the behavior was "extinguished." The latter use of the word can lead to some confusion since it is rare that a behavior is totally extinguished (i.e., reduced to zero) as fires are extinguished. The process of extinction does, however, reduce the frequency of the concerned behavior, though not always or immediately to zero.

Parents have often used the procedure of extinction to put an end to undesirable behaviors. For example, when their four-year-old learns his first curse word, everyone laughs or chuckles, even while scolding the child. The positive reinforcement this attention gives is usually immediately apparent in the increased frequency of this behavior. When the parents realize this, they decide that everyone in the family should ignore the behavior; no laughing. If indeed no one laughs, the behavior will become less and less frequent—at least in the presence of the parents. But the result will seldom be either immediate or antiseptic because extinction has some side effects.

The Frustration Effect and Spontaneous Recovery

When the child first emits a swear word and is ignored, he feels like you do when your last dime disappears into the pay telephone and you have not gotten through. He feels frustrated and may actually say the offending words more frequently or "once more with feeling." This immediate increase in frequency or magnitude of the behavior following the first extinction trial (often with accompanying kicks or shakes in the case of telephones or vending machines) is appropriately enough called the *frustration effect*.

If the parents continue to ignore the behavior despite the increased outbursts, they will eventually succeed. The frequency of the behavior will continue to decrease. But this will not be a smooth, continuous process. A *spontaneous recovery* of a higher rate may occur after a few days of decline, so named because its cause is usually hard to spot. It is probably because some subtle cue that was present when the behavior was being learned, but was absent for a while, was reintroduced. Whatever the reason, the rate will again fall with consistent nonreinforcement of the behavior.

Extinction of a behavior, then, can reduce its frequency to zero or near-zero via long-term consistent nonreinforcement. That's the good news. The bad news is that it is likely to take much longer to eliminate a habit by extinction than to acquire it in the first place. In addition, for practical use in classrooms, a teacher's use of extinction will be effective only if the other students are not reinforcing the very behavior the teacher is ignoring. A sensitive teacher may be able to ignore many of the unwanted behaviors (while attending to appropriate behaviors) of a hyperactive child, but other children may not ignore them. In making fun of the child or in striking back at him for violating their space, they may be counteracting the teacher's extinction procedures.

PUNISHMENT

Of all the types of operant conditioning, punishment needs the least introduction. It is probably the strongest and quickest way known for changing behavior, but it is also associated with the most unpleasant experiences people

71

have. As in our daily experiences, punishment is defined as an aversive consequence as a result of a behavior. Diagrammed, the situation is as follows:

$$(6a) \qquad R_{\text{breaking rule}} \longrightarrow S^{AV}_{\text{Slap}}$$

$$(6b) \qquad R_{\text{breaking rule}} \longrightarrow S^{AV}_{\text{paying fine}}$$

Slapping, yelling, or shocking a behavior or taking something away[6] (i.e., as a consequence of the behavior) usually result in an immediate suppression of the behavior. In general, the more severe the punishment, that is, the more intense and/or the longer the duration of the punishment, the greater the suppression of the behavior (e.g., Church, 1969). By suppression is meant the temporary cessation of a behavior as opposed to a permanent reduction in its frequency to zero or near-zero. There are a few strange exceptions (to be described later) to the general rule that punishment suppresses, but does not eliminate, behavior. In daily life though, the punishers that are considered legal and moral are neither sufficiently strong nor delivered close enough to the behavior to act to eliminate the behaviors or, for that matter, to deter others from doing them. Thus if you are speeding on the highway, you may slow down when you see a policeman because of having previously paid a fine or seeing others pay one. Upon getting past him, you are likely to speed up again. This is the suppression effect of punishment.

Before we ask the logical next question—namely, why aren't parents, teachers and policemen equipped with punishers that really hurt?—the truth is that stronger punishers probably do no more than suppress the behavior either, or perhaps the behavior is eliminated only in the presence of the punishing agent. Moreover, punishment has widespread side effects (as we saw in the last chapter) and, at least in humans, breeds resentment and revenge-oriented behavior. So if we did shock our students for making noise with a tetanizing voltage, so that they could not breathe and their body just shook, they might be quiet in our classes. But they would also plot how to steal our cattle prod or invent one of our own. We are existing in an interdependent, reciprocally determined world after all, and if we use greater and greater force to control students, they will have to also. And what do we do when their chemistry class gets the bomb?

DISCRIMINATION LEARNING

To learn anything implies some discrimination of the conditions under which it is appropriate. We have already seen how emotions are attached through classical conditioning to certain previously neutral stimuli—but not all stimuli. That kind of differential response according to the conditions is discrimination learning. In adjusting our operants or motions to the appropriate conditions, we are making differential responses to different stimulus

72

events. As pointed out earlier, however, those stimuli do not force the response to occur; rather they provide the occasion for the response. Thus the red light is a cue for stopping and green for going. Persons who behave in that way can be said to have learned that discrimination.

Similarly, learning to say "ess" to the printed stimulus "S" and not to the letter "R" is discrimination learning. Students learn this type of discrimination in order to receive praise or attention from their teacher (or to avoid punishment), as well as to have the capability of reading. Such positively reinforcing events control many school-learning behaviors. We have also seen how avoidance learning requires a cue so that the organism can behave in a timely fashion to circumvent a shock or other aversive situation.

The technical terms in discrimination learning are most easily learned through an example. When a baby first says "da," probably out of a maturational readiness, the significant others do not treat it so casually. Out of the many sounds the baby makes—"goo," "ga," or what have you—the parents become excited over "da" and respond to the child, "Say 'da-da,' say 'da-da'," over and over. In the presence of this kind of modeling and the actual stimulus of father, the child is expected to make the response "da-da," for which all kinds of attention is being given. As children get older, the criterion is raised and they receive attention contingent upon saying "da-da" only when father is present. They are ignored (or actively discouraged) when they call other men "da-da." We can now see that the appropriate behavior, saying "da-da" is reinforced in the presence of the appropriate cue—namely, father. That cue is technically called a *discriminative stimulus,* abbreviated S^D or S^+ to distinguish it from all other inappropriate stimuli, symbolized S^Δ (S-*Delta,* the Greek letter for d) or S^-. Discrimination learning, then, consists of reinforcement for appropriate behavior in the presence of S^D and nonreinforcement—that is, extinction—for the same behavior in the presence of any other stimulus. Diagrammed, the situation looks like this:

(7a) $S^D_{father} \longrightarrow R_{"da-da"} \longrightarrow S^{RF}_{"Good\ boy"}$

(7b) $S^\Delta_{Other\ men} \longrightarrow R_{"da-da"} \longrightarrow NoS^{RF}_{No\ attention}$

Discrimination learning is not always a part of all of the previous types of operant learning, but it is necessarily a part of avoidance learning. You can escape from a noxious stimulus, but you can avoid only if you have a reliable cue prior to the noxious stimulus (see formulas 3a and b).

Having now presented the basic types of operant behaviors, a succinct comparison of them is possible and it is presented in Table 2. The procedure or process for obtaining each type is shown along with the expected effect of that process.

TABLE 2
Summary of Types of Operant Behavior

Name	Procedure	Expected Effect	Pages Described
1. Positive Reinforcement (Reward Training)	$R \rightarrow S^{RF}$	An increase (or maintenance at a high level) in the frequency of the behavior that led to that consequence.	63–65
2. Negative Reinforcement (Escape Training)	S^{AV}—$R \rightarrow$ NoS^{AV}	An increase (or maintenance at a high level) in the frequency of the behavior that led to escaping the noxious event.	65–69
3. Extinction	(a) $R \rightarrow NoS^{RF}$ (b) S^{AV}—$R \rightarrow$ S^{AV}	A decrease in the frequency of the behavior because it does not lead to a reinforcing consequence.	70–71
4. Punishment	$R \rightarrow S^{AV}$	A decrease in the frequency of the behavior because its consequence is an aversive event.	71–72
5. Discrimination Learning	S^D—$R \rightarrow S^{RF}$ S^Δ—$R \rightarrow NoS^{RF}$	A differential response rate, with an increase of the behavior when S^D is present and a decrease of the same behavior when S^D is absent (i.e., S^Δ is present).	72–73
6. Negative Reinforcement (Avoidance Training)	S^D—S^{AV}—$R \rightarrow$ NoS^{AV}	Discriminated escape training in which an increase in the behavior occurs when S^D is present so that S^{AV} can be avoided.	65–66

GENERALIZATION AND DISCRIMINATION

We have already seen how fears (and other emotions) can generalize beyond the particular stimuli directly associated with the fear to other, previously neutral, stimuli. Analogous processes occur in operant and cognitive behavior as well. Learning concepts is a case in point.

When young children receive their first pet dog, whom they may name Snoopy, they are quite likely to generalize and call all dogs "Snoopy" for a while. If their experience with Snoopy were pleasant, they are probably also prone to approach other dogs, to the consternation of their worried parents.

The children are generalizing their behavior (naming, or approaching to pet) from one stimulus to other stimuli.

For our purposes, a technical definition of generalization of operant behavior, then, might be the following: *generalization is the performance of the same (or a similar) response in the presence of different stimuli.*[7] In the case above, saying "Snoopy" is the response that was first learned to the original pet, but is now extended to other dogs.

Generalization, of course, is a natural developmental process—as we learn new responses we consciously or nonconsciously try them out in new situations. One child, for example, was trying to describe the degree of whiteness of some object and he said, "It was pitch white." Presumably he had heard the phrase "pitch black," but associated pitch with a qualifying grammatical function as in "very" black, instead of its original usage, probably unknown to him "as black as pitch" (a black, tarry substance). Thus he generalized beyond "appropriate" usage with a humorous result.

Less humorous examples of generalizations occur in stereotyping races, ethnic groups, genders, etc., when real or imagined attributes of one person or a small group of persons are generalized to all members of that group.

When children are learning to read, there are many opportunities for stimulus generalization. For example, teach children to say "dog" to the printed stimulus DOG and then provide them with these printed words several times in random order: DOG, GOD, DOT, DUG, HOP, HAT. If, as is likely, the children respond "dog" to stimuli other than the correct one, the errors are more likely to occur to similar (e.g., GOD, DUG) than to dissimilar stimuli (e.g., HOP, HAT). The curve that can be plotted from these responses is called a *generalization gradient,* and it demonstrates that the more similar a new stimulus is to the original (reinforced) stimulus, the more likely the response will be emitted.

In the laboratory, stimulus generalization and the generalization gradient can be demonstrated more precisely by placing a hungry pigeon in a darkened experimental chamber with an illuminated disc or key on one wall of the chamber (for example, Guttman and Kalish, 1956; Reese, 1966). By pecking the key, the pigeon can obtain a small quantity of grain. After the pigeon is trained to peck the key for food when the key is a certain color (say, yellow), food delivery is stopped. Then the color of the key is systematically varied over a wide range of the color spectrum. The order of presentation of the different colors may be randomized, but each color is presented for the same duration and number of times.

The next step is to count the responses recorded for each of the different colors. The typical finding is that amount of responding follows a highly regular pattern in relationship to the different hues. The greatest amount of keypressing in this period in which food is not available occurs for the colors most similar to the original stimulus. As color of the key is changed to wavelengths further and further from the original color, responding decreases correspond-

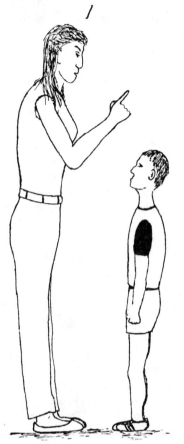

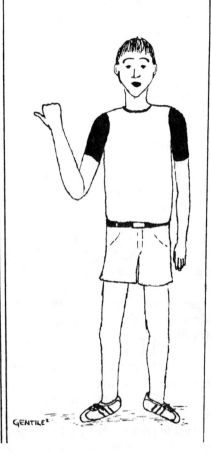

GENTILE[2]

ingly. The curve made from response rates (the generalization gradient) is found to be a function of the different test wave-lengths.

What is the significance of the generalization gradient? This gradient shows the presence of a mechanism by which the organism can respond appropriately to individual members of some response class to which it had never previously been exposed. Much of learning and experience in life has to do with identifying stimuli as members of classes, such as collies, poodles, and beagles as members of the class we call "dogs." This is a kind of cataloging process that saves us immeasurable degrees of error and helps us to master our environment more quickly.

If the process of generalization can accurately be described as a natural *developmental* process, then perhaps it is the case that discrimination—its behavioral opposite—is the major *learning* process of the developing individual. Parents and teachers seem to require finer and finer discriminations as the child ages. From the first uttered "da-da," children have to learn to say it only in certain appropriate instances. Later they learn that father is a noun, though sometimes a verb, and to discriminate nouns from verbs from adverbs and conjunctions. Where it was once appropriate to call all pets "Snoopy," Snoopy becomes a particular dog to be distinguished from cats. Cats and dogs become vertebrates to be distinguished from invertebrates, etc.

In the process of learning discriminations, the shape of the generalization gradient changes dramatically. Before the organism is reinforced for a discrimination, its generalization curve is approximately flat: in other words, the response is the same to all stimuli. As the organism is reinforced for discriminating—that is, one stimulus becomes the S^+ or S^D and all others become S^- or S^Δ—then the appropriate response occurs with higher frequency in the presence of S^+ and with less frequency to other stimuli. And the less similar the stimulus to S^+, the fewer the responses (e.g., Jenkins and Harrison, 1960).

To take a hypothetical example (see Figure 3), consider the generalization gradient for the concept of circle. As children first learn to say "circle," they may say it with almost equal likelihood to each of the symbols. As they learn to discriminate curved lines from straight lines, they may say it with less frequency to squares and triangles than to ovals and octagons. Eventually they will say it only to true circles and ambiguous circular figures.

The concepts of generalization and discrimination are also important in cognitive development, especially in relation to higher mental processes. In summary of this section, let it suffice to say that discrimination-generalization processes are integral to the teaching-learning process as well as to development.

REINFORCER EFFECTIVENESS

At various times in the preceding discussion we emphasized the importance of attention from significant others as a powerful reinforcer. Armed with that knowledge, a teacher or parent may rush right in to lavish attention on every approximation of an appropriate behavior: after all, if a little immediate positive reinforcement is good, a lot is better, right? Would that it were so. Even in training pigeons it is more complicated than that. (As W. C. Fields might have said it, "Ah yes, my little chickadee, there's many a slip twixt cup and beak.")

In this and the next few sections we shall describe some of the complications involved in the efficiency with which positive reinforcement regulates behavior.

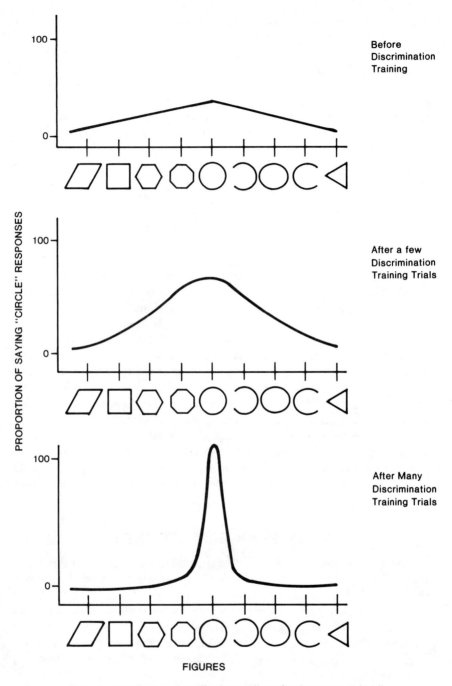

Figure 3. Hypothetical generalization gradients for the concept "circle".

TYPES OF REINFORCEMENT

Some stimuli have the power to regulate behavior from the day of our birth. This is because they satisfy a biological need; oxygen is a prime example. If oxygen were not available for a few seconds, all of our attention and behavior would be purposefully directed to finding a way to obtain oxygen. Not only would our success in obtaining oxygen maintain our life, but it would also develop and maintain the behavior that had that desirable effect. Other examples of reinforcers that satisfy biological needs are food, water, sleep, and sexual stimulation. Reinforcers of this type do not need to be learned; they are reinforcing because of the biological nature of humans and animals. For this reason they are called *primary reinforcers*.

As is well known, however, behaviors can also be affected by stimuli other than primary reinforcers, such as money, praise, or a smile. These stimuli are *conditioned* or *secondary reinforcers*, so called because they acquire reinforcing properties by being paired with primary reinforcers.

Money, for instance, is not reinforcing to a newborn baby, but it is not too many years later that money comes to be able to affect response rates. Let us consider how money may come to acquire reinforcing properties. A child in a store sees candy (the stimulus) and responds "Candy, please." The adult then provides the child with money, which he exchanges for candy (reinforcer).

Two aspects of this process should be noted carefully. First, the stimulus money became associated with the reinforcer candy by being paired with it. But second, the stimulus money not only accompanied the reinforcer but preceded it. For a neutral stimulus such as money to acquire reinforcer status, it must eventually be exchangeable for the primary reinforcer. (Notice that, if the neutral stimulus occurred after the reinforcer, the response would already have been reinforced and the neutral stimulus would be irrelevant to the process. Thus it could never come to reinforce the response.)

After many pairings of neutral stimulus and reinforcer in this manner, the previously neutral stimulus (money) acquires reinforcing properties, and people will respond in ways that will increase their chances of receiving money as a payoff. This, of course, is just another way of saying that money has acquired the defining properties of a reinforcing stimulus—it increases the rate of some kind of responding.

But what would happen if, all of a sudden, all the governments of the world decided that money would no longer be exchanged for goods or services? It would not be long before people stopped working for money. Money would have lost its secondary reinforcing qualities because it would no longer be connected with such primary reinforcers as food. The implication of this is that secondary reinforcers must be backed up by primary reinforcement, at least occasionally.

Secondary reinforcers have come to be classified into three broad classes: social reinforcers, tokens, and activities. *Social reinforcers* include attention, praise, social acceptance, smiles and other human interactional stimuli. It is

79

not actually known for sure whether many of these social reinforcers are not actually primary reinforcing stimuli, and the question will not be resolved here. For convenience, we shall include them under secondary reinforcers.

Tokens are a second class of secondary reinforcers, and they include physical objects or records that increase or maintain response rates. Examples are money, grades, points, stars, and happy faces drawn on student papers.

Activities are a third type of reinforcer, and they provide a great variety of potential reinforcers that can be tailored to individual students' preferences. Thus television-watching can be a reinforcer for doing homework, as can free time for completing an assignment. An important point to keep in mind is that any one activity may or may not be an effective incentive for a given child. The teacher or parent who wants to find effective reinforcing stimuli, therefore, will take care to find out what the child's individual preferences are at any given moment. One efficient way of doing this, often forgotten, is to ask the student what would be an adequate incentive for him to do a certain task.

More on Activities: The Premack Principle

If you think about it, an activity is a behavior, not a stimulus; thus in using television-watching as a reward for completing homework, one behavior follows as a consequence of another behavior. David Premack (1959) was the first to state explicitly how this works, in what has now become known as the *Premack Principle: of two activities, if the more preferred is the consequence of the less preferred* (e.g., if TV-watching is the consequence of doing homework), *it will act to reinforce the latter* (e.g., to increase the probability of doing homework). But not vice-versa—that is, doing homework will not be a reinforcer for watching TV.

Premack did not stop there, however. He reinterpreted the whole reinforcement relation, pointing out that it is not just the stimulus food that is reinforcing to a hungry organism, but the activity of eating. Hungry rats in a Skinner box engage in one behavior, bar pressing, in order to be able to engage in a more preferred behavior, eating. Children who are deprived of stimulation or attention will engage in behaviors that allow them to interact with other people or activities. Of course, if you have just eaten, eating will not be a preferred activity for a while. Thus the reinforcement value of a given activity shifts from time to time. In some cases, as with water for all of us, drugs for an addict, or bodily movement for a hyperactive child, the preferences may shift quickly, almost moment to moment.

For most behaviors there will be longer term preferences, which perhaps induced Premack into thinking of his principle as a theory of values (e.g., Premack, 1971a). Those behaviors in which we engage most frequently, given freedom of choice (without any coercion), are those we value most. A person who listens to rock music more frequently than classical music can be said to value or prefer rock music more than classical, given freedom of choice. (As we pointed out earlier, however, there may be considerable peer pressure to listen to rock music to the exclusion of other music, in which case the purity of the preference is questionable.)

So far we've presented the Premack Principle as a one sided case—more preferred behaviors reinforce less preferred behaviors, but not vice versa. It is actually more complicated than that. When appropriate conditions are established to make it necessary to engage in a less preferred behavior as a consequence of doing something more preferred, then the more preferred behavior is punished and becomes less preferred, (e.g., Papp, 1980; Premack, 1962; 1965; 1971a; Terhune and Premack, 1970).[8] In this light perhaps we can see how having to write a report after reading a book could be seen as a punishment for the act of reading by many children. Perhaps this also suggests how to get children to stop watching too much television: after every show, they must mow the lawn or scrub the bathtub, etc.

HOW COME YOU ALWAYS WANT TO GO OUT FOR DINNER? DON'T YOU LIKE TO COOK ANYMORE?

COOKING I LIKE; IT'S CLEANING UP — AFTERWARDS THAT I CAN'T STAND.

Some Applications

The practical uses to which the various types of reinforcers have been put are, of course, many. Praise and attention, as we have seen, have powerful effects on behavior, and unwary teachers may have their time monopolized by students. In an extreme case, which was also one of the earliest reported behavior modification studies in a special education classroom, an eleven-year-old boy of normal intelligence was able to dominate his teacher's attention during spelling by the following behavior. Zimmerman and Zimmerman (1962, p. 59) described the situation in these words:

> . . . when [he] was called upon to spell a word which had previously been studied and drilled, he would pause for several seconds, screw up his face, and mutter letters unrelated to the word. Following this, the instructor (E) consistently asked him to sound out the word, often giving him the first letter and other cues, encouraging him to spell the word correctly. Only after E had spent considerable time and attention would the boy emit a correct response.

On the assumption that the teacher's attention was maintaining this behavior, a new strategy was designed. The boy was called to the board and given a spelling word to write on the board. At first he wrote it wrong, and asked for help, but the teacher sat at the desk ignoring his request. After about ten minutes, he wrote the word correctly. The teacher said "Good, now we can go on," and gave him a second word. Similar histrionics occurred, but for a shorter period, following which the teacher went to a third word. With each successive word, up through ten, the latency of the correct response decreased along with the number of inappropriate behaviors. After the tenth correct word, the teacher wrote an A grade on the spelling chart and spent time with him on an art project. After a month of this kind of treatment—and it did take a month to break these disturbed behavioral habits—the frequency of these bizarre antics declined to a level close to zero per class session and the child was able to make better academic progress.

The effectiveness of selective attention by significant others has now been demonstrated repeatedly in many settings. As the title of an influential article by Madsen, Becker and Thomas (1968) stated it, rules, praise and ignoring are the prime elements of classroom control, at least in elementary classrooms (see also Becker et al., 1967; Hall et al., 1968; O'Leary and O'Leary, 1972; Krumboltz and Krumboltz, 1972; Madsen and Madsen, 1981; McIntire, 1970).

Attention is also important for teenagers, but often the significant others shift from parents and teachers to peer groups. This often makes teachers rely on grades as a motivator for teenagers. Grades, as we have seen, fall into the class of secondary reinforcers called tokens. But they are anything but "token" for the majority of students: the implicit economic contract existing in schools is the exchange of grades for schoolwork. Unfortunately grades are often used noncontingently, in the sense that they are not given for the performance of a particular behavior but for the relative performance of one student in relation to the norm provided by the performance of other students. This type of competitive grading means that one student can succeed only at the expense of other students, which makes the reinforcer not contingent on each student's individual performance. In addition, teachers often give grades to punish a student for behaviors that are irrelevant to the objectives of a course. Because of this, course grades are usually not a direct consequence of performance.

A better way to use tokens in the schools is like the professional football teams do. Many of these teams award stars (which are pasted on the player's helmet) to a defensive player who makes a certain number of unassisted tackles or interceptions. Each player who earns the stars receives them—yes, even some of the most macho of our idols will do almost anything for a star! In classrooms a similar use of tokens is applied with a mastery-learning approach, in which each student's grade is contingent on his own learning of the course objectives—a criterion-referenced, as opposed to a norm-referenced, grading system. (see Gentile and Stevens-Haslinger, 1983, for further discussion of this issue).

When things are going badly in secondary classrooms, it is often because students cannot perform prerequisite skills. If they are forced to compete for the teacher's praise and high grades with students who have attained the prerequisite knowledge, they are likely to come up short. This has emotional effects, of course, and also shows up in refusals to work appropriately. In such cases, an individual contract between student and teacher can be very helpful.

In one study of high school dropouts (Kelley and Stokes, 1982), thirteen students between the age of 15 and 21 were receiving $2.35 per hour on a government program for attending vocational educational classes, which could eventually lead to a high school equivalency diploma. Since their pay was not a consequence of work performed, but contingent only upon attendance, the students did the minimum work with a very low accuracy rate. When the students contracted with the teacher to receive their pay contingent upon successful completion of specified academic assignments, the quantity and quality of work increased dramatically. Analogous procedures can be followed with grades instead of money as the reinforcer.

Classroom uses of the Premack Principle are also many and varied. Many elementary teachers schedule a free play period sometime during the day. Unfortunately, it is often scheduled rigidly to occur at a certain time each day for all students. This free period could be better used by allowing each student to select activities at natural breaks in the classwork, such as when a student has successfully completed a unit of work or has been task-oriented for some reasonable period of time (e.g., Osborne, 1969).

In a variation on this idea Hosie, Gentile and Carroll (1974) observed fifth and sixth graders during free time in the classroom. From among several alternatives, several students reliably chose either painting or modeling clay on two successive days. On a third day neither of those activities was available, but in their place was a reading task on dinosaurs which included a brief written report. None of the children chose to do that report. On the next day half the students who preferred painting and half who preferred modeling were told if they did the dinosaur report, they could then paint. The other half of each preference group were promised that they could model clay as soon as they completed the dinosaur report. Of course, no one *had* to do the report at all. As the Premack Principle predicts, significantly more students completed the report when the consequence was their preferred activity than when it was their non-preferred activity.

Other classroom applications of the Premack Principle are to provide enrichment activities, such as math games, as reinforcers for completing other, perhaps prerequisite, math assignments (e.g., Taffel and O'Leary, 1976). Most current teachers use some of these approaches already, though they may not have known the name for the procedure or the research on which it is based. One of our student teachers, for example, reported the following solution to a discipline problem in an inner-city high school physical education class. The curriculum called for a unit of instruction on soccer, but the students threatened a strike if they did not play basketball instead. The teacher established a mutually agreeable contract which allowed playing basketball toward the end of each period (in some weeks at the end of the week), contingent upon their learning the soccer unit in other times.

QUANTITY OF REINFORCEMENT

We have seen how the type of reinforcer is involved in reinforcement effectiveness. The quantity of reinforcement is also important, and it can be explored through the number of reinforcements (i.e., practice trials on which reinforcement is received) and the amount of reinforcement.

Effects on Learning

Not surprisingly, the number of reinforcements affects operant behavior as it does respondent and cognitive behavior: in general, the more times the behavior is performed correctly and reinforced, the greater the strength or probability of that behavior (e.g., Hovland, 1937). The greatest increment in the probability or magnitude of the response occurs after the first few reinforcements, with each succeeding reinforced trial providing less of an increment. The last sentence describes the typical learning curve, as shown in Figure 4.

The same basic finding also applies to the amount of reinforcement. In general, the first few increments in amount of reinforcement make the biggest difference in responding, with succeeding increments having a smaller effect (e.g., Logan, 1960). In practical terms, going from zero pay to $1.00 per hour has a major effect on your behavior. So does doubling your pay from $1.00 to $2.00, or going from $2.00 to $3.00 per hour. But when you are earning $20.00 per hour, a $1.00 raise is not likely to have the same effect on your behavior that it did earlier.

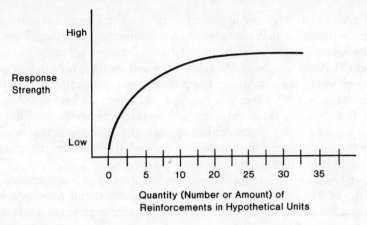

Figure 4. Typical learning curve relating response strength (magnitude or probability) to number or amount of reinforcements.

Effects on Persistence

Perhaps by now you're thankful that behavioral psychology has this nice general, uncomplicated law, given the complexities of behavior we have discussed throughout this book. If you are feeling that way, sorry, but rapanoia's got you again! The general effects described need to be qualified, especially with regard to amount of reinforcement but also, to a lesser degree, with regard to number.

The problem is that nothing occurs in a vacuum. Behavioral events have histories and each new situation is viewed by the organism in relation to that history or other events which provide a *context* or *contrast* for current behavior. Continuing with our previous example, $10 per hour is quite attractive if contrasted to your previous pay of $2 per hour, but is a punishment to someone accustomed to earning $20 per hour. Analogously, to nonhuman oganisms, the *deprivation-satiation history* of the organism and the current context make tremendous differences in performance, differences that can markedly change the shape of the curve in Figure 4 (e.g., Bower, 1961; Crespi, 1942, Reynolds, 1961). Similar effects have also been shown in respondent learning (e.g., Amsel, 1971).

Even that is not all. Up to now we have been discussing reinforcement as though it is *continuous*—that is, for every correct behavior there is a reinforcement given. In real life, as well as in many experimental studies, behaviors are seldom if ever continuously reinforced. Rather, sometimes a behavior is reinforced and other times the very same behavior is not (which is to say, it is being extinguished). This naturally occurring state of off-and-on reinforcement for the same behavior is called *intermittent* or *partial reinforcement*.

Consider what is learned in a situation in which reinforcement is delivered intermittently rather than continuously. On reinforced trials, clearly you are learning to continue the behavior and, as a side effect, you are probably feeling confident that you are doing the right thing and on the whole feeling good. On nonreinforced trials, however, you probably first feel frustrated (like what happens when you put a coin in a machine, but do not get your coffee or soft drink). But if you try again and again, getting reinforced only sometimes, you are also learning a very important lesson—namely, to engage in that behavior despite occasional nonreinforcement and feelings of frustration. Your behavior is beginning to be able to *resist extinction.*

Resistance to extinction is a topic we will develop in more detail under Schedules of Reinforcement. For now suffice it to say that if you can tolerate the frustration of nonreinforcement, you will be able to persist at a task without feedback much longer than someone who has only been continuously reinforced, thereby never learning to persist without reinforcement.

How does this relate to amount of reinforcement? Well, it turns out that in the context of prior continuous reinforcement, the greater the amount of reinforcement, the faster an organism will quit responding when reinforcement is no longer forthcoming. This lack of persistence makes sense if you consider that the organism accustomed to large rewards will have greater frustration, but will not have learned frustration tolerance.

On the other hand, if the organism has a prior history of intermittent reinforcement, then the larger the rewards obtained, the longer the organism will persist when reinforcement is no longer forthcoming (e.g., Hulse, 1958). This is because the organism had already experienced great frustration from not receiving large amounts of reinforcers, but learned to tolerate that frustration and continue with the behavior.[9]

In sum, the greater the amount of reinforcement during early stages of learning, the faster the learning. But unless some frustration tolerance is built into the training, through frequent nonreinforcement, then the experience of receiving large reinforcers could lead to a lack of persistence. Larger is not always better.

Finally, let's return to the problem of number of reinforcements. You may now be anticipating that once we get past some minimum number, it is the proportion of trials that are reinforced that is more important than the total number of reinforced trials, at least with regard to the persistence of the behavior. Since we are seldom getting reinforced by all persons in all situations, it may be that the development of persistence should be a major educational objective.

DELAY OF REINFORCEMENT

It would be difficult to imagine teaching a new response to a rat or a pigeon if the food reinforcement were not delivered immediately after the response occurred. Once the response has been learned and practiced a while, however, the reinforcement may be delayed for longer and longer periods (but there is probably always some optimal interval beyond which delays would not maintain the response).

Humans similarly need to receive immediate reinforcement, at least in the beginning of learning a new skill. Imagine a novice learning to hit a tennis ball if his instructor did not praise or correct his strokes for five or ten minutes after hitting the ball. The more reinforcement is delayed, the less effective it is. But in the more advanced stages of learning, reinforcement can and should be delayed for longer periods, in successively small steps of course. This will allow continued improvement. More importantly, it will increase persistence by allowing the student to tolerate the frustrations of waiting. In addition, it will increase generalizability of the behavior to other settings (e.g., Fowler and Baer, 1981; Kazdin and Bootzin, 1972, Renner, 1964; Stokes and Baer, 1977).

REINFORCEMENT CONTINGENCIES

When reinforcement is consistently (not necessarily continuously!) made available as a consequence of one behavior, then we say that the *reinforcement is contingent upon that behavior.* Another way of saying this is that reinforcement is dependent upon, or brought about by, that behavior. We can then speak of a causal relationship between the behavior and reinforcement as a *reinforcement contingency.* A rat who earns his food by pressing a lever is operating on contingent reinforcement. But if food were simply dropped into the cage every minute irrespective of what the animal was doing, we would say the reinforcement was *non-contingent.*[10]

Loosely speaking, it is possible to think of a reinforcement contingency as the *rule* that exists between the behavior and the reinforcement. The typical parental exhortation "no TV until you finish your homework" makes TV-watching a contingent reinforcer for doing homework. But many everyday rules are not consistently enforced and therefore lose the causal relationship implied in the word contingency. In addition, a contingency may be operating despite the fact that no rule may be able to be stated verbally, either because we are not consciously aware of the contingency or because the controlling factors have not been discovered yet. There are many species-specific behaviors that are controlled by what might be called contingencies of survival, yet the organism itself is probably unaware of the operating rule. For example, rats learn aversions to the taste of certain foods if illness is induced even up to 3 or 12 hours later. If illness does not follow, the oganism learns that the food is safe and will eat it again. Birds, on the other hand, similarly learn to avoid foods that are associated with illness, but through sight instead of taste (see, Hulse et al., 1980, pp. 65–67 for a good introduction to this topic).

Language behavior in humans offer many instances of the operation of complex contingencies despite our typical unawareness of the rules. For example, consider the following linguistic combinations (from Leeper, 1970, p. 242):

(1) old coat plus brown coat = old brown coat
(2) expensive dress plus red dress = expensive red dress
(3) beautiful sky plus azure sky = beautiful azure sky

Perhaps the linguistic rule is to place the color adjective second when combining the adjectives. But then what about these?

(4) coronation gown plus blue gown = blue coronation gown
(5) brick wall plus red wall = red brick wall
(6) utility room plus brown room = brown utility room

In these last three cases, the rule seems to be to place the color adjective first. It is grammatically incorrect in phrases 1–3 to place the color adjectives first and in phrases 4–6 to place them second. Almost all native speakers of English will agree with that—their linguistic behavior is being controlled by some contingency—yet a verbal rule is hard to come by.

Contingencies, in other words, can be simple and rule-like at times and at other times can be difficult, if not impossible, to state. Moreover, behavior can often be controlled by reinforcements which are not really causally related to the behavior, but are nevertheless *perceived* by the organism as though they were. Superstitious behavior can be produced in the pigeon by dropping food into the experimental space randomly. But many pigeons then behave as though their behavior was responsible for getting the food, and they repeat certain stereotyped behaviors over and over (Skinner, 1948). Similar behaviors occur in humans. A professional baseball player's wife, for instance, wore the same article of clothing throughout a world series because her husband hit a home run the first day she wore it. Likewise, in the *Peanuts* comic strip, Linus' belief in the Great Pumpkin is maintained by unexplained movements he perceives in his "sincere pumpkin patch." These random events serve as reinforcers for his expectation that the Great Pumpkin will appear, and they maintain his belief in the Great Pumpkin, despite the fact that he never receives any objective evidence (such as toys or candy) that the Great Pumpkin exists.

In complex school situations, teachers may often be unaware that what they do or say to a student may serve to reinforce the behavior the student was engaged in. In other words, the teacher's attention may randomly reinforce a behavior that was occurring. For example, intending to be warm and sincere, an attractive teacher may unknowingly reinforce a student's sexual advances. Such events, often leading to unpleasant confrontations later, demonstrate that the control chance reinforcement has over behavior is difficult to overestimate. The actual contingency—not the purpose of the reinforcement agent or teacher—is the important variable.

For practical purposes, few have ever stated the advantage of contingent over noncontingent reinforcement better than Benjamin Franklin (1969) in his advice to a Presbyterian minister. It seems that the enlisted men in the chaplain's outfit had been promised a gill of rum a day as an enlistment bonus. And while they were always on time for the serving of rum, few attended the prayers and services conducted by the chaplain. Franklin simply suggested that the rum be given out only immediately after prayers. The chaplain tried the idea with this result, in Franklin's words:

> Never were prayers more generally and more punctually attended; so that I thought this method preferable to the punishment inflicted by some military laws for non-attendance on divine service (p. 247).

As we have seen (and will explore further soon), contingent reinforcement does not necessarily mean continuous reinforcement, because the effects of intermittent reinforcement can be even better for maintaining behavior in the long run. Contingencies do imply that inappropriate behaviors will *not* achieve reinforcing consequences. In this sense, contingencies in the practical situation are like well-enforced rules. In dealing with humans in practical situations, therefore, it is often helpful to state the contingency as a rule. The following list may provide helpful advice in that regard.

1. Choose a rule (contingency) that can be understood and followed by the student. (Note: There is no reason why a democratic method or the student himself should not decide what the rule should be. Rules do not have to be—and indeed will often be less effective when—imposed by an autocrat.)
2. Choose a rule that can be described clearly and objectively.
3. Choose a rule that can be enforced.
4. Make sure that the reinforcement is given consistently only when, but not necessarily always when, the correct response occurs.
5. Never present reinforcement before, or without satisfactory, completion of the task.
6. Ignore irrelevant behavior that is used by the student to get you to relax the contingency requirements (he is testing the limits of the rules).
7. Do not devise or enforce unnecessary or unreasonable rules.
8. Introduce and enforce rules one by one, rather than presenting several rules at once (especially with young children).

Contingencies and Honesty

It should go without saying—but we'll say it anyway—that praise and other reinforcers should be given honestly by teachers. Many students lose respect for their teachers because everything they do receives gushing praise, ("Oh, isn't that beautiful," "aren't you doing great work," etc.) when the students know that the work was not their best, or that the teacher doesn't really mean it. Teachers establish the standards of performance in a classroom and, whether the contingency is stated verbally or not, students will adopt those standards (see next chapter) and adjust their behavior to meet those standards.

As we have seen (and will pursue further in the next section), students are not adversely affected by intermittent reinforcement. On the contrary, they develop persistence by exposure to it. Likewise, students are not harmed by teachers who withhold praise when work is shoddy, or even when it is good but could be better. When withholding praise, teachers do not need to be cold. Rather, they should provide warm attention to the students and their work and give good honest feedback on the good and bad points of it. Moreover, they should make suggestions for improving the weak points and have the students correct the work. They will then be establishing high standards as well as teaching the students to discriminate between good and poor quality work. Equally as important, they will be providing reinforcement for the student in the form of *careful, honest attention.*

SCHEDULES OF REINFORCEMENT

We have already been introduced to the concept of schedules of reinforcement in discussing persistence and frustration tolerance. Here we will discuss the topic more systematically, describing some of the major variations that have been used in the scheduling of reinforcement. The term *reinforcement schedule* means literally that—*when or how often a behavior is to be reinforced.*

CONTINUOUS REINFORCEMENT AND SHAPING

When every correct response is followed by a reinforcing consequence, *continuous reinforcement* is occurring. As we have seen, reinforcing a response every time it occurs is especially useful for increasing the frequency of new behaviors. In the early stages of learning, whether it be learning associations, concepts, or skills, immediate and continuous reinforcement allows students to repeat and improve upon correct, or partially correct, behaviors. In the very beginning, of course, the behavior is unlikely to be totally correct, and the sensitive instructor looks for approximations to the correct final behavior and reinforces those. As practice continues the instructor will raise the standard for what is correct, thereby reinforcing only *successively closer approximations* to the final correct behavior. This procedure of reinforcing only closer and closer approximations to the correct response is called *shaping.*

It is difficult to imagine most new learning occurring without such small-step improvements and continuous feedback and encouragement from a parent or teacher. But if later stages of learning required continuous reinforcement, teachers would quickly burn out and students would be too dependent, never learning-how-to-learn on their own. Besides, as we have seen, they would never learn to perform in the face of frustration and would develop no persistence. To put it another way, they would develop little or no *resistance to extinction* and would give up soon after they experienced their first occasion of nonreinforcement. How many coins do you put in a machine that does not dispense the soft drink for which you paid?

INTERMITTENT REINFORCEMENT

When a correct response occurs frequently, but it is reinforced only sometimes, we say that the behavior is on an *intermittent* or *partial reinforcement schedule*. Because organisms are not always reinforced, they come to be able to tolerate the periods of nonreinforcement and thereby maintain their behavior through extinction trials. That is, they develop resistance to extinction, or persistence. Of course, it is not as practical to teach new behaviors this way.

There are two intermittent reinforcement schedules commonly encountered, both in the laboratory and in real life. One type is based on a count of how many responses occur before a reinforcement is delivered, called *ratio schedules*. The other is based on how much time has elapsed since the last reinforcement; these are called *interval* schedules. Each of these is also broken into two basic types, *fixed* and *variable*. Once responding has stabilized on each of these types of schedules, it takes a highly consistent stylized form, which can easily be identified and distinguished from the pattern of responses generated by other schedules of reinforcement (e.g., Ferster and Skinner, 1957).

Ratio Schedules

Under ratio schedules, reinforcement is contingent on the number of responses performed, without regard to the amount of time taken to perform the response. The two major types of ratio schedules are the fixed-ratio schedule and the variable-ratio schedule. With a *fixed-ratio schedule,* the number of responses required to obtain reinforcement is always the same. For example, reinforcement may be given after every 5 responses. This would be called a fixed-ratio; 5 (FR:5) schedule. An FR:10 schedule would provide reinforcement after every 10 responses. The number of responses necessary for reinforcement then, is specified in the fixed-ratio schedule and it is always the same.

With the *variable-ratio schedule,* the subject still has to perform some number of responses to obtain a single reinforcement. However, the exact number of responses required is varied, so that the subject never knows the exact number required for reinforcement. Variable-ratio schedules are described in terms of the average number of responses required for reinforcement. A variable-ratio: 20 (VR:20) would dispense reinforcement after 20 responses *on the average.* The exact number of responses might vary from one reinforcement after every 5 responses to one reinforcement after every 40 responses, but the number of responses necessary to receive a reinforcement would average 20 over some sequence. Such a sequence of responses necessary for a reinforcement might be the following: 18, 27, 12, 23, 10, 20, 30.

Because ratio schedules reward the number of responses, persons or animals working under the control of ratio schedules respond at a high and fairly steady rate. A rat on a fixed-ratio: 50 schedule soon learns that he must press the bar 50 times before he earns a reinforcing pellet of food. His rate of responding is therefore quite high—that is, he usually emits all 50 responses

91

very quickly and in a highly rhythmic form. If he takes a break, it is likely to be right after a reward, the so-called post-reinforcement pause. Similar behavior is emitted by factory workers or salesmen on a piece rate, or by students on a timed test.

On a variable-ratio schedule, the response rate is also very high but slightly more steady. This is because the subject can never determine exactly when reinforcement will be delivered. An example of a variable-ratio schedule maintaining a high and consistent rate is that of a gambler playing a slot machine. He does not know how many coins he must put in the machine before his next reinforcement. It is always possible that the next response will be reinforced. Therefore he responds at a high, rhythmic rate, with very little pausing, except to pick up the coins delivered by the machine.

Persistence, of course, is unquestionably high in gambling behavior of all sorts, in part because ratio schedules (even fixed ones requiring large numbers of behaviors without reinforcement) condition tremendous frustration tolerance. When you use the variable schedule, so that one cannot count how long it has been since the last payoff, behavior becomes quite stable. The gambler is eagerly anticipating that the next bet will provide the payoff. But the gamblers' behaviors are being so persistently maintained by the VR schedule on a slot machine that they may go through a whole tray of coins and never discover that a machine was broken.

Interval Schedules

With an interval schedule, reinforcement depends on the amount of time that has passed since the last opportunity for reinforcement; that is, after the prescribed time interval, the next correct response will be reinforced. Note that if a correct response were not required, then non-contingent reinforcement would be occurring. Thus reinforcement is contingent on the first correct behavior following the prescribed time interval.

The two basic types of interval schedules are called fixed interval and variable interval. A *fixed-interval schedule* is based on some constant unit of time between successive reinforcements. For example, a fixed-interval: 1 (FI:1) schedule would dispense reinforcement after the first correct response occurring 1 minute or more following previous reinforcement. A FI:10 schedule would provide reinforcement for the first correct response following a 10-minute interval since the last reinforcement.

A *variable-interval schedule* provides reinforcement intermittently following the first correct response after a specified time has elapsed. The subject can never anticipate when the next reinforcement is due. Variable-interval schedules are described in terms of the average interval programmed between successive reinforcements. For example a variable-interval:5 (VI:5) schedule would be one in which a reinforcement would be made available for a correct response after every 5 minutes on the average. The exact spacing of reinforcements would sometimes be less and sometimes be more, as in the following

THE WORK HABITS OF CONGRESS: THE EFFECTS OF A FIXED-INTERVAL SCHEDULE

It is a striking phenomenon that the plotted behavior of various species on the same reinforcement schedule is so similar. We have already noted the characteristic high and steady rates of behavior evidenced both by pigeons and by human slot-machine players on ratio schedules—both peck away at a high rate, pausing only to collect their rewards or to collapse from fatigue. It is humorous to note that even some of our venerable institutions are controlled by their reinforcement schedules.

Weisberg and Waldrop (1972), for example, showed that the United States Congress is controlled by a relatively pure case of a fixed-interval schedule. In this case the powerful reinforcer of vacation time (among others) is contingent on appropriate work behavior, which for Congress is acting on bills. By tradition, congressional sessions begin and end within a relatively consistent time span. Thus the defining characteristics of a fixed-interval: 9 months' schedule are present—namely, a fixed month of adjournment and recess contingent on appropriate work (defined as deliberating, filibustering, and referring to committees, in addition to passing bills).

When Weisberg and Waldrop plotted the number of bills passed by eight Congresses from 1947 to 1968, they found in each case the characteristic fixed-interval response rate. In each of the two sessions of every Congress, relatively few bills are passed during the first 3 or 4 months after the Congress is called into session, followed by an increasing acceleration in the number of bills passed up until the day of adjournment. As many people have suspected, Congressmen and rats have something in common.

sequence: the first correct response after 2 minutes, 7 minutes, 10 minutes, 1 minute.

Because interval schedules do not depend on the number of responses given, but only on the amount of time that has passed, a rat will emit many fewer responses in a given time under an interval schedule than under a ratio schedule. On a fixed-interval: 10 schedule, for example, an experienced rat would probably not respond at all for the first 5 minutes following reinforcement. Then his response rate will slowly increase as the end of the 10-minute interval approaches, because after 10 minutes his next response gets reinforced.

This is similar to the behavior of an individual who is waiting for a bus. If he knows a bus comes every 10 minutes, his looking-down-the-street response will become more frequent the closer it comes to the end of the 10-minute interval. If a bus comes by but is full, he will stop looking for a while, then start looking more and more frequently when the next bus is due. Both the rat and the man were responding under fixed-interval schedules.

Under variable-interval schedules, the rate of response is also lower than under ratio schedules. However, the rate of response is more consistent under a variable-interval schedule than under a fixed-interval schedule. This is because the individual never knows exactly when his next response will be reinforced. Contrast the man watching for a bus with the man watching for a taxi. Since taxis come at variable intervals (not on the relatively fixed-interval schedules of buses), the man must keep looking for the taxi, but not necessarily at a high rate, since he cannot predict exactly when a taxi will pass by.

SHAPING FROM CONTINUOUS TO INTERMITTENT SCHEDULES

Attention Spans

A common problem for teachers, particularly teachers of special education classes, is the student with a short attention span. Most often a male child, he is usually easily distracted from what he is doing, and overly active or restless. Without getting into diagnosis or labeling at this point (as Juliano and Gentile, 1974, asked, "Will the Real Hyperactive Child Please Sit Down?") it may be instructive to consider that there is only so much time for behavior. Then the bigger the slice of time taken up by inappropriate behavior, the less time there is for appropriate behavior. Conversely, if you can increase the attentive behavior, the proportion of behavior left for inattentive behavior must decrease accordingly. We mention this because when the typical classroom consequences of the child's (let's call him Johnny) short attention span are analyzed, they usually show aspects of the following:

1. Johnny attends to some task, at which time the teacher is happy that he is occupied, since now she can work with some other children. Thus Johnny is being ignored; the consequence of Johnny's working is to be ignored by the teacher.
2. Johnny stops working at the task and does something else, at which time the teacher reminds Johnny that he should be working and often takes him by the hand and leads him back to his work space. Thus the consequence of Johnny's not working is to receive the teacher's attention.

Looked at in this way, the first step in increasing Johnny's attention span is to have the teacher attend to his working behavior—not his inappropriate behavior. At first, the teacher will have to praise Johnny (or find some other effective reinforcer) for working for very short periods of time. The schedule of reinforcement here will be short intervals—very nearly continuous reinforcement. As the child begins to attend to his work for longer periods, the teacher can then lengthen the intervals between reinforcements. But consistent with the principles of intermittent reinforcement, she must attend to Johnny's appropriate behavior. Instead of catching the child being bad, she must *catch the child being good*. By considering the problem as one of shaping to an intermittent reinforcement schedule, the teacher can slowly increase Johnny's attention span.

94

One way this has been done in special education classes (e.g., Alexander and Apfel, 1976; Wolf et al., 1970) is to use a simple timer, such as a kitchen timer, and set it for, say, two minutes. When it goes off, the teacher praises the student if he is working appropriately, or ignores him if he is not. The timer is again set for two minutes and the procedure is repeated. The schedule for reinforcement is therefore FI:2. (Some teachers have used more tangible reinforcers in token economy systems and were able to record data on several children, or a whole class, when the bell sounds.) As the child begins to respond appropriately, the teacher then may set the timer for varying times, sometimes two minutes, sometimes five minutes, etc; the schedule is becoming longer and more variable, until it reaches a VI:5 or VI:10.

With many special education classes or other severe behavior problems, a discrete event such as the timer bell is useful to remind both the teacher and student of the new reinforcement contingency in the classroom. In more regular classes, a teacher can often achieve a similar result by nonobtrusively walking over to a disruptive student at increasingly longer intervals when he or she is behaving appropriately. Just a look and a smile, sometimes a touch or a few words, can increase the attention span of a disruptive student.

Student/Teacher Ratios

From the previous example, it is obvious that one teacher would not be able to deal effectively with a class of 30 Johnnys. Since Johnny needs to be on a continuous (or nearly continuous) schedule of reinforcement at first, it will be physically impossible for the teacher to be adequately spread around to more than a few such students. Except in the generally smaller classes for exceptional children, this fact is often ignored in schools today. Class size is usually determined for fiscal and administrative convenience and not for the recognized educational needs of students and teachers.

This fact is recognized in programs for disadvantaged learners, such as Headstart, where there is a very small student/teacher ratio. When the students graduate into regular classrooms, however, they are competing with a greater number and variety of learners for the teacher's attention. If they have not been properly shaped from the relatively continuous reinforcement of the special program classroom to the much less frequent intermittent schedule of the regular classroom, they may not be resistant to extinction. Their lack of persistence will show up in a variety of ways: extreme teacher dependence, no frustration tolerance, short attention spans, and little work output, to name a few. Inadequate provision was made for the generalizability of the student's behavior from the training environment to the regular environment. This is the "Train and Hope" method of preparing students for the real world (Stokes and Baer, 1977).

We are not naive enough to expect that the schools will ever reduce the teacher/student ratio to some optimal level—it will probably always be less than optimal. What teachers need to do, therefore, is to recognize the problem in terms of reinforcement schedules, recognize their own limitations in providing more than a few students with nearly continuous reinforcement, and get help. Surprisingly, help is almost always available for the asking. Paid teacher aides and student teachers are one source. Parents as classroom helpers are another. Older or more advanced students in the school system are yet another. Finally, perhaps the least tapped resources in our society are senior citizens. If we had our way, senior citizen housing would be built on the premises of schools, perhaps as high rise apartment complexes on the upper floors of elementary and middle schools. Under programs managed by teachers, old folks could help students practice their assignments and could provide more frequent reinforcement. There would also be benefits for the senior citizens in giving them something worthwhile to do with their time, and the students could do things for them, as adoptive grandparents.

Adjacent facilities exist in only a few places, but it is still possible for inventive teachers to reach out to senior citizens and others for help.

PATTERNED SEQUENCES OF REINFORCEMENT

The four types of reinforcement schedules discussed in some detail above—namely, FI, VI, FR and VR—are not the only ones possible, though they seem to be the most common. Multiple, concurrent and sequential schedules and interactive combinations of schedules and amounts have also been studied in laboratory settings. In the complexities of human daily life, of course, combinations and inconsistencies abound, so it is important to take a broader look at schedule effects where the data allow.

One interesting series of studies concerns patterns of reinforcement schedules, arranged sequentially. Many investigators had shown that, compared with continuous reinforcement, intermittent schedules produce great persistence in responding through periods of nonreinforcement. Some studies went beyond that to show that such persistence could be maintained despite continuous reinforcement, if the organisms were given prior experience with intermittent reinforcement trials (e.g., Jenkins, 1962; and Theios, 1962). It was as though the organism learned to tolerate frustration while responding during the early intermittently reinforced trials; that experience then provided a psychological immunity to an experience of continuous reinforcement, because the organisms showed great resistance to extinction.

Before we go on, it is well worth noting the parallel of this psychological immunization against giving up to Seligman's (1975) immunization against learned helplessness. In the latter case, an experience of competently dealing with the environment (through avoidance learning during contingent punishment) prevents learned helplessness despite a subsequent experience of noncontingent punishment (in which the behavior is irrelevant to the outcome). The prior learning provides a context against which current experiences can be interpreted.

Suppose, to make things even more complex, the following three different reinforcement schedules were arranged in sequence: (1) continuous reinforcement; (2) alternating intermittent reinforcement, in which each reinforced trial was followed by a nonreinforced trial; and (3) VR: 2 intermittent reinforcement, in which every other response was reinforced on the average. If you consider this sequence carefully, you will note that reinforcement becomes less and less predictable from condition (1) to (2) to (3). An organism exposed to this sequence, therefore, ought to be learning persistence through a shaping process of successive approximations. What about the opposite sequence? An organism going from condition (3) to (2) to (1) is finding events becoming more and more predictable, again through a kind of shaping process. Persistence should be dissipating.

Hulse (1973) actually conducted such a study on rats and indeed found that the 1-2-3 sequence produced great persistence, at least as much as produced by exposure to VR:2 schedules alone. He also found that the 3-2-1 sequence produced a super-extinction effect: the rats exposed to this increasingly predictable series of reinforcements showed even less persistence during nonreinforced test trials than rats exposed to only continuous reinforcement.

It is always somewhat risky to speculate on the cognitive processes rats and other animals might be using while producing behaviors such as those just described. It seems clear that they have abstracted some features of the changing environment, though it is not clear exactly what cognitive processes they are using. Humans, on the other hand, are known to be quite capable of abstracting rules from sequences of events. As more is learned about such sequence and pattern effects, we may come to be able to explain more complex behaviors and thinking patterns, not only of rats, but of humans.

REINFORCEMENT SCHEDULES AND CARTOONS

It has been a number of pages since we had a cartoon or a joke. If you were wondering why, you now know: if the cartoons act as reinforcers for your reading the text, then your persistence in reading will be better strengthened by random intermittent cartoons than by cartoons presented at regular intervals.

TOKEN ECONOMIES

In a nontechnical sense, almost all schools are already token economies, since grades are dispensed as a result of classroom achievement or other behaviors. Grades, however, are not strictly contingent upon day-to-day behaviors; are often given days or weeks after the behaviors; and are often contingent upon a student's performance relative to others, instead of an absolute performance. In a more technical sense, then, grading systems do not qualify as token economies.

What does qualify as a token economy is a system in which tangible secondary reinforcers are distributed immediately following and contingent upon certain prescribed behaviors. Those secondary reinforcers, usually plastic tokens or points, are exchangeable at a later date for a wide variety of other reinforcers, such as privileges, activities, foods, grooming aids, etc. The advantages claimed for token reinforcers used in such a system are the following (e.g., Kazdin and Bootzin, 1972): (1) they bridge the delay between the behavior and the eventual reinforcement; (2) they allow reinforcement at any time during any activity, including sequences of behaviors; (3) they can be parcelled out when back-up reinforcers are unavailable; (4) they are not subject to deprivation or satiation states; (5) they provide the same reinforcer for individuals who may choose very different back-up reinforcers; and (6) since, like money, they become associated with a wide variety of other reinforcers, they may take on a greater incentive value than any single back-up reinforcer.

When such advantages get translated into advice for teachers they often take the form of the following kinds of rules for implementation (e.g., Stainback et al., 1973, Chap. 4);

1. Learn behavior modification techniques, both general and those specific to token economies. The message is that a little learning can be a dangerous thing.
2. Arrange the setting so that you can observe students' behaviors no matter what you are doing, and so that you can distribute reinforcers quickly and easily (without, for example, tripping over desks).
3. Obtain tokens which are appropriate, not easily counterfeited or stolen. If actual tokens are not desirable, it is possible to have a personalized card taped to each child's desk or notebook, on which a tally mark can be placed for appropriate behavior.
4. Establish a store, in which tangible items (e.g., foods, school supplies) or items or activities are for sale, or can be rented (e.g., tapes and tape recorders, games, free time). Pricing must be done with attention paid to the desirability of the objects or activities.
5. Collect other necessary materials which will assist the implementation of the program (e.g., banks to store tokens).
6. State the rules of the class on which contingent reinforcement will be based. These should be few in number and should be written clearly and positively—i.e., tell what behavior will be reinforced, not what behavior is undesirable.
7. Determine the specific behaviors of individuals that will also be reinforced with tokens—that is, develop individualized goals for behaviors to be modified to complement the classroom goals in point 6.
8. Collect baseline data on the frequencies of the behaviors to be modified (i.e., those in points 6 and 7), so that the results after implementation of the program can be compared to the behaviors prior to implementation.
9. Secure trained help to implement the system.

Perhaps the most obvious feature of the above list is the immense behavior modification required on the part of the teacher. For most teachers, a token economy requires a substantial change of roles and daily activities, so much so that it is tempting to attempt to implement tokens as an afterthought to the ongoing activities. Such an approach will probably contribute further evidence on "How to make a token system fail" (in the apt title by Kuypers et al., 1968). Stainback and colleagues (1973, p. 5) made the following point in that regard:

> It is discouraging when some teachers remark that they have tried a token system and it didn't work, when later we find their idea of a token system was handing out a token a week, or at best, a token a day for good behavior or for completing the arithmetic assignment. One of the first things that must be perfectly clear is that if you have not given out *at least*[11] twenty-five tokens per child per day, you haven't used a token system. In order for the token system to work, you must communicate and communicate often. The same is true with praise.

It may indeed be the case that the major effect of a token economy—or perhaps of any school behavior modification program—is on the teachers. To the extent that teachers are re-educated to pay attention to students' positive, normal and achievement-oriented behaviors instead of to the negative, disruptive and achievement-evading behaviors, then the token economy is probably half-way successful already. For those teachers who need such redirection of their attention, a considerable investment in time and effort is required.

Often no reinforcement is offered the teachers for this changed behavior, or the decision to implement a token economy is imposed from the top. It is easily understandable when teachers' behaviors do not persist through these periods of nonreinforcement. A few programs have recognized the token economy staff with reinforcers such as increased pay, vacations and workshift preferences (Kazdin and Bootzin, 1972). One study even reinforced teachers with tokens that, at the end of the day, were exchangeable for beer (McNamara, 1971).

An extensive literature now exists on token economies, their uses and misuses, in educational and other settings, and with various categories of people from elementary school children to adults, and from normal to retarded, hyperactive and emotionally disturbed (Kazdin, 1982; Kazdin and Bootzin, 1972; O'Leary and Drabman, 1971). Most research on classroom token systems has been done with special education students. There is now evidence that such programs are effective in (1) decreasing disruptive behavior, (2) increasing study and attentive behavior, and (3) to a lesser extent increasing academic achievement (O'Leary and Drabman, 1971). If it seems "obvious" that these behaviors should change together, it turns out to be not necessarily so. A study by Ferritor and associates (1972) suggests that the relationship between task attention and correctness of performance is not that simple. In their studies of arithmetic-drill exercises in third-graders, they found that (1) reinforcing attending behavior alone increased attending and decreased disruptions but had little effect on correctness of work; (2) reinforcing correctness of work alone increased accuracy with little positive effect on attending and disruptions; and (3) reinforcing both attending and correctness was necessary to improve accuracy, increase attention, and decrease disruptions. Thus reinforcement effects may be more specific than we would hope for, and, in order to understand the behavior, strict attention must be paid to the actual reinforcement contingency operating.

Regarding the effects of token systems on academic behaviors, O'Leary and Drabman (1971), p. 385) had this to say:

> If token programs serve as a priming or incentive function, one would certainly expect academic behaviors to be more difficult to change than social behaviors, since children in token programs frequently have the appropriate social behaviors in their repertoire but not the academic skills necessary to progress without considerable instruction.

They then went on to make these the first three of their ten recommendations:

1. Provide a good academic program since in many cases you may be dealing with deficient academic repertoires—not "behavior disorders." (p. 395)
2. Give the child the expectation that he is capable of doing well by exaggerating excitement when the child succeeds and pointing out that if he works hard he *can* succeed. (pp. 395–396).
3. Have the children aid in the selection of the behaviors to be reinforced, and as the program progresses have the children involved in the specification of contingencies. (p. 396).

TOKEN ECONOMIES: FOR "ORDINARY" CLASSROOMS?

Token systems, in sum, have been shown to be successful for a variety of purposes. But they are not without their problems, two of the most difficult of which are staff training and transfer of behaviors beyond the environment of the token system (Kazdin, 1982; Resnick, 1971). Transfer can be resolved by shaping to intermittent schedules (a point discussed earlier in this chapter), by training parents and significant others to use similar techniques in other environments, by teaching students how to transfer their behaviors (e.g., by teaching self-control), and by weaning students from tangible reinforcers to the more wide-spread social reinforcers (Stokes and Baer, 1977). There is even a report of a system allowing persons to earn their way off the token system by meeting high standards of performance (Kazdin and Mascitelli, 1980). While this should help transfer behaviors, it nevertheless strikes us as strange that an incentive system should provide negative-reinforcement through "earning your way off."

Kazdin (1982, p. 432) also makes another point that is troublesome to us, to wit:

> A significant development over the last decade is recognition that lack of responsiveness to the token economy may reflect more on the program than on clients who fail to respond. Lack of responsiveness usually refers to the failure of some clients to respond to a set of contingencies that is standardized across all clients.

Clients sometimes fail to respond, but often they actively resist. Precisely because a token economy restructures the extant system of reward, ". . . the potential for coercion is great," as Kazdin (1982, p. 434) cogently argues.

It is for reasons such as these that we agree with Ryan (1979), that token economies and other explicitly extrinsic reinforcement systems should be avoided in the "ordinary" classroom.[12]

If token systems are helpful with special classes, it is often because (1) the teachers are more likely to have been properly trained to use these techniques; (2) the main target behaviors are usually disruptive or attentive behaviors and not achievement per se; (3) most, if not all, students in the class are in need of immediate tangible reinforcers and specific contingencies in order to show improvement; and (4) most students in the class have known academic deficits which need correction before regular classroom objectives can be attained.

None of these four problems is true of the vast majority of "ordinary" classes. Each class has its clown, its disruptive student, its underachieving student, etc., but teachers can deal with these individual problem cases with special contingency contracts. The majority of students will respond to a teacher's attention, praise, corrections and grades if provided in appropriate ways (such as suggested in the rest of this book). Thus, while token systems can be useful, we would recommend their adoption only in special circumstances.

PUNISHMENT AND ITS AMAZING EFFECTS

MASOCHISTIC BEHAVIORS

Earlier in this chapter we defined punishment as an aversive consequence of a behavior (R→S^{AV}), pointing out that its usual effect is to suppress behavior, at least temporarily. Suppose, however, that you visited a laboratory in which you witnessed an organism behave in the following strange way. A green light goes on, the organism quickly presses a bar, and then receives a strong shock (S^D—R→S^{AV}). The light goes on again, the bar is pressed and the shocking consequence is repeated. For the next hour, this sequence of events is repeated with no diminution in the organism's response rate or latency. This is truly masochistic behavior since the organism is causing itself to be shocked by pressing the bar. It is also opposite to what is expected from punishing consequences: the organism should stop pressing the bar—if it is followed by strong shock. What is maintaining this behavior? How did the organism acquire this self-punitive behavior?

Consider possible answers to the question before we provide a likely behavioral history. The behavioral episode in question is of potential importance as a prototype for studying masochistic behavior in humans, though it is also of interest in comparative psychology. As Seligman (1975, p. 29) quipped, ". . . some experimenters will not believe that a phenomenon is real until it has been demonstrated in the white rat."

The answer, or at least one simple answer,[13] to how to induce the masochistic behavior described above is to have the green light go on, *followed ten seconds later by a strong shock.* This establishes conditions for avoidance learning, so that the next time the light goes on, the organism will do all sorts of things that might work to keep the shock from arriving. Finally the organism will stumble on the bar press, the consequence of which will be to receive a *mild shock,* but avoid the strong shock that would have followed within ten seconds. The organism will now perfect his avoidance behavior, responding more quickly and vigorously each time the light goes on, accepting the mild shock.

But the story does not end there. Through a process of *habituation,* we become more tolerant of noxious stimuli. For example, if you work near loud noise, you begin to adapt to the noise and it is not nearly as bothersome after a while. Similarly, the organism adapts or habituates to the mild shock. Thus the voltage can be slowly increased over several trials until, after some time, the organism is now pressing the bar and receiving the consequence of considerably more shock then he originally learned to avoid. In other words, he would be much better off not pressing the bar, but—and this is a critical point— he will probably never find out because, without some other kind of intervention, his avoidance bar pressing behavior will be extremely persistent. How persistent it will be depends on a number of factors, the most important of which is probably the severity of punishment.

Before going into specific effects of variables like severity of the punishment, consider another example of masochistic behavior. An organism is trained to leap a barrier from one side of a small room to another. If he does so within ten seconds of the onset of a green light, he avoids the shock; of course, he learns this avoidance response very quickly. But now lets reverse things. If the organism crosses the barrier, he receives shock; but if he stays where he was, he avoids it. After their first experience jumping into the shock ($R{\rightarrow}S^{AV}$), organisms stop jumping and simply stay put when the green light goes on, right? Wrong. There is now considerable evidence (.e.g, Church, 1963) showing that few organisms learn to reverse their behavior. Instead, they punish themselves by continuing to jump the barrier into the shock. In fact, jumping into punishment produces more persistence than continuing to jump into a safety zone after shock has been removed from the original side of the room.

What is going on here? Conventional or common sense explanations might stress the fear factor (e.g., Mowrer, 1960). If the original shock was severe enough, avoidance would occur and be maintained because whenever the S^D (the light) came on, the conditioned fear would recur and the organism would respond. Then why doesn't the organism have even more fear when jumping into shock and stop jumping? Because, it seems, there is more to it than that.

For one thing, there are apparently *species-specific defenses* that impel organisms—in different ways for different species—into "flight or fight" behaviors whenever they are punished (e.g., Bolles, 1975). Shock, loud noises, and other aversive stimuli seem to propel organisms into action, rather than into passiveness, as a survival mechanism. Sometimes, if another organism is present when shock is delivered, the action will take the form of aggression.

In addition to fear and species-specific response patterns, there is also a more cognitive factor—the necessity of learning the particular contingency involved. Organisms whose emotions and motions are so fully engaged (i.e., they are fearful *and* running or jumping) are less likely to be cognizant of

DON'T JUST DO
SOMETHING,
STAND THERE.

which event predicts safety and which predicts danger, a finding which is as true of humans as other organisms (see Hulse et al., 1980, for a good review). Thus punishment may produce cognitive confusion, especially when the conditions under which it is administered are changing.

FACTORS CONTRIBUTING TO PUNISHMENT'S EFFECTS

The above examples require some moderate to severe pain to produce such bizarre effects. A mild reprimand would surely not produce such masochistic behavior in normal humans, though it might produce conditioned emotional responses and other side effects. But painful shocks or other physical blows might if conditions were confusing as in the cases above. In this section, however, we shall consider the more straightforward case of punishment—namely, the case in which an aversive stimulus is delivered following a behavior $(R \rightarrow S^{AV})$.

Severity of Punishment

The first factor contributing to the behavioral effects of punishment is its severity. In general, the greater the intensity and/or duration of punishment, the greater and more permanent the suppression of the punished behavior (Church, 1969).

As usual, this general statement must be qualified according to the context provided by past history. Prior exposure to punishment of a certain type and severity affects how organisms will respond to subsequent punishment. Church (1969) summarized the research on this problem and concluded that organisms tend to persist in the performance of what they have learned in their previous exposure to noxious stimuli. This may help explain the masochistic tendencies we just discussed. If organisms learn vigorous escape or avoidance responses after exposure to a punishing consequence, then they are likely to persist in that behavior. The stronger the original punishment the less likely they are to discover that their behavior is no longer adaptive.

Delay of Punishment

Analogous to the effect of delay in reinforcement, the more immediate the punishment, the greater the suppression of the punished behavior. This can also be extended to sequences of behavior. Church summarized the research evidence as follows (1969, p. 154): "Punishment of the first response in a behavior sequence produces greater response suppression than punishment of later responses in the behavior sequence."[14]

Punishment Contingencies

Punishment that is contingent upon a response produces greater suppression of the behavior than the same punishment provided noncontingently, or randomly according to time. In addition, if a discriminative cue is presented prior to the noxious stimulus, the suppression becomes limited only to that condition. That is, there is little or no suppression of the behavior in the absence of the warning signal (Church, 1969). Neither does it seem to produce as much emotional behavior, such as generalized anxiety, depression and helplessness, as is likely in noncontingent punishment (see Seligman, 1975, and our discussion of learned helplessness in Chapter 2).

PUNISHMENT AS A CUE FOR REINFORCEMENT

As a final amazing effect of punishment, let's consider what happens if punishment and positive reinforcement are sequentially related. But first, let's review. The procedure for positive reinforcement is to present a desired stimulus contingent upon performance of a behavior ($R \rightarrow S^{RF}$), with the expected effect of increasing the probability of the behavior. The procedure for punishment is to present an aversive stimulus contingent upon the behavior ($R \rightarrow S^{AV}$), with the usual result of suppressing, or decreasing the probability of, the behavior. Now, let's combine these so that a behavior receives the consequence of an aversive stimulus followed by a desired stimulus, diagrammed as follows:

$$(8) \qquad R \rightarrow S^{AV} \rightarrow S^{RF}$$

Will the behavior increase or decrease in frequency? There is some evidence in animals that, at least for mild to moderate shock as the S^{AV}, behavior under $R \rightarrow S^{AV} \rightarrow S^{RF}$ occurs almost as frequently as under $R \rightarrow S^{RF}$ (Church, 1963).[15] It is, in other words, as though the aversive stimulus acts as a signal or as feedback that reinforcement is coming, so your response is correct. It certainly does not deter the response.

Extrapolating from such results to difficult and complex human situations is always risky, but we see a parallel that is so striking that it should at least be mentioned. First an example from a typical adult-child supermarket interchange. The child, reaching from the shopping cart seat, grabs a package of candy from the just-reachable shelf. The parent takes it from the child and scolds or slaps, following which a tantrum ensues. This embarrasses the parent sufficiently that a deal is made and the child receives candy, gum, or something equally desirable.

A more serious human problem may also be considered via the $R \rightarrow S^{AV} \rightarrow S^{RF}$ prototypic model. This is the battered child syndrome. In some of these cases, children seeking attention (often in less-than-desirable ways, but perhaps the only ways they learned) receive physical beatings way beyond what is justified by their behavior. Immediately following the attack, the parent feels guilt and remorse and then lavishes attention and love on the child. This may also be one of the few times such children receive that kind of warmth and they may come to accept it and even feel that the beatings are proof that the parent loves them. If others of us do not understand the attachment of child to parent (or wife to husband, or pet to master) in wanting to return for

105

more abuse, because we do not have similar behavioral histories, we can at least understand their behavior through the metaphor of the punishment-reward sequence research.

PUNISHMENT: THE MORAL OF THE STORY

There are three stories about punishment we are particularly fond of. The first is about the teenager who comes to breakfast and says to his father, "Pass the goddamn cereal," whereupon his father slaps him across the face and says, "What did you say?" So the kid says, "I said, pass the goddamn cereal." His father slaps him again and says, "Now what do you want?" The kid says, "Well, I sure don't want any of the goddamn cereal."

The second story, from a Peanuts cartoon, has Charlie Brown explaining to Linus that the best way to teach a dog is to punish him with a rolled up newspaper. His dog Snoopy, overhearing the conversation, thinks "Sure, but it also tends to give you a rather distorted view of the press."

The third story is about the behavioral psychologist who was trying to toilet train his new puppy. But everyday when he came home from work there was a mess on the living room carpet. So he stuck the dog's nose in it, then threw the dog out the window. This went on for thirty days without any change. But on the thirty-first day, do you know what happened? The psychologist opened the door and the dog ran over to the mess he had made, stuck his nose in it, and jumped out the window.

The morals of these stories are, first, that punishment teaches what not to do, but does not teach what to do. Second, punishment has emotional side effects. Third, punishment may have quite varied and unexpected effects or, as Guthrie (1935, p. 160) put it, "To train a dog to jump through a hoop, the effectiveness of punishment depends on where it is applied, front or rear." Guthrie's comment, like the above jokes, are humorous, but not frivolous. Punishment may suppress behavior, but probably only if the aversive stimulus produces behavior that is incompatible with the punished act. If the aversive stimulus releases behaviors similar to the punished act (e.g., hitting a child for fighting), punishment may facilitate the act (Church, 1963). When we strike children to suppress their fighting behavior we are also providing models who physically strike others to suppress annoying behaviors. What are we teaching?

Indeed, what *are* we teaching by punishment, especially revengeful, retribution-types of punishment? Does discipline require us to pay attention to every inappropriate behavior, or does such attention simply increase the frequency of inappropriate behaviors? If it is clear that punishment has quite varied effects, it should be equally clear that humans are too quick to use it to the exclusion of other methods of control. We are not just trying to control children's behaviors; we are trying to teach them how to learn, how to control

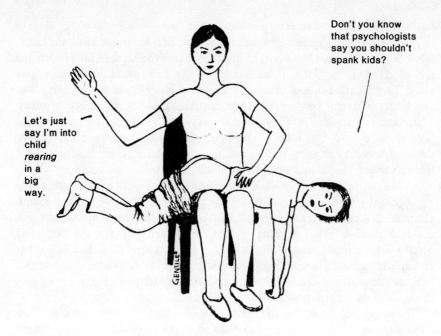

themselves, how to create, how to love, etc. We are trying to "influence" them, to use Friedenberg's softer words (1959, p. 59):

> But influence does not mean pushing people around; it means leading them to want to do what you want them to do . . . it requires real awareness of what other people need and some skill in helping them get it. More than anything else, it requires a clear understanding of what is going on and how things actually work. An influential person is no bully; he is a sculptor who works in the medium of human situations. He must respect his tools, his materials, and his market.

In this chapter, we have explored "what is going on" and how behaviors "actually work." In the next chapter we will broaden our outlook to include imitation, among other topics, and in Chapter V we shall draw practical implications from all of this and apply them to problems of discipline.

EMOTIONAL AND COGNITIVE INTERACTIONS WITH OPERANT BEHAVIOR

Operant conditioning in both basic and applied research settings is probably the best studied field in behavioral research. So perhaps it is fitting to end this chapter with an emphasis on the interdependence of the operant level of behavior with the respondent and cognitive levels.

Dealing first with the operant-respondent or motions-emotions interaction, there have been innumerable variations of cartoons and jokes on the following basic theme. A secretary, sitting at her desk when a man walks by, says to her office mate, "I can't imagine why I like Mr. Peterson. He's not handsome or rich, and he's not my type at all. But just the sight of him makes me feel good." And, of course, it turns out that Mr. Peterson is the company pay clerk. The negative side of that is even more compelling because we are usually better aware of people or settings that make us fearful, angry or guilty. The point is that it is probably impossible to be emotionally neutral about people and events. Our mutual interdependencies of behavior not only condition observable physical and verbal operant behaviors, but also condition feelings to the people and settings in which our interactions occur.

Vis-a-vis operant-cognitive interactions, it is also quite improbable that any operant conditioning—whether it be positive or negative reinforcement, extinction, or punishment—can occur without also setting many thought processes in motion. What is going on here? How can I change the situation? Shall I hit the other person, ignore him or explain something to him? What extenuating circumstances might be causing him to act as he is? Thoughts such as these occur, sometimes in parallel and sometimes as interacting processes with our operant behaviors.

Consider the following discrimination-learning problem: train a chimpanzee (or even a lower animal) to respond to the larger of two squares until the subject comes to respond correctly 90 or 100% of the time. Now give him a new discrimination, with the previously correct stimulus having to be compared with a still-larger square. Which stimulus will the organism judge to be the correct one?

This is an old problem in psychology, known as a *transposition* experiment. What is the answer? The chimps choose the larger of the two stimuli. Despite being positively reinforced for choosing a specific stimulus, the organism was learning a *relationship* between the stimuli. In other words, if the chimps could think aloud, we might have heard them saying, "the larger one is correct" instead of "that particular one is correct."

While this problem and its other like it were much debated in the literature, the debate centered on theoretical explanations and whether chimps and rats become lost in thought over such problems (e.g., Krechevsky, 1932; Spence, 1937; 1940). What was never at issue was the following: *when a specific behavior is reinforced, the organism learns to perform that behavior, but it may also learn more than that specific response.* What the more is, is often difficult to specify, especially in nonhumans, but it falls under the category of cognition.

More recent and quite exciting extensions of this point have been seen in the literature on teaching chimpanzees to use sign language or communicate in other ways (e.g., Gardner and Gardner, 1969; Premack, 1971b). In these studies the chimps were positively reinforced for using appropriate symbols. For example, the first chimp to use sign language, Washoe, had to use the American Sign Language sign for "more" before the consequence of more food or more play was achieved. But much more than this was learned by the chimps. Once they learned the appropriate responses (via operant conditioning), they combined the symbols in grammatical or logical ways beyond the specifics taught. Washoe, for example, after separately learning the words for bird and water, signed "water bird" when she saw a duck (described on Public Broadcasting's TV show Nova entitled, "The First Signs of Washoe").

In sum, while much of our teaching/learning goes on at the operant level through the social learning and feedback of student-teacher interactions, parallel analytical and synthesizing activities are going on within the student. Those cognitive, emotional and motivational processes, meanwhile may be manifesting themselves in verbal and nonverbal interactions between students and teacher.

NOTES

1. A Phrase coined in song by Kay Johnson-Gentile (1978).
2. It is sometimes said that this definition is circular, to wit: a reinforcer is something that increases the frequency of a behavior; thus if a behavior is followed by something that increases the frequency of a behavior, then that behavior will increase in frequency. This statement of the "law of effect" or the principle of reinforcement does indeed sound like a vacuous tautology. But more is implied than that.

   For one thing, as implied in our definition, any reinforcer is transituational (as first demonstrated by Meehl, 1950). This means, for example, if money reinforces the study behavior of an individual, it will also reinforce another behavior. More generally, it is always possible to demonstrate the effectiveness or noneffectiveness of a reinforcer in a given situation by the proper experimental design, in which a targeted behavior is monitored to prove that only that behavior is affected by the treatment. The interested reader is referred to Cooper (1981) and Kazdin (1973) for some of the issues involved.
3. This incident was reported by Margaret L. Zabranskey and first published in Gentile, Frazier and Morris, 1973, pp. 1–2.
4. In contrast to this most typical of American experiences, I like to consider the time I spent with a Japanese father, and his son (aged 13) and daughter (aged 12) on a long drive in their car one evening. He and I were talking in the front seat. After a while it dawned on me that the children in the back seat were totally quiet, just sitting. They weren't hitting each other, insulting each other, etc.—just sitting quietly. Finally, I questioned my host why the children were so quiet. His matter-of-fact answer was that they were quiet because the adults were talking.
5. S^D = Discriminative Stimulus, or Cue
6. To be technically complete, we should call attention to the fact that some investigators define two types of punishment analogous to the two types of reinforcement—namely, *positive punishment* and *negative punishment* (Boe, 1969). Positive punishment is the case we have described in which a behavior has the consequence of receiving an aversive stimulus $(R \rightarrow S^{AV})$. Negative punishment is the withdrawal of an available attractive stimulus contingent on the behavior $(S^{RF} - R \rightarrow NoS^{RF})$, which is similar, but not identical, to extinction. This usage is not widespread and we have chosen not to adopt it.
7. To be more technically accurate, this is a definition of *stimulus generalization* and should be labeled as such to distinguish it from *response generalization*. The latter is the performance of different responses to the same stimulus, such as shutting a certain door with varying degrees of force. For our purposes, we are not very concerned with these slight differences in responses, and we shall therefore describe only stimulus generalization.
8. The Premack studies demonstrating this punishment effect were all done on animals. Klara Papp (1980) was able to demonstrate this effect on children, aged ten to fourteen.

9. Hulse (1958) was the first to demonstrate this phenomenon experimentally, though others have replicated it. The frustration explanation builds on Amsel's theory (Amsel, 1958; 1962), though the results can also be explained in other ways. The reader who wishes to pursue the topic further would be advised to begin with Hulse, Egeth & Deese, 1980, Chap. 5.
10. We have already seen the words noncontingent and contingent punishment in Chapter II in the context of learned helplessness.
11. Emphasis in the original.
12. See also Balsam and Bondy (1983) and Lepper and Greene (1978) for cases of how inappropriately used tangible rewards can prove troublesome.
13. For example, Sandler and Quagliano (1964).
14. At home, as in Church (if you'll excuse the pun), it is good advice not to say to your child, "Wait till your Daddy gets here—you're going to get a spanking."
15. There is also a smaller amount of evidence on humans using noise as the aversive stimulus (Johnston, 1972).

CHAPTER IV
Modeling and Social Learning

INTRODUCTION

1. "By not exalting the talented you will cause the people to cease from rivalry and contention.

   By not prizing goods hard to get, you will cause the people to cease from robbing and stealing.

   By not displaying what is desirable, you will cause the people's hearts to remain undisturbed." from the Tao Teh Ching, "The Way" in Murphy and Murphy, 1968, p. 158)

2. "There is only one way to improve ourselves, and that is by some of us setting an example which the others may pick up and imitate till the new fashion spreads from east to west. Some of us are in more favorable positions than others to set new fashions. Some are much more striking personally and imitable, so to speak. But no living person is sunk so low as not to be imitated by somebody."

   (James, 1904, p. 142)

3. "Parents who beat their children for aggression intend to "stamp out" the aggression. The fact that the treatment does not work as intended suggests that the implicit learning theory is wrong. A beating may be regarded as an instance of the behavior it is supposed to stamp out. If children are more disposed to learn by imitation or example than by "stamping out" they ought to learn from a beating to beat. That seems to be roughly what happens. . . ."

   (Brown, 1965, pp. 394–395)

4. On one of her daily runs to the junior high school, schoolbus driver Gloria Arsenault caught the aroma of marijuana. She told the children to stop smoking. When they did not, she drove directly to the local police station who found two joints and two hashish pipes among the students. None of the students confessed to smoking and no one "squealed." Appearing to have no other recourse, town officials and the police suspended the bus service for three days.

   Did the students—some of whom lived as far as six miles from school— have to walk as a consequence of their behavior? None did. Their parents, many of whom "complained loudly about the suspension," drove them to school.

   (*Time,* January 17, 1983)

In a strange way each of the above four items, from the Taoist philosophy of ancient China to a relatively current news item, is an example of and helps define the scope of the concerns in this chapter. We are not only affected by the direct antecedents and consequences of our behavior, but we are also greatly affected by the behaviors of others. Humans are social beings—survival of the species depends upon social interactions—and it is therefore not surprising that our most efficient way of learning to approximate complex behaviors at any age is imitation. The phrase "Monkey see, monkey do" is probably at least as apropos of humans as monkeys.

Consider how much more efficient it is in teaching someone to hit a golf ball by demonstrating it and saying do that, compared to trying to describe all the facets of the stance and swing. Even more preposterous would be to treat the various facets of the golf swing as operant chains of behavior (which they nevertheless are) and positively reinforce each successive approximation of the correct behavior. Bandura (1962) humorously described the hypothetical application of shaping principles to teaching a person to drive a car. This is not to say that the operant and respondent principles we have studied in the last two chapters must be discarded; rather, it is to say they must be viewed in a larger context, that of groups.

Indeed, the fourth item above is a case in point. The breach of discipline would have been unlikely to occur if each student had been separately driven to school in their own individual school buses. People behave differently in groups than they do as individuals for a number of reasons, among which are the following: (1) there is a lower likelihood of any person's behavior being directly related to a consequence—a factor of anonymity; (2) there are competing reinforcement contingencies—some persons will be reinforced for breaking the rules; and (3) powerful peer pressures can be brought to bear on anyone who opposes the behavior of a subgroup—the negative reinforcement of avoiding the censure of peers can be much stronger than the positive reinforcement from authorities for "squealing." As if this were not sufficient to describe a no-win situation for such law-abiding citizens as the bus driver, the parents protested the action taken and the students received none of the aversive consequences intended for them by the authorities.

Whatever your thoughts on the merits of this relatively innocuous case, similar principles operate in more severe cases as well. A news item that hit the national press in 1981 (e.g., Buffalo Courier-Express, November 25, 1981), for example, reported that a teen-ager murdered his 14-year-old girl friend and then took a procession of more than a dozen of his schoolmates to view the corpse. After the police were finally notified, twenty-four hours after the first "viewings," a policeman interviewed thirteen of those who viewed the corpse. He said that none of them reported the murder because their primary objective was "to cover up their friend."

From minor disciplinary incidents to covering up a murder, from selling toothpaste to status symbols, from learning sex roles to learning to be violent—all these involve models to be imitated and/or other social complexities. This chapter will focus on these topics and, to bring some order to them, we begin with some basic definitions and principles involved with learning by imitation.

MODELING

Mark, a ten-year-old, had been occupying the attention of his visiting aunt and uncle for the better part of an hour with his postcard collection, a good portion of which had been sent to him by them over a period of three or four years. His sister, Sara, aged four, sat with them throughout. As the last cards were being inspected, Mark pointed out that he had a duplicate of one and might give it away. Sara immediately said, "I'll take it, Markie," and announced that she would add it to her postcard collection. Of course, when Mark obliged by making her a gift of the duplicate, her collection consisted of that one card.

This common developmental process, known to every parent, serves to illustrate the basic components of a modeling episode, as well as providing some glimpses of the factors controlling such behavior. Mark was, of course, the *model* (M) whose behavioral interaction with aunt and uncle was being witnessed by the *observer* (O), Sara.[1]

VICARIOUS CONSEQUENCES

The behavior of both children is easily understandable, at least at the general level of parental discourse. Through his postcard collection, Mark was monopolizing the adults' attention—his behavior of showing his postcards was being *directly reinforced* by that attention. And promises of future reinforcers were made for additions to the collection on the aunt and uncle's current trip. During this period Sara was observing the reinforcement her brother was receiving and was therefore being *vicariously reinforced*. Vicarious means through someone else's experience, in the same way that we say we had the vicarious experience of seeing China by viewing a friend's pictures of China. In symbolic terms, the model (M) received direct reinforcement, while the observer (O) received vicarious reinforcement. Despite the fact that O did not personally engage in M's behavior, the probability of O's performing that behavior has increased as a result of witnessing M's behavior and its attractive consequences. Vicarious learning of this sort, since it requires no performance by O, is a case of what Bandura (1965) called "no trial learning."

The fact that modeling can occur with no-trial learning requires that we introduce a distinction, long recognized by learning theorists, between learning and performance. Important research by Bandura and his associates (e.g., Bandura, Ross and Ross, 1963c; Bandura and Walters, 1963) demonstrated that children observers learn many of the details of a witnessed act, though they may suppress performance of such imitated behaviors until they are more likely to be reinforced than punished for emitting M's behaviors. Those research studies typically showed children observers a film in which some M engaged in unique kinds of aggressive-destructive behaviors against, for example, an inflated Bobo doll. A third of the subjects saw a film in which M's aggressive behaviors were severely punished, another third saw M lavishly rewarded for the same behaviors, while the film shown to the remaining third saw no consequences of M's behaviors. Later the subjects were placed in a setting just like that in the film and were scored on which behaviors of M were imitated, how frequently, and under what conditions. As expected, when O witnessed M's behavior being punished, there was little imitation in the real-life situation. This would be suppression according to a *vicarious punishment* effect.

However, there was no difference between the no-consequences and positive reinforcement groups in performance of the behavior. Apparently they *learned* and *performed* the behaviors equally well. Most importantly, when all O's were asked later to reproduce the behaviors they saw in the film and were given attractive rewards for doing so, there were no differences among any of the groups. All groups including those who witnessed M being punished, had *learned* the acts equally well. Whether they would *perform* the acts depended upon the situation. Vicarious reinforcement and vicarious punishment, in other words, have their effects on subsequent performance of behaviors. The behaviors will be learned observationally so long as they are novel and appropriately attended to.

Bandura (1965; 1969) has gone further in explicating *three effects of modeling.* First, there is the *learning effect,* as we have just seen. New behaviors, never before occurring in O's repertoire, may be acquired as a result of witnessing M. Second, there is an *inhibitory* or *disinhibitory effect* of modeling. O is likely to inhibit or suppress the performance of a behavior as a result of M's being punished for the same behavior; in contrast, if M's behavior was reinforced, O's performance of a similar behavior may be disinhibited, or increased in probability. Third, there is a *response facilitation effect,* in which M's behavior simply serves as a signal (a discriminative stimulus, or cue) to facilitate the performance of a behavior already learned and socially sanctioned. Examples of the response facilitation effect of modeling are applauding after someone begins to applaud, trying new foods when others do, or pledging money to a benefit fund because others are doing so.

REINFORCEMENT RECONSIDERED

On the basis of what we have now discovered about the relationship between modeling and reinforcement, it is worth spending a moment to reemphasize the definitions of reinforcement and punishment learned in the last chapter. Positively reinforcing and punishing consequences were defined as increasing (or maintaining) or decreasing, respectively, the frequency of a behavior. This can now be seen to imply that such consequences affect performance of an already acquired behavior more than they teach a behavior. Learning can occur in the absence of a reinforcing consequence, as has been widely known for many years.[2] Learning can also occur, as we have just seen, without any overt performance and therefore with no direct consequence to O. In fact, it may be impossible not to learn things if conditions are properly arranged. For example, DO NOT LEARN WHAT FOLLOWS:

"COLORLESS GREEN IDEAS SLEEP FURIOUSLY."

Chances are, unless you covered the line, you learned that infamous nonsense statement even if you tried not to.

To say that learning occurs whenever we pay proper attention to something is not to say, however, that reinforcement and punishment cannot facilitate or hinder the learning. The consequences of a behavior often help make the learning more memorable cognitively and affectively. Thus while learning can occur in the absence of reinforcing or punishing consequences, such consequences may facilitate (or hinder) the learning and will certainly affect when and whether the learned acts or facts are performed. Another way of saying this is that reinforcing and punishing consequences are sufficient but not necessary for learning. They primarily affect the performance of behavior once learned.

WHOM DO WE MODEL?

Often to the chagrin of the parents, children model their behaviors too well as, for instance, when they are frustrated or hurt themselves and utter a parent's favorite expletive. Children obviously model their parents, older siblings, and significant others with whom they interact in person or on television. As children grow older, teachers become dominant models and are then displaced by peers and media and sports personalities.

To say that such factors as age, sex, prestige, wealth, talent and/or popularity of models affect the likelihood of observers reproducing their behavior is probably true, but not very informative. Only Charlie Brown of the Peanuts

cartoon strip has a baseball hero—Joe Shlabotnik—who was a major league failure. Other children identify with and model their baseball swings after successful players and "superstars."

Why is that? What are the factors responsible for the efficacy of a model in inducing imitative behaviors? Bandura, Ross and Ross (1963b) again provided a cogent experimental analysis of the problem. Children observed an adult model who had a wonderful collection of toys. That adult later gave some of those toys to a second adult or, in a different experimental condition, to a child. All of these characters were models who then each acted in striking and unique ways that later might be imitated by the observers. The question of interest was would the observers imitate the adult model (A) who controlled the resources, the adult model (B) who was the beneficiary of A's generosity, or the child model (C) who also was a similar-aged recipient of the gifts?

Bandura and his colleagues found that the observers most frequently modeled A, the person who *controlled the resources*. For these children it was clearly more important to be able to give than to have to receive (to paraphrase an old aphorism): they understood the advantages of social power and that seemed to dominate the modeling situation.

Perhaps there is a relatively clear message from this study—namely, that persons will be more effective models if, whatever else they are, they are in control of desirable resources. This fact seems not to have been lost on advertisers, a point to which we will return later. Nor has it been lost on women's rights or minority group advocates who promote a greater number and variety of women and minorities in positions of power and competence on television shows.

But all modeling is not based on the power of the model. As William James said in quotation 2 at the outset of this chapter, no one is so low as to be imitated by no one. We imitate the behaviors of siblings younger than we, if they may be getting some attention we are not ("Mommy always liked you best!"). We may even imitate siblings of the opposite gender, even if we are not being reinforced for such behaviors.[3] Moreover, we may model aggressive behavior even if the consequences of it are negative—a point we shall turn to next. It is not yet entirely clear, in summary, whom we model or why, though social power of the model, vicarious consequences of the model's behavior, and the likely consequences of performing the model's behavior are three important determinants of modeling.

MODELING AGGRESSIVE BEHAVIORS AND TV VIOLENCE

From time to time a unique suicide will occur and soon afterwards be followed by several more, enacted in a strikingly similar manner. In parallel fashion the evening news is semi-regularly dominated by a bizarre murder or other aggressive act that was almost a carbon copy of a TV or movie scene, or a recent real-life crime. Such bizarre episodes reach the point that the police and others worry continually that publicity for a crime may have the unintentional side-effect of stimulating a rash of "copycat" duplications of the feat. It seems that no matter how insane an act or actor appears to the general public, there always seems to be someone who will imitate the behavior.

Aggressive behaviors, in particular, are extraordinarily ripe to be modeled from sources such as movies and TV, as well as real-life persons. Or so it seems. From time to time, therefore, there are investigations into the effects of TV violence on aggressive behaviors, some of which have been sponsored by the U.S. Senate.[4] Before delving into the findings and implications of these studies, let's become a subject in one of the most famous of the experiments.

If you were a three-to-five year old attending the Stanford University Nursery School in the early 1960's you may have participated in this study. A female experimenter escorted you from your classroom to a special room. On the way in you met another adult who was also invited to come along and join the game. You were then seated at a table which contained such artistic materials as potato prints, stickers, and colored paper, and given instruction on how to create pictures with those materials. The other adult, the Model, was taken to a table at the far corner of the room to play with tinker toys, a mallet, and a 5-foot inflated Bobo doll. Then the experimenter left the room.

After about a minute of tinkering with the tinker toys, M spent the remainder of the ten-minute period aggressing against the Bobo doll in a number of highly novel ways, including sitting on the doll and punching it in the nose, pommeling it on the head with the mallet, and tossing it in the air and kicking it around the room. M repeated these acts in sequence about three times interspersed with verbal comments appropriate to the acts—e.g., "Sock him in the nose," "Kick him," and "Pow."

Following this, the experimenter returned and led you to another room full of a number of attractive toys to play with. But shortly after you became involved with one of more of the toys, she announced to you that because these were her very best toys, she decided not to let you play with them and to keep them for other children. Then she took you to a third room, which included a wide variety of toys, like a 3-ft. Bobo doll, a mallet and peg-board, dart guns, a tea set, crayons, dolls, stuffed animals, and so forth. She stayed inconspicuous in the room and let you do whatever you wished. In this third room, unknown to you, you were being observed through a one-way vision screen and scored every five seconds for various types of aggressive behavior.

Before telling you the results, we'll now introduce you to the other conditions in this study. You were in the Real-Life Model condition. Other children witnessed the same aggressive acts by the same model, but shown on a ten-minute Movie in the same room. Still other children saw the same behaviors performed by a cartoon figure called Herman the Cat. The last fourth of the children were a control group who did not witness any modeled aggression, but went directly to the second room. Finally, half of the subjects in the Real-Life and Movie conditions observed a male model, while the rest observed a female model.

The results were quite convincing in showing that over all, the real-life, human film and cartoon film Models induced approximately equal amounts of aggressive behaviors by the child observers and that amount was almost twice as much as that which occurred in the control group. The effect was even greater for the imitative aggression scores—that is, the specific acts of aggression performed by the models. Clearly, the observers learned the aggressive acts.

Other notable findings concerned the gender of both M and O. Boys exhibited more aggression than girls, especially of the type that involved hitting and gun play. Girls, in contrast, sat on the Bobo doll more frequently. This tendency was even more pronounced when sex of M was taken into account. Boys who observed the female M were more likely to sit on the Bobo doll without punching it, while those who observed the male M were more likely to punch it. Girls, on the other hand, were likely to imitate the male M's sitting on the doll, but less likely to punch it. Thus even for three-to-five-year-old youngsters there is a "sex-appropriate" behavior pattern that makes a model more or less likely to be imitated.

Bandura, Ross and Ross (1963a), the authors of this famous study, contrasted their design and results with some other conceptions of aggression and modeling. One important aspect of their experimental design was the inclusion of a frustrating experience in the denial of opportunity to play with the attractive toys in the second room. They reasoned that people would be more likely to reproduce aggressive responses if they had encountered a frustrating experience, based on Dollard and colleagues' (1939) *frustration-aggression hypothesis*. Since they were not concerned with a frustration vs. no-frustration comparison, they did not include a no-frustration control group in their study. Their control group experienced frustration equal to the other groups, but did not witness the prior aggressive acts by a model. As a result, they did not act nearly so aggressively when presented the opportunity.

The Bandura et al. results also contrasted strongly with other alternative explanations of the effects of filmed and real-life aggression on modeling. There was, and perhaps still is, a view that filmed violence has a cathartic effect, allowing observers to vent their frustrations vicariously (e.g., Feshbach, 1955, 1970). While there may indeed be occasions on which violence fantasized or observed vicariously produces a reduced tendency to be aggressive—the so-called catharsis effect—most researchers in the field would agree with Huston-Stein's assessment (1978, pp. 80–81):

> . . . the results of the theory-based laboratory studies of Bandura and Berkowitz[5] do apply to the naturalistic effects of television violence on real aggressive behavior. Heightened aggression occurs after children or adolescents watch violent television under many conditions; such aggressive behavior can be suppressed by situational constraints, but often it is not. Other factors related to television viewing, particularly deprivation of programs that children like to watch, can also lead to aggressive behavior. Finally, aggression is especially likely to increase for children and adolescents who are already aggressive. The net result is that the people with the greatest potential for harm to other people are the ones most likely to be inspired to violence by television.

Lest you draw the conclusion that it is only a "violence-prone personality type" who succumbs to the aggression portrayed by television or other models, consider that the nursery schoolers at Stanford were not a particularly violent or deviant group. And besides, whenever we are labeling a group for research purposes as "more aggressive," that is simply their current status. We do not know how they developed that status, which may also have been influenced largely by modeled violence. We do know that there is evidence from naturalistic settings which shows (1) that violence at school is correlated with the amount of violence watched on TV at home, and (2) that television viewing at primary school age predicts later aggressive childrearing practice on any other family characteristics studied (Huston- Stein, 1978).

Modeled aggression, on TV or elsewhere, can indeed be a dangerous commodity. Even when the "bad-guy" gets caught and punished in the end, the aggressive acts are learned by the observer. Even when the modeled aggressive acts can be rationalized by laudatory motives, as when superheroes punish villains, the aggressive acts are learned by the observer. Whether these aggressive behaviors are subsequently manifested or suppressed by the observers depends, among other things, on the similarity of the modeled and real situations and the likelihood of positive or negative consequences in the current situation. Nevertheless, the models—villainous or pious—of these aggressive behaviors are teaching the moral equivalent of "might is right."

MODELED PROSOCIAL BEHAVIORS

To be fair to the television industry, there have been shows developed especially for children that attempt to model pro-social behaviors such as cooperation, empathy, sharing, tolerating frustration, and so forth. Sesame Street and Misterogers' Neighborhood on Public Television come to mind first, but there are other shows on both public and commercial TV which model socially sanctioned behaviors. Incidentally, most shows model some pro-social and some anti-social behavior, including Sesame Street, though the ratio and vividness of violent acts is usually of concern to critics.

As might be expected, there is considerably more research on TV violence than on TV pro-social behavior. The evidence that exists indicates that the observers of programs like "Misterogers" do indeed model some of the pro-social behaviors, and perform fewer aggressive acts than control groups of children not watching the show (e.g., Friedrich and Stein, 1973; Stein and Freidrich, 1972; Shirley, 1974).

It is ironic that pro-social behaviors such as cooperation are not as vivid as many aggressive acts. Thus they may not be as easily recalled or modeled.

120

On the logic that that is essentially accurate, Friedrich and Stein (1975) added role playing and verbal labeling of the pro-social behaviors being modeled on TV to enhance the probability that the acts would be recalled and imitated. They concluded that each enhances a different aspect of behavior: role playing increased the probability of the behavior in a test situation, while labeling (e.g., "helping") facilitated subsequent recall of the concepts modeled, but did not affect their behavior.

A TENTATIVE CONCLUSION

More needs to be learned about the effects of modeling on behavior, but much is already known. A report written for the Scientific Advisory Committee of the Surgeon General on Television and Social Behavior inferred from the available data in 1972 that viewing violence on television can induce aggressive behavior in adolescents (e.g., Chaffee, 1972). We must concur. While TV violence is obviously not the sole cause of aggressiveness, modeling in general is perhaps the primary means of learning specific aggressive behaviors, verbal and non-verbal. It is therefore very difficult to overemphasize the importance of modeling. Thus the parent or teacher who spanks or yells at a child for not sharing may be modeling the very behaviors intended to be stamped out (see also quote number 3 by Brown, 1965, in the beginning of this Chapter).

Moreover, if models appear to be deriving pleasure from the act of punishing then they may be instigating vicarious emotional conditioning in observers for such feelings. Aggressive behavior may or may not be ubiquitous in this world, but in species other than humans it is almost always the means to a nonaggressive end, such as protection of offspring or the need for food. But as Feshbach pointed out (1964, p. 264).

> The derivation of satisfaction from eliciting pain and suffering in others is a peculiarly human phenomenon. . . . The motivation to injure others—or aggressive drive—which can be influenced by anger is, according to the present theoretical analysis, an acquired motivation based upon the internalization of a standard which the child acquires from exposure to particular cultural values and from his own concrete experiences.

We shall have more to say about internalization of standards later in this chapter. Meanwhile, even if we are wrong and aggressive behaviors occur for other reasons, what do we as parents and teachers have to lose by modeling the behaviors we are attempting to induce?

ADVERTISING

P. T. Barnum was reputed to have said that a sucker is born every minute. If you watch commercial television long enough, you'll not only overdose on violence, but you'll come to understand why it is called "commercial" television. TV is not the only medium for advertising, of course, and modeling and vicarious reinforcement are not the only selling techniques used. For example, coupons and rebates that come with the purchase of certain products are designed as direct positive reinforcements for behavior that is loyal to the sponsor. On top of that, some supermarket chains double or triple the value of product coupons to reinforce the behavior of shopping at their store. But if modeling is not the only psychological technique used to modify the behavior of generation after generation of "suckers," it is nevertheless a major technique.

A sexy movie star slinks into view, runs her hands over fanny and thigh and, in appropriate bedroom voice, whispers "Nothing comes between me and my _____", advertising a brand of designer jeans. A small, average looking man in a locker room full of big, handsome, muscular jocks announces that he has an advantage over these guys: his advantage is not looks or brains, but the razor blade he uses. Sure enough, up comes a beautiful blonde in a sports car, to whisk away our frog-transformed-into-a-prince-by-the-kiss-of-a-razor, as he announces smugly to the jealous macho-men, "So who said life was fair?" If most reasoning can be said to use either inductive or deductive logic, much current advertising seems to rely on seductive logic.

Famous people—sports figures, film and TV personalities, musicians and artists—are shown using "the only" product able to stop their hemorrhoidal itch, relieve their headache without stomach upset, or transport them to their party in a car sporty enough to maintain their glamorous lifestyle. Ordinary people who use the advertised product are the envy of the neighborhood for their shiny floors, the absence of ring-around-the-collar, or their newly discovered attractiveness to the opposite sex. The formula is the same: a model uses our product and is highly reinforced. We observers should be vicariously reinforced and, therefore, ever so slightly more disposed toward purchasing the product.

The story, however, does not end there. Advertisers also have access to other techniques such as direct operant reinforcement, as mentioned earlier, as well as respondent conditioning. In the latter case, they use music and jingles that may come to be uniquely associated with and evoke certain feelings appropriate to the product. They also associate their product with words and emotional states of the actor/models that will elicit the feelings desired for their product (see Higher-order Conditioning in Chapter II). Finally, they advertise on programs that fit the image they are trying to convey: beer is advertised most often on sporting events, cereals on cartoon shows, gospel records on religious shows.

Observer/consumers are often unaware of the many ways they are being manipulated, but products, musical groups, and styles begin to capture larger shares of the market as a result of these techniques. Walt Disney was a master of similar techniques in creating lasting positive feelings toward his creations. For example, in the Hall of the Presidents at Disneyland and Disneyworld, a very patriotic feeling is induced in the observers as they watch various life-like versions of the presidents move and speak. But as the show climaxes with Lincoln giving a stirring address, the sunset in the background slowly changes to a red, white and blue American flag while appropriate patriotic music fills the theater. For those old enough to recognize the music and know what the flag is, hardly an eye remains dry.

We mention these techniques for two reasons. First, all of us are subjected to such behavioral manipulations whenever products, lifestyles, ideas and beliefs (yes, even religious, educational and political products and beliefs) are being sold.[6] Thus, we can better understand our own feelings and behaviors by learning about how others attempt to manipulate us. Second, it helps us understand our children—why they "desperately need" certain sports shoes, jeans, rock records, and hamburgers, but would rather die if seen by their peer group with the wrong brands. The advertisers create a "need" for their product through media models and, if successful, peers follow through by using the product, providing models closer to home as well as differential consequences to those who conform and those who are too different.

A nagging question may remain: why don't advertisers (and others) simply provide us with a logical presentation of the facts to convince us to use their product? The answer is that such "convincing" does not work and often gives rise to counterarguments that, if anything, make it harder to change the belief and behavior. Facts contrary to one's beliefs create what Festinger (1957; Festinger, Riecken and Schachter, 1956) called *cognitive dissonance,* which people can resolve to cognitive consistency by changing their beliefs or, more likely, by marshaling support—social or logical—for their current beliefs. Try to convince a smoker to give up smoking or a "junk-food junkie" of the benefits of broccoli. Behavior change by persuasion seldom works though it is universally and repeatedly attempted. As Varela (1978, pp. 121–122) described such direct persuasion,

> All the arguments favoring a certain position are marshaled as strongly as possible, the dire consequences of not following that course of action also being presented. The target of our persuasion attempt usually proves to be very refractory, something that leaves us nonplussed. "How is it," we wonder, "that in spite of all these clearly logical reasons, our subject remains, if anything, more adamant in what is often a pigheaded position that is not only wrong, inconsistent, inconsiderate but often damaging to him as well?" We focus the problem on the subject, seldom doubting that perhaps what needed improvement was the procedure that we used.

If we observers/consumers still haven't learned that convincing and persuading is an inefficient means of changing attitudes and behaviors, the message has not been lost on those forces—companies, promoters, certain religious organizations and politicians—whose livelihood depends on shaping our attitudes and behaviors. And so, to paraphrase the Taoist verse (No. 1 in the Introduction to this chapter), they display what is desirable and cause many people's hearts to become disturbed.

VICARIOUS EMOTIONAL LEARNING

The vicarious learning processes we have discussed so far have been mostly concerned with behaviors most observers would call operants—aggressive acts, purchases, imitations of a model's motions. But emotions and respondent conditioning can also occur via the indirect route of witnessing a model.

Our common experiences tell us that this is true from observing actors portray various emotions which induce observers into a similar emotional state. Often, however, we observe not only the actor portraying the emotion, but also other situational cues that may directly induce the emotion in the observer. For example, if an actress playing a mother begins to scream and cry just after her child falls off a bridge into the river, the audience may feel a similar emotion, too; however, it may not be the excellence of the acting that induced the observers' reaction, but the horror of seeing a child fall from a bridge. The most convincing evidence of vicarious conditioning of emotions, therefore, occurs when the only stimuli available to the observer are those of the model.

Fortunately or unfortunately, life is full of such situations.[7] If young observers see a parent react with intense fear to an unseen something they later learned was a spider, it is not surprising if the observers develop a fear of spiders. Through the vicarious experience of witnessing a model's fear, the observer associates a similar reaction to the feared object, even though that object has never been directly experienced.

As described, vicarious and direct classical conditioning are governed by the same processes (as Bandura, 1969, cogently argued). In fact, the process looks remarkably like higher-order conditioning (see Chapter II). Consider its likely history. The initial experiences children have with parents showing fear reactions may have occurred in the presence of an actual US for fear, such as fire, falling, or some other pain-producing consequence for the children (observers), as well as the parent (model). Then the parent's emotional reaction can become a CS for producing that reaction in the child. As we know, once a stimulus becomes a CS_1, it can be used to condition other stimuli via second-order conditioning. In the above example, the spider is a CS_2 which gains its strength to elicit a fear reaction by being paired with the CS_1—namely, the parent's emotional reaction.

Similar but more subtle vicarious respondent conditioning may occur in children learning to feel tense and uneasy with, say, mathematics through a parent's, teacher's, or peer's dis-ease. Attractions to rock music, for example, may also be learned this way: an older sibling's or friend's facial expressions and emotional reactions appear to be happy and excited after listening to a new musical group. The younger child then takes an immediate liking to the group, though there was no direct experience with the music.

It is possible that this kind of vicarious emotional arousal is the basis for understanding how others feel—a process usually called *empathy*. Observers are not intuiting what another feels; they actually feel, or can at least imagine how they would feel, if they were in the same situation as the model (Bandura, 1969).

THE DEVELOPMENT OF SELF-CONTROL

At a typically American birthday party for a one-year-old, all will be amused when the guest of honor literally digs in to the cake with both hands. The same observers would be much less amused if their children attacked the cake in the same manner at their fifth birthdays. By this time children are assumed to have acquired the means to control their own immediate impulses in the interests of propriety. But how do they learn such behavioral self-management or, as it is usually called, self-control?

Before attempting an answer to that question, let's define more precisely what we mean by self-control and then consider a typical adult's reaction to a determined need for self-control. *Self-control is displayed when, in the relative absence of immediate external constraints or reinforcers, a person engages in a behavior which was previously less likely than some alternative available behavior.* This definition, which is based on that of Thoresen and Mahoney (1974), can be better understood through an example. A person who was trying to lose weight would demonstrate self-control if he or she ate fresh garden vegetables and skipped the fattening foods and desserts at a buffet luncheon when dining alone. In this case, the unlikely behavior is eating the vegetables, the alternative and perhaps more probable behavior is eating the fattening foods and desserts, and the absence of immediate constraints is given by no one else being present and lots of other available foods.

It would be sensible to advise an adult with a self-control problem to do three things (e.g., Gross and Drabman, 1982, Kanfer, 1970): first, to *self-monitor* the behavior of interest, in this case, eating; second, to *self-evaluate* the behavior in terms of some standard of performance; and third, to *self-reward* for meeting the behavioral standard. Self-monitoring might take the form of observing and recording how often, what and how much you eat, by counting calories or even by counting bites of food in a day.[8] To evaluate your own performance you need a standard. This might be derived from some optimal number of calories per day for your height suggested by a nutrition expert or some other model. Then, when you meet this standard each day you reinforce yourself with praise or some special activity you reserve for that occasion— hopefully the reward is not eating a big piece of chocolate cake.

Using these three components of self-control in this order is a logical and oft-suggested intervention technique to effect change in behavior. But now let's return to the question of how self-control behavior is learned by normally developing children. Clearly young children do not learn to monitor, evaluate and then reward their own behavior in that order. The sequence is the reverse, as Harter (1982, p. 173) cogently argued using a real example of a young girl whose mother is trying to teach her to pick up after herself:

> She has previously learned to imitate mommy's approval in the form of "good girl," which leads to an experience of positive affect. However, she next must learn to discriminate between those actions which are good and those which are bad; she must learn how to evaluate her behavior. Mommy initially serves as

the evaluator, telling her that she is a good girl when she puts her dirty clothes in the hamper, and that she is not a good girl when she doesn't. The child internalizes these standards for self-evaluation. As a next step in the process, Mommy begins to set the stage for self-monitoring, by initially monitoring the child's behavior.

Mommy, as monitor says things like "Now *you* know what you are supposed to do with your dirty shirt," setting the conditions for the child. Eventually, this component of the process becomes internalized, such that the child can monitor her own behavior. The developmental acquisition sequence then is self-reward, self-evaluation, and then self-monitoring.

What Harter is describing is the natural process of acquiring self-control or, more generally, what might be called self-motivated behavior. It is *internalized* by the child as a result of social interaction with significant others. Moreover, in her view, it is a parallel developmental process to the kind of competence motivation (e.g., White, 1959) that we mentioned earlier as the cure or prevention for learned helplessness. Internalized control of one's own behavior is a form of mastering skills and controlling environmental consequences and, therefore, it is a prime component of purposeful behavior.

What is important to remember—and why this discussion is occurring in this chapter on modeling—is that the acquisition process for this kind of self-regulation moves from external to internalized control. Children first self-reinforce by modeling the way they are reinforced by their parents (and how they reinforce each other and themselves). Next, children self-evaluate according to the internalized standard they model from the parents. Finally, they can monitor their own behavior to remain consistent with that standard.

ADOPTING STANDARDS

Another series of research studies by Bandura and his colleagues explicates the process of internalizing standards. In four studies using a miniature bowling game,[9] elementary school children observed models playing the game, expressing self-evaluations and giving themselves rewards (e.g. of candy). In some cases the model was adult; in some cases another child. In some cases the model imposed a strict standard (e.g., a high score was required before the model said, "That's a great score. I deserve some M & M for that score" and had some candy); in some cases a lenient standard (low score) was adopted for the same verbal praise and material reward.

The results of this series of studies showed the importance of models on self-imposed standards. Compared to control subjects who did not witness models playing the game, children generally adopted the standards of the model they observed. Observers were more likely to adopt high standards for their own behavior if M had a high standard and if M consistently applied that standard both to him- or her-self and to others. Observers were also more likely to internalize the standards if M's performance and standards were moderately high, but not too high. Presumably an expert is too advanced to be a believable model for a beginner.

These studies and others which replicated and extended the findings have now accumulated a considerable amount of evidence on the importance of models on setting and maintaining performance requirements, the acceptable standard for the performance, and how much material reinforcement is appropriate to a given level of performance. As children continue to develop they internalize more and more of the standards of significant others. What is more is that they are largely unaware that they are doing so.

CONFORMITY

THE INDIVIDUAL VS. THE GROUP

Perhaps it is not too big a leap from models, internalized standards and self-control to a more obvious way in which we humans are susceptible to the influences of others—namely, the pressures of a group to conform to their behaviors and standards. Some famous studies have been done in social psychology to uncover how group consensus and norms become established (e.g., Sherif, 1947), the impact of group norms on an individual's behavior (e.g., Asch, 1956; Krech et al., 1962) and the impact of authority on obedience (Milgram, 1963).

To make the point most vividly, assume that you are a subject in Dr. Asch's experiment on visual judgment. You are brought into a room, seated as the seventh of eight subjects and told that you will be seeing a card (A) with a vertical line drawn on it. Next to it would be another card (B) with three vertical lines on it. The job of everyone is to decide which of the three lines on card B is the same length as the standard on card A. Furthermore, you are to state out loud your opinion in turn. After everyone agrees to participate and understands the directions, the first trial begins.

Card A's line is 10 inches and the lines on card B are 8 3/4 inches, 10 inches and 8 inches. It is apparently an easy judgment for all, because each subject in turn (the six before you and the one after you) all state that the middle line matches the standard. On the second trial there is also unanimity. On the third trial the match appears to you to be as easy as the first two and you are all prepared to say it is the third line on card B which matches the one on card A. To your great surprise, however, the first subject calls out "number 1." You double-check your perception and conclude he must have made an error just about the time the second subject also says "number 1." In fact, all six subjects before you agree that number 1 matches the standard. It is now your turn. What do you say? Do you conform to the others or do you continue to trust your own judgment and resist the temptation to be agreeable?

As you may have gathered, the other seven subjects were stooges following a script of the experimenter. You were the only real subject, being tested not on visual judgment, but on resistance to conformity. Would you have conformed? You were, as Asch's title suggests, a minority of one against a solid majority of seven who were obviously wrong; and yet one-third of the 50 subjects tested yielded to the social pressure and agreed with the majority on at least half of the test trials.

The results of variations on this type of research show that the amount of conformity is markedly decreased when there is just one other person who disagrees with the majority and when the judgments can be made privately or anonymously. Conformity can be increased by increasing the difficulty of the test items or judgments and by having the reference group be significant others (e.g., colleagues or supervisors). The extent to which yielding to pressure can go is seen by some comparisons on opinion items using Crutchfield's variation on Asch's procedure (e.g., Krech, Crutchfield and Ballachey, 1962). Military officers, for example, all disagreed with the statement "I doubt whether I would make a good leader" when tested privately; under group pressure, however, 37% agreed with the statement. Only 19% of college students privately agreed that "Free speech being a privilege rather than a right, it is proper for a society to suspend free speech whenever it feels itself threatened;" when confronted with unanimous group pressure on that point 58% agreed. The same technique can induce people to agree to such facts as "male babies have a life expectancy of only 25 years," "the USA stretches 6000 miles from San Francisco to New York," and "men are 8 or 9 inches taller than women on the average."

GUARDS VS. PRISONERS

If you were too young to be recruited for Asch's study and/or you think those findings ancient history, perhaps you might have responded to an advertisement for male college students to participate in a two-week mock-prison experiment in the early 1970's. If so, you would have been extensively interviewed and tested to assure that you were more-or-less normal. Then you would have been randomly assigned to be either a guard or a prisoner. If you were a guard, you were randomly assigned to one of three eight-hour three-man shifts and were outfitted in appropriate uniform and night stick, which you were told was not to be used but was just for "show." If you were one of the twelve prisoners, you were unexpectedly "arrested" at your home by regular police officers who transported you to the make-shift jail in a 35' corridor in the psychology building at Stanford University. Upon arrival, you were stripped of your clothes, sprayed for lice and made to stand in the cell yard alone naked for a while. Then you were given a prisoner's uniform and a cell.

When all were there, the warden came to greet all prisoners with the standard speech of your lack of responsibility and citizenship in the real world, which the prison staff would teach them. He then read you the rules of the prison which, if followed along with the proper penitence for past misdeeds, would lead all to get along fine. Some of the rules follow:

1. Prisoners must remain silent during rest periods and meals and whenever they are outside the prison yard.
2. Prisoners must eat at all mealtimes and only at mealtimes.
8. Prisoners must call guards "Mr. Correctional Officer."
16. Failure to obey any of the rules is punishable.

Except for the admonition not to use physical punishment, the guards were given no other specific instructions, but were told only to carry out whatever activities were necessary to interact with the prisoners and staff members.

Haney and Zimbardo (1977), who conducted the study, described the results in the context of socialization of roles. Their results were classical examples of the ways institutions and environmental settings shape behavior into the stereotypical behavior patterns expected for the role. The guards gave directives and became physically and verbally abusive in the name of maintaining "law and order." Macho exercises of power by guards were respected and modeled by other guards. Prisoners, on the other hand, resented their treatment and sometimes rebelled. The guards taunted and harrassed them more. The prisoners became angry, even enraged at each other when, for example, guards took privileges away from the group because of defiance by one. Eventually most of the prisoners became passive, initiating no activity, and reflecting symptoms of learned helplessness. One even had to be released on the second day because of stress.

In this experiment no one was told how to behave. Assumption of roles led to one social group reinforcing its own members for struggling against the other group. That increased the other group's conformity to perceive the situation similarly, to become more cohesive as a group, and to resist the other group. In addition to the dynamics within a group, pressures from outside groups increase conformity. Ironically, in Haney and Zimbardo's words (1977, p. 219).

> Because they have been socialized to see each other exclusively as 'enemy,' guard and prisoner groups cannot appreciate the degree to which their individual plights are actually common ones.

AUTHORITY VS. MORALITY

Perhaps the most vivid experimental example of conforming behaviors occurred in a study by Milgram (1963), which was an attempt to understand the kind of obedience which allows crimes to be committed by people who were just "following orders." Had you been one of the paid subjects, you would have been told you were to help the experimenter administer a study of the effects of punishment on learning. Your job was to read a list of word pairs to another subject (a confederate of the experimenter's), whose duty was to memorize them. The latter was taken to another room where he would be out of sight and strapped into what resembled an electric chair. Whenever the learner made an error, you were to administer a shock to him from a real shock-generator. After each error, the voltage of the shock was increased one level (from a low of 15 to a high of 450 volts). Unknown to you, the shock was not connected to the learner in the other room.

The learner, of course, made many errors and you were told by the cold, matter-of-fact experimenter to increase the level and administer the shock. The learner regularly screamed and, by 300 volts, pounded on the wall and then fell silent. The experimenter nevertheless told you to treat the silence as an error and press on. If you complained and asked to discontinue in the experiment, the stone-faced experimenter told you to please continue.

If the study does not sound sufficiently convincing to believe that the shocks were real, you should read Milgram's report. The subjects administering the shocks were not only convinced that they were hurting an innocent subject, but many were highly stressed themselves, muttering such phrases as "Oh, God, let's stop." And yet—and this is the frightening result—26 of 40 subjects showed continued obedience until the end.

As in conformity to other norms, yielding to pressure to obey can be reduced if the experimenter were not an authority figure (in this case he wore a white laboratory coat of a scientist or physician), or if he were not in the same room as the subject, or if the learner receiving the shocks were in closer proximity and visible to the subject.

While such research would not be permitted under the current strict guidelines for human research, it was then supported by grants from the National Science Foundation and Yale University. Its procedures and results are

MORE ON MILGRAM'S OBEDIENCE STUDY

Milgram's (1963) experiment had some other interesting features and results. For example, Milgram asked 14 Yale seniors in psychology to predict how 100 subjects age 20–50 would respond when asked to administer shocks. The unanimous prediction was that only 0–3% would "obey" to the end and administer Very Strong Shocks.

Regarding the belief that shocks were painful, the subjects rated the shocks they believed they were administering on a 14-point scale from "Not at all painful," the lowest rating, to "extremely painful," the highest. Their modal response was the maximum 14, with the mean (average) being 13.42.

Subjects' emotional behavior was consistent with their belief that they were administering painful shocks. One sign of their tension was nervous fits of laughter shown by 14 of the subjects, with 3 of them having uncontrollable seizures of laughter. In the post-experimental debriefing these subjects were embarrassed by their laughter and took pains to point out they were not sadistic and did not enjoy administering the shocks.

If we can be excused for a bit of black humor, Milgram's experiment was truly a case where the punisher could say to the victim, "This is going to hurt me more than it hurts you."

significant for helping us understand the subtle and not-so-subtle pressures we are under to conform. These studies also show how difficult it is to resist and remain independent of such pressures.

If there is good news from these studies, it is that not everyone succumbs to the pressure. Thirty-five percent of Milgram's sample, for instance, were able to resist obeying the experimenter's orders because they felt the orders were wrong. But it would be a much too simplistic conclusion to draw from these studies that there are simply two kinds of people in this world—those who blindly obey and those who don't.[10] The impelling conclusion from these studies in our view is that pressures from our reference groups can be very powerful determiners of our behavior in given situations.[11] It is simply not a viable notion that evil is perpetrated by evil people and that good people are not perverted or sadistic. Good people can become sadistic and perpetrate evil when they are placed in a situation which expects, requires and reinforces otherwise unthinkable acts. One reason that this can occur is because the socialization process into accepting one's own unacceptable behavior occurs gradually ("and besides, everyone else is doing it!").

None of us is immune from such pressures, though some have learned how to assert our independence in ways that are self-protective and still supportive of the best interests of the group. It is also true that group pressure is not always subversive of the individual: sometimes it is clearly in the interests of the individual. In either case, we will better understand ourselves and the people with whom we interact if we can properly assess the group pressures under which we are all acting.

NORMS AND CLASSROOMS

In one of our classroom observations in Japan in 1976, an interesting discussion occurred in an eighth grade girls classroom. It seems that a discipline situation had occurred: two of the girls had skipped classes early to meet boyfriends but told their parents they were in school. As a result, they had to stand in the teachers' room instead of going to class until the class decided what needed to be done. Thus one class period was set aside for class reflection on the problem.[12]

A student led the meeting, with the teacher sitting to the side taking notes, but otherwise not commenting. The two "deviants" were in class to present their side of the issue and to comment on agreements. After a short presentation by the leader, the class broke up into five groups of 6 or 7 members each. After a few minutes, the large group was formed again and spokeswomen from the groups presented arguments. Popular views were greeted with spontaneous applause. Formation of small groups occurred twice more for a minute or two each time. The total time for the meeting was about 30 minutes, during which time the "deviants" presented their side, all arguments were heard, and an agreement was reached.

The observer was not privy to the solution reached; but that is not the point here. The situation is in itself interesting because it is an overt demonstration of group norms in operation. By having individual or small group views expressed, debated and eventually adopted by the larger reference group—in this case the class—we have the process of norm-building occurring before

our eyes. *Norms, at least in classroom settings, have been defined as ". . . shared expectations or attitudes about what are appropriate school-related procedures and behaviors."* (Schmuck and Schmuck, 1983, p. 198).

The Japanese are justly famous for their attempts at reaching consensus in all parts of their society. Here we see how they build a consensus, which in no uncertain terms informs all what the classroom norms are. It can build an esprit de corps for all the participants in the group, since each individual contributes to and is affected by the eventual agreement. It also applies direct group pressure on any "deviants" in the group to conform.

If Japanese groups are often more overt in their group processes, group pressures in western societies are just as real. Deviates from reference group norms can receive much pressure to conform, followed by outright rejection and hostile criticism if they do not conform (e.g., Schachter, 1951). Of course, if there are several deviates who have been rejected from a group, they may now have a common enemy which can form the basis for a new group with its corresponding set of norms.

Tracking systems, undertaken with the best of good will by teachers and administrators, can also fall prey to this adversarial group norm problem. Like the guards and prisoners in the Zimbardo-Haney (1977) study, the students in the "fast lane" will develop shared expectations and behaviors that are different from those in the lower tracks. Life would be simple if all these groups could be kind to and tolerant of each other, but often that is not the case. It is never the case when one of the groups is given the label "buzzards," as described in the preface of this book.

GIVEN THE EXISTENCE OF A GENERATION GAP, AND DIFFERENT CONFLICTING NORMS AMONG THE GENERATIONS, THEN WHY IS IT THAT CHILDREN WHO DON'T GET ALONG WITH THEIR PARENTS GET ALONG SO WELL WITH THEIR GRANDPARENTS?

SIMPLE. THE CHILDREN AND GRANDPARENTS HAVE A COMMON ENEMY.

CLASSROOM GROUPS

SOCIOMETRY AND INTERPERSONAL RELATIONS

It may strike you that the previous section on groups and their conflicting norms paints a rather dismal picture for a teacher who wants to see both individual achievement and cooperation in the classroom. Looked at from a different perspective, however, perhaps it is not so dismal. Each student, like each teacher, wants to be considered a normal person, possibly better than average in some ways, but still a normal, not too deviant person. To be normal is to be like the others and also to be liked by the others.

Unfortunately, the number of friends and amount of respect people have are not equally or even randomly distributed. Rather, this *sociometric wealth* (the *sociodynamic law* as it is called by Moreno, 1953), is distributed much as economic wealth is distributed: a few are wealthy and many are poor. Likewise with friends: when students are asked to name the three classmates they like the most, a few students will be chosen as friends by many other children. Unfortunately, the least popular children are not just ignored or isolated, though that is often the case; they are also, in contrast to popular children, more likely to be frequently mentioned in a list of the three persons disliked most. To give an example, Bill will choose Harry as his most-liked classmate, while Harry will not mention Bill in any of his most-liked choices, and may even place Bill at the top of his personal least-liked list.

Research by Dilendik (1972) in two sixth grade racially integrated classrooms confirmed this basic pattern. In one of the classes none of the isolated students—those at the bottom of the sociometric ladder—chose their "best liked" people from within their group. All chose upward and, of these, only 19% were chosen reciprocally by their more popular peers. In contrast, of the popularity leaders 78% named friends from within that clique, with 71% success. The other 22% chose downward with reciprocity of liking returned at 100%. The data from the other class were similar.

This situation can be bad enough for the individuals involved. For the group, however, it can have other implications. In Moreno's words (1953, p. 705):

> . . . conflicts and tensions in the group rise in proportion with the increase of the sociodynamic effect, that is, with the increased polarity between the favored ones and the neglected ones. Conflicts and tensions in the group fall with the decrease of the sociodynamic effect, that is, with the reduction of the polarity between the favored ones and the neglected ones. This hypothesis has been brought to an empirical test and confirmed by many investigators.

No classroom is so cohesive that it has no cliques and 100% reciprocity of friendships. The social world in which we live is much too complex for that. Friendships and cliques are often in existence from previous years and they may carry over into a current classroom. Norms and values of one group may be quite different from those of another and, as we saw in the prisoners and guards study by Haney and Zimbardo (1977), members of one group may reinforce each other for giving the other group trouble. Moreover, there is a tendency to overgeneralize on the good points of the group of which you are a member as well as on the bad points of a separate group. Heider (1958) makes this perceptual principle a central part of the balance or homeostasis of an individual when he says,

> For instance, liking and admiring go together; the situation is unbalanced if a person likes someone he disrespects. In other words, the unit of the person tends to be uniformly positive or negative. This is known as the halo phenomenon. To conceive of a person as having positive and negative traits requires a more sophisticated point of view; it requires a differentiation of the representation of the person into subparts that are of unlike value. (p. 182)

Groups are often formed for the purpose of being different from others. Thus their norms will emphasize the similarities of their members and the differences between them and everyone else. Thus the "best sorority" at a college has the prettiest, brightest, most desirable women on campus as members (by their own definition) and tremendous group pressures are placed on the sorority sisters never to date men who are not fraternity members, but rather to date only the BMOCs[13] from the most exclusive fraternities.

135

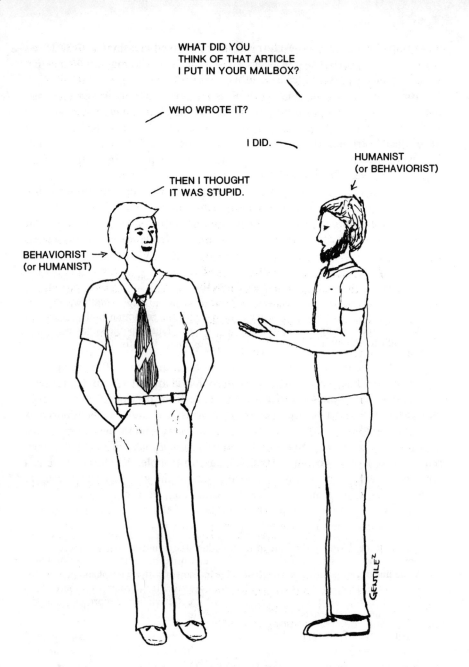

In these gestaltist tendencies to oversimplify our relationships with others, however, also lies a solution to the problem. To paraphrase an example of Heider's, where are you most likely to find a Kansan boasting about the Empire State Building?

      a. in Topeka
      b. in New York
      c. in Tokyo
      d. in Chicago

The obvious answer, Tokyo, implies that Kansans can overcome their regional competition with New Yorkers when they are representatives, not of Kansas, but of the USA. Similarly Democrats may vehemently criticize a Republican administration in Washington when discussing politics with other Democrats or Republicans; but they will temper their criticism with praise when having such a discussion with a Communist party member.

As the cartoon suggests, psychologists are not above these group dynamics games either. But the situation is not hopeless; we've already seen that people can view themselves as members of a small separatist group or of a larger group, inclusive of the smaller factions. Teachers can take advantage of this fact in planning their approach to the classroom, the topic to which we shall turn now.

TEACHERS AND GROUPS

Teachers do not create in their classrooms the kinds of group dynamics we are discussing; rather they inherit them. Teachers nevertheless can facilitate group cohesiveness or contribute to factionalism by their reactions to the different individuals and groups in a classroom. Factionalism becomes a de facto part of classroom life when ability grouping is instituted. It is further encouraged when the groups are given "good" or "bad" labels, or when teachers treat the students differently on the basis of their group membership.

Beyond grouping, however, there is a more general point to be emphasized. Teachers model respect or disrespect for various students by what they say to them or about them in front of others. We have witnessed the kinds of "death at an early age" that Kozol (1967) described in classrooms—namely, children hearing teachers make derogatory statements about them within earshot of others. Aside from the direct devastation that such behavior has on the affected child, the teacher is additionally modeling how other students may behave toward that person. Moreover, if the object of the teacher's comments is a social isolate, it will further isolate the child. If the object of the criticism is a member of an alienated group, it will tend to further alienate the group to treat the teacher and those students who receive the teacher's favor as the enemy.

Fortunately few teachers are as insensitive as portrayed above; but all of us are prone to momentary lapses which may produce the same unwanted effects unintentionally. Good and Brophy (1978) provide an interesting example of this under the topic "teacher expectations." The teacher asks a complex question of the class, pauses, and then calls on Johnny Bright. Johnny remains silent, scratches his head, and wrinkles his brow, behaviors the teacher interprets as "working out the problem." When Johnny asks for the last part of the question to be repeated, the teacher happily obliges on the assumption that the Bright boy has the problem partially worked out, and then waits patiently for the answer. "If someone interrupted the teacher at this point to ask him what he was doing," says Good and Brophy (1978, p. 89), "he might respond that he was 'challenging the class to use creativity and logical thinking to solve problems!" If the teacher had called on Sammy Slow, on the other hand, the same silence, head-scratching and furrowed brow might be interpreted as further evidence of Sammy's being hopelessly lost again. After a short pause, the teacher may say, "Well, Sammy?" to which Sammy may request to have the last part of the question repeated. But this might only serve to confirm the teacher's suspicion about Sammy and he might have the student sit down and call on someone else. In Good and Brophy's words (1978, p. 89), "If interrupted at this point and asked what he was doing, the teacher might respond that he was 'making it clear that the class is expected to pay close attention to the discussion, so that they can respond intelligently when questioned!"

Such subtleties of differential treatment are not lost on the students as individuals or as classroom subgroups.

COOPERATION, COMPETITION AND INDIVIDUALIZATION

. . . in the first few hours of a game as played in the land of After-Africa both teams were engaged in a desperate attempt to establish . . . "a monotheistic lead." The ultimate ambition was to separate oneself from one's opponents by a single goal. In the first few minutes of a game therefore, attack was the imperative. But once the goal had been scored, the victorious team then shifted its entire strategy to defense. The commitment was a commitment against equalization. A small margin of superiority by one team over the other was supposed to be aesthetically more satisfying than a wider measure of separation.

But the defeated team had to attempt equalization whatever happened. If the defeated team succeeded in establishing parity with its opponents, both teams resumed attack as the strategy of action on the field. Both teams became once again engaged in the relentless pursuit of a 'monotheistic lead.' The lead was still monotheistic if one side had two goals to its credit and the other had one. But the totality of three goals was at a lower level of purity than the single match goal. (Mazrui, 1971, pp. 35–36).

The conception of a competition as a dedication to win without humiliating the opponents is not something with which most people grow up in the United States of America; perhaps nowhere, since the event Mazrui described occurred in African Heaven.[14] It is used to introduce this section because it may serve to induce a reconceptualization of competition.

Sport, of course, exists for the primary purpose of competition between individuals or groups (secondary purposes might be competition against oneself or physical fitness). But contrary to many of our aphorisms about the "dog eat dog world" we live in, each culture socializes its citizens to be cooperative for the most part. Competition is reserved for special occasions and then usually based on strict regulations or norms of fairness.

Schools, in contrast to sporting events, exist for the primary purposes of the improvement of individuals and of socializating those individuals to society's goals—a cooperative venture. Secondarily they have the goal of teaching people to compete better, but that is intended to be a consequence of the individual growth and within the cultural norms of cooperation. Few would dispute this and yet many of the teaching methods and events in classrooms appear designed to foster competition: grading on the curve, homogeneous groupings, and recitations based on the game "who knows the answer?"

One analysis of the problem suggests that we have not adequately attended to the student-student interactions in developing our teaching plans. As Johnson and Johnson (1975) see it teachers must not only specify their instructional goals, but they must also specify the *goal structures,* defined as the type of interaction that will exist among students while working to attain the goals. Three types of goal structures cover the range of school situations—namely, cooperative, competitive and individualistic—each of which is described next.

Cooperative Goal Structures: require that individual student behaviors are coordinated to achieve the educational goal; if one student in the group succeeds, all succeed.

Competitive Goal Structures: require that an individual student's success comes at the expense of the others; if one student succeeds, others cannot, at least not relative to the best.

Individualistic Goal Structures: require that students achieve goals without interaction with others whether the goals are the same or different for each individual; if one student succeeds it has no bearing on another's success.

Learning specific knowledge and skills is an individual process. Each person's nervous system, conditioning history, and manner of interacting guarantees that that is so. When one member of your group learns something the learning does not transfer to the other members by osmosis. Teachers teach groups, but individuals learn. Having said that, however, does not imply that each individual in the group is independent from the others, even in individualized instruction. This chapter in particular, and this book in general, has presented evidence to the contrary: we are all interdependent, reciprocally determining each other's behavior and highly influenced by the groups of which we are members.

Thus we must concur with the claim that there are indeed some times in which individualized or competitive goal structures are desirable in class, but that "Beyond all doubt, cooperation should be the most frequently used goal structure," (Johnson and Johnson, 1975, p. 66). To decrease classroom anxieties, to encourage creativity, to bring social isolates into the mainstream of the classroom, to encourage friendships, to reduce the felt need for cheating, to encourage adoption of modeled standards, to reduce aggression and discipline problems, to encourage students to encourage each other—all these and more require a cooperative classroom climate.

Providing specific research evidence on such claims is beyond the scope of the present treatment,[15] but it should be clear from the thrust of this chapter that these claims must be generally true. When people feel alone and against the group they are anxious and easily manipulable (e.g., the Asch studies). They are easily distractible and therefore less frequently on task. They have little opportunity to discuss ideas with peers, to clarify and elaborate what they have learned in part because helping another student might be at their own expense, and thus their learning retention, and transfer of training cannot help but suffer.

This does not make cooperative learning a panacea. It does not guarantee that students will not compete at times. Nor does it guarantee that learning and retention will be maximum, that all regardless of race or creed will be friends, and that there will be no discipline or motivation problems. What it does is allow more possibilities for these desirable outcomes. And the teacher sets, by establishing either explicitly or implicitly, the kind of goal structure that will exist in the classroom.

MODELING AND SOCIAL LEARNING: SOME RECOMMENDATIONS

It should be obvious by now that difficult problems such as racial integration and equality do not disappear simply by desegrating classrooms and busing poor black children to affluent white neighborhood schools. The racial attitudes of all can change in positive, accepting directions, but they do not just happen because the children are in the same classrooms. If, in fact, each separate racial group becomes cohesive but antagonistic to the other group, then the social experiment of busing can be a social disaster. Academically it will also likely be a failure since the higher achieving, but socially antagonistic students, are unlikely to be models the lower achievers will want to imitate.

On the other hand, there is some evidence that integrating classrooms can bring about better academic performance by the minority group, but only when they are accepted as friends by the majority group (e.g., Lewis and St. John, 1974).

It is true that problems of racial, sexual, or other kinds of equality have political, legal and economic overtones in this society, and thus the schools cannot be held totally responsible for solving them. It is nonetheless equally true that schools—and more specifically teachers—do immensely affect student interactions and behaviors in classrooms. They do this by the academic standards they set for the class, by how they treat students in class, by how they allow students to treat one another, and by how they practice what they preach. To be more specific, let's review some of the major points of this chapter and infer some recommendations for classrooms.

1. Teachers, by virtue of their position of knowledge and authority in the classroom, can be powerful models for students. The students will likely learn to adopt the teacher's standards in the level of performance required for self-reinforcement and will likely model the teacher's treatment of others (e.g., whether teacher's comments are kind, honest and constructive; or whether they are destructive or derogatory).

2. Teachers not only model social and emotional behaviors, but also model cognitive behaviors, such as logical thinking and problem-solving. Thus if teachers speak of encouraging creative thinking and problem-solving but ask only "Who knows, or what is, the answer?" they are modeling "answer-grabbing" (to use Holt's (1964) terminology). To be a model of process instead of only product, they must ask "How can we find the answer?" (e.g., Good and Brophy, 1978) and think aloud whenever possible for the students, as well as encourage it among the students.

3. If teachers want cooperative behaviors in classrooms they cannot model competitive behaviors by rewarding one student at the expense of another. Thus grading on the curve is incompatible with cooperation. So is ridiculing a student's contribution, or calling on a student whom you suspect is unprepared to answer, and then moving to another student who appears to succeed at the first student's expense.

4. Teachers can reduce the sociometric distances in the group by reinforcing the natural peer group leaders (those who are liked by more isolated students) for modeling appropriate academic and social behaviors. Some of these natural leaders can also be peer tutors (with appropriate training) who may also help others increase their academic performance. This will also relieve the teacher from being the sole person in the classroom reinforcing goal-oriented behavior.

5. Teachers also model emotions and how they can be controlled. Honesty in expressing these emotions is important both for the teachers own mental health and for the student observers. Thus if certain behaviors are making you angry, say "What you are doing is making me very angry. What can we both do to keep this situation from getting out of hand?" The feeling is thus expressed in a nondestructive way and the students observe a self-controlled, honest model of how that can be done without an aggressive confrontation.

6. Teachers and parents should recall that witnessing violence on television, or perhaps elsewhere, is unlikely to have a cathartic effect of "draining people of their aggressive energy" (to use the apt phrase of Berkowitz, 1962). Rather it may (1) teach techniques of aggression, (2) provide cues for arousing previously learned aggressive behaviors, and (3) affect an individual's cognitive justifications for aggression.

7. Aggressive acts—by children or adults—against the cause of someone's frustration can reduce hostile tension, but only if the other person does not counter-attack. In any case, the act of aggression, if repeated and practiced often enough to the exclusion of other ways of solving interpersonal conflicts, can become a dominant habit. An "aggressive personality" is being formed. As Berkowitz (1962, p. 256) proposed, ". . . frequent aggressive behavior can be regarded as arising from aggressive habits and that such habits may be strengthened by whatever rewards the attacker receives through injuring others." Adults, therefore, need to model and systematically to teach cooperative ways of resolving conflicts.

8. Teachers may often be able to turn interpersonal conflicts, peer pressures, or group rivalries into instructional training exercises by encouraging role-reversals and honest evaluations of what is going on. This is not to say that teachers should step into each controversy. Many controversies, especially young children's, are short-lived and may actually be prolonged by adult attention. But in some cases students can learn to analyze their own and others' feelings and behaviors with a little help from role-playing and teacher behavior as a model.

As with other topics introduced in this book, much more could be said. The interested reader is encouraged to consult some of the original experiments cited to find out for themselves how the information we have was generated. In addition, the following texts are recommended for further information and practical advice on the issues mentioned: Darryl J. Bem's *Beliefs, Attitudes and Human Affairs* (1970), Thomas L. Good and Jere E. Brophy's *Looking in Classrooms* (1978). David W. and Roger T. Johnson's *Learning Together and Alone* (1975), Vernon F. and Louise S. Jones' *Responsible Classroom Discipline* (1981), and Richard A. and Patricia A. Schmuck's *Group Processes in the Classroom* (1983).

NOTES

1. We are adopting the terms imitation and modeling as synonyms because of the relative simplicity they provide in describing common situations. Other terms have also been used as labels for the imitation process, the most common among them being "identification" which usually implies that O is strongly attracted to M for various reasons. In the example of the big brother-little sister given above, that was probably operating. But in other situations such strong attraction may not be obvious. Thus we shall use the more neutral terms modeling and imitation. For further discussion of definitional issues, see Bandura (1969) and Flanders (1968).
2. The famous experiments on "latent learning" were some of the first strong evidence on that (e.g., Tolman, 1932, 1959).
3. Brim (1958) gives some evidence that boys with a sister as their only sibling manifest more feminine traits than those whose only sibling is also male.
4. Huston-Stein (1978) provides a very readable review and bibliography of both the anti-social and pro-social effects of television.
5. She is speaking here primarily of the following publications of Bandura and Berkowitz: Bandura (1965b); Bandura and Huston (1961); Bandura, Ross and Ross (1963a, 1963c); Berkowitz, (1962, 1964, 1970); Parke, Berkowitz, Leyens, West and Sebastion (1975).
6. We haven't even told all of the story. Some advertisers use techniques that are usually only perceived subliminally, if at all (e.g., Key, 1976). That is, messages (such as the word "sex") or figures (such as a skull, a shark, or penis) are hidden in the advertisement (often in the ice cubes of liquor adds). Some controversy exists regarding this. Although we believe that Key has evidence that the practice does occur, it is not clear what effect, if any, it has on observers. The mechanisms for the above techniques, in contrast, are well-known and effective.
7. There are also experimental analogues of such situations (e.g., Berger, 1962; R. E. Miller, 1967), but real life examples are plentiful and perhaps more vivid.
8. In a self-study by H. D. Kunzelmann reported by Thoresen and Mahoney (1974) daily bites of food was indeed the behavior of interest.
9. Bandura, Grusec and Menlove (1967); Bandura and Kupers (1964); Bandura and Whalen (1966); and Mischel and Liebert (1966).
10. And besides as we pointed out earlier, the only two kinds of people we recognize are those who divide the world into two kinds of people and those who don't.
11. This is not to say that group pressure is the only determiner of such behavior—there are also, as we have seen, developmental histories and other situational factors that contribute to conformity behaviors.
12. This type of meeting is called "hansei kai" in Japanese.
13. Big Men on Campus
14. Ali Mazrui's book, *The Trial of Christopher Okigbo,* begins with the untimely death of the Igbo poet Okigbo and follows him to heaven where he is put on trial for betraying his art by becoming involved in the politics of the Nigerian civil war. Along the way Mazrui expressed some utopian views. We highly recommend it. The passage cited here is intended to show that our conceptions of competition are culture-bound: there are alternatives to what we usually take for granted.
15. See Johnson and Johson (1975) and Slavin (1980) for references on the research evidence.

CHAPTER V
Discipline: Motions, Emotions and Commotions

INTRODUCTION

"If I ordered a general to fly from one flower to another like a butterfly, or to write a tragic drama or to change himself into a seabird, and if the general did not carry out the order that he had received, which one of us would be in the wrong?" the King demanded. "The general, or myself?"

"You," said the little prince firmly.

"Exactly. One must require from each one the duty which each one can perform," the King went on. "Accepted authority rests first of all on reason. If you ordered your people to go and throw themselves into the sea, they would rise up in revolution. I have the right to require obedience because my orders are reasonable." (from the *Little Prince* by Antoine de Saint Exupery, 1971, p. 45).

From all that we have learned so far about (1) the interactions of emotional, motivational and cognitive processes within individuals; (2) the social interactions between people on all of these levels; and (3) the influences of groups and models on all of these social learnings, it should be clear that discipline problems are just special, and perhaps more complicated, cases of normal interactions among students and teachers. As such, we should be able to analyze some of the interaction patterns with the hope of discovering what conditions are maintaining the behaviors of each person involved. Thus, after a definition of misbehavior, this chapter will explore the social learning of some prototypical discipline problems, provide a cross-cultural perspective in which to view misbehaviors in schools, survey some of the analyses that others have made to prevent or solve discipline problems and suggest some viable, field-tested techniques for dealing with actual or potential discipline situations.

A DEFINITION OF MISBEHAVIOR

First, a definition is in order. *A discipline problem, a misbehavior, or a case of indiscipline* (We have always favored this British term) *shall be considered to be "any action taken where it is not wanted"* (following Gnagey, 1968, p. 5). This definition avoids questions of moral transgression, safety, courtesy, etc., which are often bound by culture, social class, or religion and which therefore lead to disagreement. For example, one teacher may find classroom talking to be objectionable and another may find the same level of noise to be a sign of contented and constructive activity. Who is to say what absolute standard is to be imposed on all classrooms or all teachers?

If a discipline problem is simply any action taken where it is not wanted, then such an action is like a weed: any plant growing where it is not wanted. A dandelion in a lawn is a weed to some homeowners, but so may be a rose in a wheatfield to a farmer. It depends on the context, the purpose, and the preferences of the person(s) responsible.

DISCIPLINE SITUATIONS: INTERACTIONS GONE SOUR

Given this, classroom rules serve to establish the context in which interactions occur. If a teacher (perhaps along with the students) has established a rule of no talking unless called upon by the teacher, then any student talking is likely to be viewed as an annoyance—at least by the teacher. Of course, students may find reasons to talk anyway: to make fun of the teacher who is writing at the board, to get a laugh out of another student, to ask for an interpretation of what was said, or for many other reasons. When the talking first occurs, it may be diagrammed as follows for teacher and student:

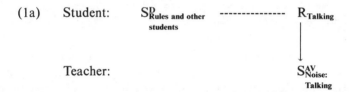

In the presence of the classroom rules and other students the student should not talk. But he does anyway and his talking serves as an aversive stimulus for the teacher.

The teacher angrily acts to correct the situation by yelling at the student, which has the effect of punishing the student, as follows:

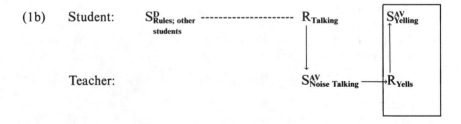

Now the effect of a moderately aversive punishment like yelling is usually to suppress the behavior, so the student immediately stops talking. As we know, however, punishments of this small magnitude do not serve to eliminate the behavior forever; rather, they suppress the behavior only for a short while in the presence of the punisher. This immediate suppression, nevertheless, has an effect on the teacher, diagrammed as follows:

(1c)   Student: $S^D_{\text{Rules; other students}}$ ---------- R_{Talking} S^{AV}_{Yelling} ——→No $R_{\text{Stops Talking}}$

        Teacher: $S^{AV}_{\text{Noise Talking}}$ ——→R_{Yells} No S^{AV}_{Quiet}

This is a classic case of negative reinforcement (i.e., escape) on the teacher's part. That is, the teacher finds that yelling removes the aversive stimulus, as aspirin removes a headache or pulling a plug removes shock. The student is negatively reinforcing the teacher for yelling.

What we have in this mutual interaction, then, is the teacher punishing the student, while the student is negatively reinforcing the teacher. The punishment has no long-term effect on the student. The negative reinforcement, on the other hand, has a great effect on the teacher: the frequency of yelling in similar situations is likely to increase.

At first the student would not plan this effect; nor would the teacher. But if it continues and becomes a reaction pattern, the teacher is likely to be yelling more and enjoying it less. In fact, it won't be too long until the students notice how emotionally upset the teacher becomes (and how much entertainment value that can hold, especially if they are not interested in, or prepared for, class) and begin to plan how they will get the teacher angry each day. When the situation reaches this sorry state, the teacher has lost any semblance of control over the class.

Consider the example mentioned earlier (Chapter III) about the student thrown out of math class, which he hates. Chronic discipline cases can be a thorn in the side of a teacher. Another way of saying that is that they are aversive stimuli. But the class or the teacher is likewise an aversive stimulus to the student. Diagrammed, it looks like this:

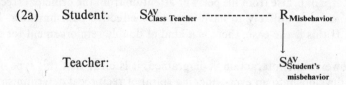

(2a)   Student: $S^{AV}_{\text{Class Teacher}}$ --------------- $R_{\text{Misbehavior}}$

        Teacher: $S^{AV}_{\text{Student's misbehavior}}$

There is only so much teachers can take, so after the final straw is dumped on them, they send the student out of class (to go to the principal or stand in the hall). This has the immediate effect of escaping from the aversive stimulus for the student, providing negative reinforcement (like escaping a fire). He is likely to behave that way again if he wants to escape the class. Extending the diagram, it appears as follows:

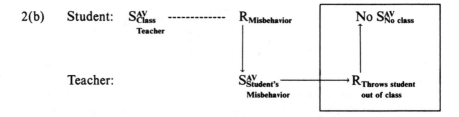

The effect is not only on the student, however, because as the student escapes the class, he removes himself from the teacher—another instance of negative reinforcement as follows:

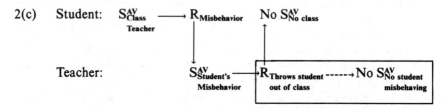

This is a classic case of mutual interaction based on negative reinforcement. It is very destructive of any potential for teaching or relating, but it is nevertheless a very strong pattern of interaction since each person is reinforcing the other. The student is being conditioned to misbehave in the presence of the teacher and the teacher is being conditioned to do something to get rid of the student.

There may, in fact, be more going on than this. Often a student who is sent out of class, in addition to escaping the teacher, receives positive attention in the form of praise from his peers or attention from the principal (recall that the principal is unlikely to have any really effective punishment at his disposal). If this is the case, there is a kind of double reinforcement for the student.

However the interaction is diagramed, it is clear that this type of interaction develops into an ever-widening spiral of reciprocal determinism which degenerates rapidly. To develop a positive teacher-student relationship requires that this interaction pattern be interrupted in some way. In an Adlerian

148

That Jones Kid is so obnoxious . . .

How obnoxious is he?

TEACHER'S LOUNGE

He's so obnoxious that even encyclopedia salesmen and airport evangelists leave when he comes in.

KOHRN/GENTILE

approach to this sort of problem, Dreikurs (1968, p. 47) analyzed this type of interaction in the following way:

> It requires alertness not to succumb to the child's goals when he expresses them through disturbing or inadequate behavior. Yet if the teacher falls for the child's provocation, she plays into his hands and fortifies his belief that his methods are effective. When in doubt about a child's goal the teacher can find a helpful guide in watching her own reaction to his behavior. It is good policy not to do what the child expects; this means not to follow one's first impulse, but to do the opposite. Such a procedure is particularly helpful if a teacher does not know what to do. Then she can simply watch herself and see what she would first be inclined to do—and do something else.

Dreikurs makes it a major principle of his approach to discipline that the teacher must be sensitive to his or her own bodily responses to the interaction. The teacher verifies the child's goals in part by observing the teacher's own affective behaviors, both operant and respondent. What the teacher feels inclined to do, "almost with impulsive coercion," is the behavior the student would like as a consequence of the misbehavior. If the teacher feels annoyed and feels inclined to scold or coax, the child is probably seeking attention. If the teacher feels challenged or threatened and feels like authority must be invoked, then student and teacher are probably in some kind of power contest. If the feeling is one of "I don't know what to do with you," the student is probably trying to get the teacher off his back by behaving as though he has no ability or willingness to do the tasks assigned. For these reasons Dreikurs concludes (p. 45) that,

It is of great importance that the teacher learn to observe her own emotional response to the child's disturbing behavior. Not only does such observation provide her with a training in understanding the child's goal, but it is an indispensible prerequisite for a more adequate approach to the child. For as long as the teacher gives in to her impulsive reaction, unaware of its meaning, she will fortify the child's mistaken goal instead of correcting it.

The previous two discipline examples are of the acting out variety. A common problem, especially for elementary teachers, is the case of the student who does his work, but too quickly and, almost invariably, inaccurately. There may be several complex factors operating here, and one of them may be that assignments have come to produce conditioned emotional responses. If this is plausible, then whenever and however the respondent conditioning occurred, it is reasonable to expect that assignments (math ditto sheets, tests, writing assignments) are conditioned stimuli. That is,

(3a) $\qquad CS_{\text{Assignment}} \text{ -----------------} \rightarrow CR_{\text{Emotional Response Anxiety}}$

On the operant level that same assignment may be an aversive stimulus and lead to any behavior that reduces the anxiety (an interpretation originally suggested by Mowrer, 1960), in this case, escape or avoidance. If avoidance is precluded—after all, there are only a few excuses for missing school or skipping class without getting into big trouble—then escape is all that is left. One way of escaping is to do the work, but quickly to get it over with. In symbolic form, the two levels of behavior interact as follows:

(3b) Respondent Level:

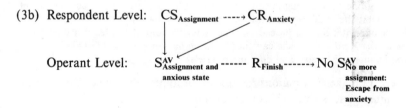

To solve a problem like this probably requires much shorter assignments, but with an emphasis on correct behavior, not fast behavior. But if this escape condition really exists it is unlikely that simply being correct will act as a positive reinforcement for completing the behavior (this was one of the myths of programed instruction!). To complicate matters further, if there is anxiety attached to such assignments, then direct intervention may be in order for that problem. For instance, relaxation training may be helpful: the teacher can work with the child to do deep breathing exercises, or to take a short break from the assignment to tense and relax muscles at his or her seat, then to return to the assignment (see Chapter II for other suggestions).

As these examples show, often what seems to be a misbehavior is a complex interaction between person and environment, or between levels of behavior within a person. The teacher's own behavior and feelings play a large role in discipline incidents because teachers are as much controlled as they control. Nevertheless teachers are responsible for the classroom and must remove themselves from the fray at times to interrupt negative interaction patterns or to recognize that there are often anxious students beneath those cases of indiscipline.

A CROSS-CULTURAL PERSPECTIVE

One of the wonders of the educational world is what happens at the end of the school day in many (if not all) of the classrooms of Japan.[1] When the last lesson has been completed, one team of students move the desks and chairs, and clean the classroom from top to bottom. They wash the blackboards, wash the floors, realign the desks, and then rearrange everything to be ready for the next day. Meanwhile other teams of students wash the hallways, stairs, toilets, and other common areas.

An American visitor, after recovering from the initial shock, may have had several reactions. One negative reaction might have been "Aren't there any child labor laws in Japan?" Another, more positive, reaction: "Gee, they must save a lot of money on janitorial staff." After some reflection a quite different reaction may have emerged: "Students are unlikely to write on the walls, litter or otherwise vandalize their school if they are responsible for cleaning and repairing it later the same day. Ingenious, those Japanese."

152

What about the rest of the school day? In some ways it was just as remarkable. Before school students could be seen milling around the school building talking or playing sports or games. Particularly in the elementary schools, the children were likely to be engaging in a game of dodge ball or the ubiquitous jump rope games they play. When the bell rang, all ran—they seldom walked—in total disarray to their classrooms to take their seats. A few minutes later their teachers entered and signaled to the class leader to call the 30–40 students to attention. The leader then said something to the effect that, "We are all ready for the lesson, Sensei."[2] This was followed by "Oneigaishimasu" or "Hajimemasho" ("let's begin") and "Rei" the command for all to bow to the sensei and sensei to them. Then classes (or homeroom activities) began.

When the bell rang to signal the end of the class period, perhaps 40 minutes later, the teacher again nodded to the class leader who called all to attention, thanked the teacher for the lesson, and initiated the bowing. Class was then dismissed for ten or fifteen minutes and all hell broke loose. Children grabbed their sports or play equipment and ran outside, or they stayed inside and played musical instruments, talked, or whatever. The teachers meanwhile took their own break or talked with individual children. They did not monitor halls or playground activities, at least not in any active way. When the bell rang, the whole process repeated itself.

Lunch was a similarly interesting experience, with lunches served in classrooms by students (often draped in white coats and surgical face masks). The teacher ate with the students. After all had eaten and cleaned up the food and dishes, which might have taken 30 minutes, the remainder of the lunch break (30–45 min.) was available for more free activities.

Chinese schools had many similarities to what has been described in Japan. There classes were even larger, in the 40–50 range. Each class began with a formal greeting from the teacher, standing and bowing. This was followed by the lesson. When the bell rang after 40 minutes or so, again students ran everywhere to play games or sports (in China table tennis, basketball, and a different kind of rope game are popular activities). When the next bell rang after 10–15 minutes, the students scrambled back to class to repeat the sequence. In addition to these regular interclass interludes, exercise periods were scheduled twice a day, once in the morning and again in the afternoon. These were held in the playground/sportsfield with the entire school, teachers included, in attendance. Then to the cadence of a recorded voice and background music, calisthenics and eye exercises were done for ten to fifteen minutes. (Such exercise periods were also common in factories and other institutions in China.) At the end of the day student clean-up crews cleaned the building.

Contrast the above Japanese and Chinese school routines with a current typically American school routine. Students sit on a bus on their way to school, get off the bus and are expected to go fairly directly—quietly and without running—to their classrooms. When they arrive they must sit at their desks and be silent or talk quietly in approved ways. Between classes they may have 3–5 minutes during which (if they change classes) they must *walk* relatively quietly until the process repeats at the next class. At lunch time they must walk to the cafeteria, supervised by teachers or others, stand in line quietly, and sit at their (often) prescribed place at the table until dismissed, often to return to the classroom within 30–40 minutes to begin the afternoon session of more sitting.

In which culture do you think the diagnosis of hyperactivity has reached almost epidemic proportions? In which culture is there an all-day school rule against running? against play? against physical activity? In which culture is school vandalism rampant? In which culture is "teacher burnout" a major concern?

Granted there are other reasons for the differences between oriental and American discipline problems than the ones just presented, such as differences in respect for teachers, involvement of the parents (in fact, the extended family and even the police) in the schools, and totally different political and economic policies for education. In addition, Chinese teachers at the secondary level teach only two or three classes per day six days a week, although their class sizes are close to 50. This is only half the class periods most American teachers must handle in a day, though their class sizes are likely to be considerably smaller and they have Saturdays off.

Nevertheless, we have seen that if you randomly assign people to be prisoners or guards (Haney and Zimbardo, 1977), they assume their roles. And compared to Japanese and Chinese schools, American schools have many unnatural rules for children and adolescents against physical activity. Moreover, we have assigned our teachers the role of policing those unnatural rules. And as we learned from The Little Prince in the opening quote, "I have the right to require obedience because my orders are reasonable." But if the orders are not reasonable can we expect them to be obeyed? If school is perceived as a jail and teachers as guards, will not students adopt the norms and behaviors of prisoners? If students do not have to repair or clean up what they destroy or make dirty, and in fact adults (parents and taxpayers) make reparations for them, what consequences are controlling their behaviors?

THE SCOPE OF THE PROBLEM

Sometimes one can see one's own culture best by visiting another. This vicarious excursion to other cultures may help us understand why discipline continues to raise such problems in American schools and suggest some of the issues that must be faced if these problems are to be solved. But what is the magnitude of the discipline problems American schools face?

Problems prominently mentioned in reviews are truancy, lateness to class, profanity, fighting, disruption, drugs and alcohol, violence, vandalism, assaults on students and teachers, rape and robbery (e.g., Feldhusen, 1978). Interestingly, the severity of the problem is in the eye of the beholder. Teachers, administrators, students and parents are likely to perceive different problems as those of prime importance. Predictably they would be those that most directly affected their own lives (e.g., absenteeism would be of much concern to teachers, vandalism to administrators, and robbery or fighting to students, with some overlap, of course). All would probably agree that there is a problem. Certainly many polls echo the concern that we hear directly from teachers that discipline is their number one problem, though few would go as far as DeCecco and Richards (1975) who speak of "civil war in the high schools."

In historical perspective it is possible to see that discipline was of equal concern to teachers around the turn of the century. Doyle (1978) surveyed recent and 1890-era educational literature and found many problems common to the list above. However, he also pointed out that in that age (a) less than 50% of the total school-age population enrolled in schools; (b) anywhere from 25–50% of those enrolled were absent for substantial portions of the year; (c) enrollment was highest in the first four grades, with fewer than 40% of those who finished eighth grade going to high school and only 10% of those graduated; and (d) the poorest of society, including immigrants and blacks, were most likely to be truant. In short, the students most likely to cause discipline problems or commit crimes were least likely to be in school.

Compulsory attendance laws, designed to bring universal literacy and accessibility to the American dream, ironically also took crime off the streets

A TEACHER'S FIRST DAY

Herbert Foster, in his book *Ribbin,' Jivin,' and Playin' the Dozens* (1974, pp. 7–8) describes his first day teaching mechanical drawing and blueprint reading at Haaren High School in Manhattan (where the movie for Bell Kaufman's *Up the Down Staircase* was filmed.) After being interviewed by the department chairman, he was escorted to his class and told (1) not to give the students too much work since they were slow and (2) that he was the sixth substitute for the class since the regular teacher resigned a few weeks previously.

The day went more or less smoothly until the first period after lunch. During that period a student ran out of the back door of the class. When Mr. Foster closed that door a student ran out the front door. Soon it was clear it was the same students running in and out of the doors. Not knowing what to do about that, another problem arose. A student said "Hey, teach, we work a period, read comics a period, and then take the last period off—OK?" Foster, realizing he was being tested, replied that he was the teacher now and that work would be going on all three periods. We'll continue in Foster's words:

> From then on everything seemed to happen at once. Someone crumpled up a piece of paper and threw it at me with a near miss. I thought of my Psychology I and II courses ("make a joke out of things"—or— "decontaminate through humor") so I said, "If that's the best you can do, you better hang up." Whereupon all hell broke loose. The class was going to show me they could do better!
>
> Students ran across the table tops throwing T-squares and drawing boards. Others ran in and out of the room. The noise was deafening. T-squares and drawing board missiles flew through the air. The classroom was not only noisy but dangerous. And do you know what I did? You know that section that is cut out of the teacher's desk where the teacher puts his legs when he sits down? I hid there—in the kneehole.
>
> Suddenly, five or six teachers stuck their heads into the room to see what was going on. I looked up sheepishly from my shelter without saying a word. Since the din continued even with their presence, they threw both doors open and my students took off.

To find out what Foster did the next day, consult his book.

---

and brought it into the schools. This may have been done somewhat consciously since Americans often expect the schools to solve broader social problems. Thus "incorrigibles," who were dealt with by the police before universal education, became the province of school personnel once education became the primary occupation of youth. Doyle (1978) concluded that, in the aggregate, youth of today are no worse than they have ever been. However, the venue has changed: violent and criminal behaviors that occurred in the streets now occur also in the corridors and classrooms.

Teachers and other school personnel are seldom trained to handle even minor discipline problems, let alone crime. The first day of class is perhaps even more traumatic for teachers than for students (e.g.; Foster, 1974). Teachers' goals seldom even include questions of discipline—they want to teach skills and knowledges in their subject matter specialities. But as we have seen in this book, cognitive learning cannot occur in the absence of emotional and motivational learning and, in some cases, cognitive learning may only be possible once the other threats and disruptions are removed. Safety and self-esteem, after all, take precedence over learning, self-improvement and other motives for self-actualization (Maslow, 1954).

NATURAL CONSEQUENCES AND REALITY THERAPY

Case 1. Psychotherapist to patient who has delusions of being Adolf Hitler: "I've been told you have experience hanging wall paper."
Patient (taken aback): "Yes."
Therapist: "Good, we're decorating the dayroom and need experienced help."

Case 2. Psychotherapist to patient who has delusions of being Jesus Christ: "I've heard you're quite a good carpenter."
Patient: "Yes"
Therapist: "Good, then you won't mind building a bookcase for me."

Aside from the productive labor involved in assigning the above psychiatric patients to useful jobs, the therapist was making the patients accept the natural consequences of their behavior, albeit unexpected consequences.[3]

As Dreikurs (1968) explained, *natural consequences* emphasize the power of mother nature or the social order, not the power of a particular authority. The teacher simply makes the students responsible for their behaviors, both verbal and physical. For example, a student was constantly getting out of his seat, leaning on his desk in a half-standing position in such a way as to bother the teacher. Rather than reprimand the child, the teacher asked whether he would prefer to sit or stand while working at the desk. He said he preferred to stand, whereupon the teacher said, "Then the seat would no longer be needed," and removed it from the room. The next day the teacher asked his preference again and he chose to sit. According to Dreikurs (1968, p. 103) this solved the problem.

Glasser (1965) gave s similar example, all too well recognizable by parents. His five-year-old was asked whether he wanted to bathe in the regular bathtub, which was full and ready for him. He said, "No," preferring to assert his independence and bathe in his own tub. At that point his ten-year-old sister took over the ready and waiting water. Little brother immediately became incensed, wanting to take the big tub. Glasser bodily picked up his "fifty pounds of tantrum" and placed him in his own tub. After the tantrum was spent and all was quiet the psychiatrist Glasser said to him (1965, pp. 17—18): " 'Let me give you some good advice. Do you know what advice is?' He did, so I told him, 'Never say no when you mean yes.' "

Glasser's advice is sound for all ages. Responsibility is learned by accepting—sometimes suffering—the consequences of our choices. Unfortunately parents and teachers often want to spare children the negative consquences of their own behaviors. Many would give in to the child's tantrum and let him take his bath in the big tub despite his earlier negativism. But what they would be teaching, if giving in to the child's tantrum were a frequent occurrence, would be (1) that what you say doesn't matter very much, since you can always reverse yourself; and (2) that tantrums get you what you want.

Glasser's behavior as a parent, at least in the above instance, is true to his advice to other parents, teachers and psychotherapists. He calls his method *Reality Therapy* (1965) because it emphasizes the client's own behavior and its consequences in the here and now. Glasser believes that all psychiatric patients and chronic discipline problems have a common characteristic—namely, that they deny the reality of the world around them and the part they play in making their world.[4] Their own behavior is not just willful self-destruction or wanton aggressiveness, however. Rather it derives from unsuccessful efforts to fulfill their needs.

In Glasser's view there are only *two basic human needs: the need for love* (to love and to be loved) *and the need for self-worth* (to feel worthwhile to ourselves and others). The differences between humans, then, are conceived not as differences in our needs, but differences in our ability to fulfill those needs. When we have someone who cares about us and we about them, then the love need is satisfied. But we must also behave at a high standard (in terms of competence and values), according to Glasser, or we will not fulfill our need to be worthwhile.

In applying his ideas to classrooms, Glasser suggested that the two needs for love and self-worth are really so intertwined as to be inseparable, being reducible to what we usually call *identity;* "the belief that we are someone in distinction to others, and that the someone is important and worthwhile" (1969, p. 14). Then love, which in schools is really social responsibility or the golden rule, and self-worth become two pathways to an identity. Self-worth in school means academic success. A student who does not achieve success in school must find it elsewhere, possibly through withdrawal, through delinquency, or power games.

If you have survived to this point in the book, Glasser's ideas should sound like variations on the litany of recommendations we have already made on the basis of what is known about emotions, motivation and social learning in general. But Glasser's work provides a fitting framework for dealing with these concepts in a discipline chapter because he takes an additional, practical step— namely, *accepting no excuses.* No matter what terrible conditions children grew up under, from poverty to broken homes, this does not excuse unsuccessful behavior. The schools must help the children learn successful, responsible behavior.

> In helping children, we must work to make them understand that *they are responsible* for fulfilling their needs, for behaving so that they can gain a successful identity. No one can do it for them. If they continue to choose pathways that lead to failure, that diminish their self-worth, that are without love, they will continue to suffer and continue to react with delinquency or withdrawal. (Glasser, 1969, p. 16)

In reality therapy approaches, then, there is little interest in the client's past history, family background, or the reasons for the unsuccessful behavior. The therapist *does not ask why* the behavior is occurring. The question, rather, is *what*. What are you doing? How is that helping you satisfy your needs? This focuses the question on the behavior in relation to the person's goals. Focusing on why, in contrast, usually leads people to find excuses for the behavior (e.g., "He made me do it," or "I was bored," "The teacher's a jerk," etc.) Being in touch with reality means accepting no excuses for a failure— just commit yourself to a new, better behavior and try again.

If the responsibility of students is to make a value judgment about their inappropriate, unsuccessful behaviors and commit to new, better behaviors, then school personnel have a parallel responsibility of not holding a students' past negative behaviors against them. The title of Glasser's book, *Schools Without Failure* (1969, p. 20) emphasizes that point as follows:

> The only worthwhile information . . . to be gleaned from the past concerns the child's successes; this knowledge can be used to help him in the present. The past of people who fail is filled with failures. It is useless to work with failure because the teacher (or the therapist) and the child become deeply involved with failure . . . By ignoring the past failures, we encourage the child to change his present behavior.

SPECIFIC RECOMMENDATIONS BASED ON REALITY THERAPY

Consistent with his approach for dealing with unsuccessful student behaviors, Glasser (1977) recommended ten steps for teachers to follow in solving discipline problems. In a very important sense these steps are really changes in teacher behaviors. The steps teachers should follow are these.

1. Consider a specific child with whom you are having a difficult problem and make a list of what you do when the child disrupts. Don't ask "why," just ask "what" do I do?

2. Consider each behavior on the list and ask "Is this technique working?" It is likely that it isn't or you would not be worrying about the problem. (If you're not sure, you may want to do a social learning analysis as suggested earlier in this chapter). Resolve to stop responding in the ineffective ways.

3. Commit yourself to making the student's life better in class, being warmer, finding appropriate behaviors to reinforce, and special things for the student to do that can show his/her self-worth. Whether or not this makes an immediate change in the student's behavior, which is unlikely, resolve to continue this behavior for the long-term.

4. When problems arise, as they inevitably will, do not behave in ways which you've shown don't work (steps 1 and 2). Instead, recall your newly developing relationship with the student (step 3) and ask "What are you doing?" If the student responds by blaming someone else, press on in a matter-of-fact manner until the answer includes a statement of the actual behavior, at which time simply ask that the student stop it. Recognition of the problem by the student is often sufficient to engage self-control and the problem may disappear. This is especially true of a student with whom the teacher has a good relationship.

5. If the problem persists, follow the question "What are you doing?" with "Is it against the rules?" and then with "What should you be doing?" (Glasser, 1977, p. 62) The matter-of-fact manner of the teacher should convey warmth and helpfulness, but also firmness.

6. If the problem still persists, again ask "What are you doing? and "Is it against the rules?" but then tell the student that we need a plan to work out this problem. The student must come up with the plan of positive action that includes specific behaviors over a short time period. Resolving never to forget my homework again, for example, is not specific, not positive and unrealistic (never is a long, long time). Resolving to do my homework as soon as I get home and then placing it at the door of the house for the next three days is specific, positive and short-term. Part of the plan is a natural consequence of what should happen if the student violates the rule again. This plan for direct positive action and the consequences of not fulfilling the plan constitutes a *contract* between teacher and student. No excuses can be accepted for not fulfilling the contract. The students must suffer the consequences they agreed to and must recommit to a new plan. Note that the teacher does not "punish" the student—just enforces the contract.

For almost all problems, steps 1–6 will provide an adequate solution. For severe and chronic disruptions additional steps may be needed. Glasser recommends the following:

7. You may need to have an in-class suspension, or isolation of the student from the rest of the ongoing activities. This "time out" tells the affected students that they have not responsibly carried out the contract and may therefore not participate in class until they have devised a totally new plan to which teacher and student can agree. When the new contract is approved, the student can rejoin the class.

160

8. If recommitment in the class does not work, in-school suspension is the next step with the plan being made by the student with the principal, psychologist, or other school personnel. As soon as the new plan is developed, the student is readmitted to class.

9. Students to whom recommitment to plans is taken too lightly, who refuse to draw up a plan, or who are otherwise totally out of control must be suspended to go home with their parents for the rest of the day. But tomorrow is another day and they may return with a plan.

10. Students who cannot learn to be responsible for successfully meeting their needs in these ways (Steps 7–9) may have to be barred from attending school or referred to other agencies until at that level commitment to a whole new contract can be made.

REALITY THERAPY AND SOCIAL LEARNING

Glasser's system has become quite popular through his best-selling books, films and articles. Apparently many schools have adopted many of his ideas. In this section we will further analyze his suggestions in light of other principles in this book and other methods of solving discipline problems.

Reasonable Rules, Responsibility and Reinforcement

Glasser's first steps ask teachers to deal with defining a real problem in light of the classroom rules and the ultimate goals. If there are too many or unreasonable rules, then there will be much conflict. If the rules are few and reasonable, then students and teacher will have fewer conflicts by definition.

While students who break rules may be technically in the wrong, teacher reactions set the stage for the long-term relationship. Glasser's advice in step 3, therefore, is to commit to making the student's life better tomorrow. Though teachers seldom[5] start a discipline problem, they have the power to defuse it, maintain it or aggravate it by their reactions. Through their reactions they also model the actual contingencies of reinforcement and punishment in the classroom as well as the norms and standards for treating others. Perhaps more importantly, they have the capability by their reactions of helping students get through minor problems or see their problems spiral into larger crises.

For example, when a student is late, some teachers might say, "Why are you always late? Why can't you get here on time like everyone else?" A more productive response might be, "We're on page 256." Of course, if this is a chronic problem, then it may be necessary to confront the student *individually* and have the student commit to a new behavior. During the individual conference teachers may also assert their own feelings on the topic: "Although I try not to show it in front of the class, it really annoys me when you come to class late." This honest and fair response is much better than, "Why do you constantly disrupt the class by coming late?"

Glasser's procedure, then, has the goal of making students responsible for their behavior. It does so by neither adding to an already emotional situation nor by denying honest emotions. It simply moves on to having the student commit to a new, better behavior and the teacher commit to looking for the student's appropriate behavior, not dwelling on past errors. This procedure is not unlike suggestions made by others (e.g., Canter and Canter, 1976; Charles, 1981, Dreikurs, 1968; Dreikurs et al.; 1971; Ginott, 1972; Gordon, 1974). Ginott (1972, pp. 15–16) summed it up in his own personal philosophy:

> I have come to a frightening conclusion. I am the decisive element in the classroom. It is my personal approach that creates the climate. It is my daily mood that makes the weather. As a teacher I possess tremendous power to make a child's life miserable or joyous. I can be a tool of torture or an instrument of inspiration. I can humiliate or humor, hurt or heal. In all situations it is my response that decides whether a crisis will be escalated or de-escalated, and a child humanized or de-humanized.

Punishment, Retribution and Restitution

In earlier chapters we have seen some of the problems with punishment, some of which are worth reiterating in the present context. First, punishment has emotional by-products, including classically conditioned feelings to subjects, situations and people. Second, it seldom works to eliminate the behavior it is intended to stamp out; rather it suppresses it for a while usually only in the presence of the punisher as a cue. Third, punishment informs the victim what not to do, but does not teach what the appropriate behavior is. Fourth, if punishment is followed by reinforcement, it may act as cue for reinforcement and increase the probability of the subject working to attain punishment (e.g., masochistic behavior). Fifth, if nothing the subject does can avoid the punishment (noncontingent punishment), learned helplessness can result. Sixth, punishment delivered by a teacher or other significant person provides a model for the observers of how to treat others and solve problems. Seventh, punishment for an act does not correct the problem for which the person was punished—that is, there is no restitution. Finally, punishment engenders revenge, especially if a group reinforces its members for retaliation against the punisher.

Given all the above, it is no wonder that authors on the topic of discipline argue for nonpunitive resolutions to conflict. As the cartoon portrays, the ultimate punishment at the teacher's disposal is to stop trying to teach the students who make trouble, though the students are more likely to appreciate the holiday (escape from distasteful work) than to consider that punishment.

Punishment, in sum, seems to serve only two purposes—namely, to stop inappropriate behavior and to vent the punisher's anger. It can eliminate behavior, but only if the punishment is strong (in which case it is outlawed by civilized societies) and the victim cannot escape or reduce its effects. But even rats learn how to reduce the effects of aversive stimuli. One rat, pictured by Azrin and Holz (1966, p. 385), learned to lie on its back to distribute strong shocks across his entire furry back instead of on his sensitive feet, all the while pressing the bar to continue receiving his food as if having "Breakfast in Bed."

$1 \times 1 = 1$
$2 \times 2 = 4$
$3 \times 3 = 9$
$4 \times 4 = 16$
$5 \times 5 = 25$
$6 \times 6 = 36$

$7 \times 7 = 49$
$8 \times 8 = 64$
$9 \times 9 = ?$
$10, ?$
$11, ?$
$12, ?$

Since you have not responded to my other discipline techniques, I shall fall back on my ultimate punishment: I shall teach in such a way that you all remain ignorant!

If rats are intelligent enough to dilute the effects of punishment, can we expect less of students? The only punishments we are left with, in other words, are ineffective. That leaves the second purpose of punishment—venting anger—also unfulfilled, since the problem will not have been eliminated and there will be a continual need to vent anger.

Why, then, do teachers and others continue to punish? The answer, it would appear, is that they mistakenly believe it works. More likely, as we have seen earlier in this chapter, the teacher is being negatively reinforced for punishing behaviors and those behaviors are simply becoming habitual, as smoking or drinking can become habitual responses to stressful events.

In light of this, advice on how to avoid punishing is welcome indeed. Natural consequences, such as those involved in suspending students (Glasser's Steps 7–10) for not keeping their contracts are much preferable to punishments or continual arguments. The teacher is simply enforcing a contract suggested by and agreed to by the student.

In cases when students lose control and become aggressive, *physical restraint* may become necessary (e.g., Foster, 1974). It differs from corporal punishment in the following ways: (1) its intent is solely to cease the aggressive behavior of the child; (2) it uses the minimum force necessary to stop the behavior; and (3) it is used only during the behavior for as long as needed. As described, physical restraint is useful to a teacher when students are aggressing against each other. Like football team members "holding back" an enraged teammate from fighting against an opponent, there is no enmity built up between the aggressor and the restrainer (e.g., the teammates or teacher). The intent is important here.[6] Were the teacher to punish the student instead, the force would likely be greater than necessary and would continue after the aggressive behavior ceased. This would likely maintain hostility in the form of "getting even."

The final point to be made in this section concerns the distinction between retribution and restitution (e.g., Gnagey, 1968). *Retribution* can be thought of as retaliation— "an eye for an eye;" "don't get mad, get even." It is very difficult to punish someone in such a manner and keep the immediate problem from growing since the loser of the battle will harbor resentment and plot a new retaliation. The problem may also grow in another way, by spreading out to include the observers in the class if they feel the punishment was unfair or too harsh (what Kounin and Gump, 1956, dubbed "the ripple effect.") *Restitution* on the other hand, is making right what is wrong. If you have broken a window, restitution is repairing it or paying for it. If you have broken a contract or commitment, restitution is completing the contract even though late and/or recommitting to a new contract.

Restitution strikes people as being reasonable, as being a logical and natural consequence of an inappropriate behavior or error. Therefore, it is not likely to engender revenge. It is not even likely to be considered punishment. Moreover, it is effective in teaching people to be responsible for their own behavior.

Time Out

Glasser called his in-class suspension (step 7) a brief "time out," whose purpose was to have the student devise a new plan before rejoining the class. In essence this provides a reinforcement contingency between fulfilling the contract and participating in the class activities: if the appropriate behavior occurs, participation follows; if inappropriate behavior occurs, participation is not allowed until the student is ready to behave appropriately.

Time out, as used by Glasser, is quite a sensible and useful procedure. But no behavioral procedure has been more mis-used in practice, in our opinion, than time out. Thus it is not uncommon to visit schools or other institutions in which a time out box or room is proudly displayed. Students who break a rule or annoy the teacher are sent there as a kind of solitary confinement. And since it feels so good to the teacher to have miscreants out of their sight, it is easy to keep them out of mind and forget about them for 30 minutes or, in some cases, much longer. This long time period is a mis-use of the "time out" idea.

Originally known by its longer title, *time out from positive reinforcement,* the procedure was first used in pigeon training experiments as an alternative

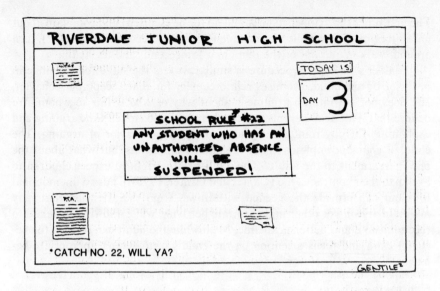

RIVERDALE JUNIOR HIGH SCHOOL

TODAY IS.
DAY 3

SCHOOL RULE #22
ANY STUDENT WHO HAS AN
UNAUTHORIZED ABSENCE
WILL BE
SUSPENDED!

PTA.

*CATCH NO. 22, WILL YA?

GENTILE²

to punishing incorrect behaviors. In discrimination learning studies, for example, correct choices led to food, while incorrect choices delayed the next problem to be presented and thus delayed the availability of food (e.g., Ferster and Appel, 1961). In variations of the procedure used on humans institutionalized delinquents, who were fighting or otherwise breaking rules, were briefly isolated to interrupt the attention they were receiving for this inappropriate behavior (e.g., Brown and Tyler, 1967). Time out lasted from half a second to ten minutes in prototypical pigeon studies and less than 15 minutes in corresponding human studies.

Time out was made contingent on a response in such a way that when the undesired behavior occurred, all stimuli that might be reinforcing that behavior became unavailable for a time. Since it is not always clear in practical situations what reinforcers are maintaining the behavior (e.g., other students' attention, etc.) isolation to a somewhat stark room can be effective. *But the isolation must be brief.* In fact, it will be less effective if it has durations beyond 15 minutes (Johnston, 1972) and is likely to be (perhaps accurately) perceived by the student as a retributive act by the teacher if it is longer than a few minutes. Then students may spend the extra time plotting revenge. Hall and Hall (1980, p. 14) advise that a "time out period should last from two to five minutes and certainly no longer than a minute for each year of the person's age."

Time out was very effective when used in the following way to teach good manners in the Gentile household:

Doug (aged 4, speaking in a nasty tone of voice): "Dad, get me a drink."

Dad (calmly): "Doug, please go back to your room. And when you can ask me nicely, come back and ask me again."

The first times this happened he would go (or be escorted) and complain about unfair treatment. Later, he would smile (Dreikurs' "recognition reflex"?), turn around, walk in and out of the room in a few seconds and try again.

Glasser's time out procedure is similar. It sets the stage for a change in behavior by the child, promises reinforcement for that acceptable behavior, and does not get into an argument about why or who is fair to whom. We believe that American parents and teachers spend too much time arguing and explaining, thereby reinforcing and modeling the behavior of arguing. The child, of course, complains about the adult's unfairness, but what about the unfair treatment to the adult? The adult has the right to expect children to live up to their contracts, too (Canter and Canter, 1976). Thus an unemotional time out can provide the needed withdrawal from the attention that may maintain arguing or other inappropriate behavior, while allowing the child to recommit to doing better next time. Meanwhile the adult can remain (or become) calm and focus attention on the child's forthcoming appropriate behavior.

Contracts

Dr. Haim Ginott once relayed in a lecture that the best way for solving student-student problems was for the parent to act as arbitrator with a rule that only written complaints would be accepted. Thus if one of your children whines, "He hit me," you say "Here's some paper and pencil. Write down everything that happened." If the child does so, then you show the other child the written accusation and ask the other child to respond in writing. What happened almost always, in Ginott's story, was that after one trial with this procedure, the kids would say to each other, "Let's make up 'cause if we complain, we'll just have to write it all down." Ginott was also fond of advising parents not to try to "get to the bottom of a problem" because there is no bottom—everyone just sinks into a murky abyss.[7]

The moral of the story is that putting behavior—whether past, present or future—into writing may solve most of the problem without involving the teacher or parent in emotional conflicts. The act of writing out a plan committing oneself to a new behavior does several positive things: (1) it makes people aware of their behavior and its consequences, (2) it provides a permanent record of the new agreement, so that (3) the consequences of the successful or unsuccessful behavior can occur in a manner that is productive for the future relationship between the parties to the agreement.

Written agreements or *contracts* are already widely used in education and behavioral self-management (e.g., Jenson, 1978; Sulzer-Azaroff and Reese, 1982). They always include a statement of the objectives, often include a recording technique for monitoring the person's behavior, and usually include consequences for appropriate and inappropriate behaviors. They are especially useful for persons over twelve years old because, properly negotiated, they provide informed consent and maximum participation of the students in learning responsibility for their behaviors. At the same time they prescribe certain behaviors for the teacher.

Some commonly stated rules for contracts include the following (not all of which are necessary for all contracts).

1. Specific objectives must be stated clearly so that both student and teacher (and perhaps administrator and parent) will know exactly what the goal is.
2. The behaviors wanted (and perhaps not wanted) must be specified clearly. Emphasis should be placed on what to do instead of what not to do.
3. The time frame (usually one week or less) and conditions within which the behaviors are expected to occur must be specified.
4. For many problems records should be kept by both students and teachers vis-a-vis the behaviors.
5. The consequences of completing appropriate behaviors as well as engaging in inappropriate behaviors must be specified.
6. The consequences must occur as specified.
7. If there are several behaviors that are targeted for change, it is probably best to deal with one at a time with others added later. This may be stated at the beginning so the student knows what he or she is getting into.
8. The student must agree to the contract, should write the contract or at least contribute to the wording of it, and all parties to the agreement must sign it.

Many of us are mostly unaware of our own behaviors, their frequency, the conditions under which they occur, and their effect on others. Until we systematically count the number of mouthfuls of food we take each day, for example, we may not be aware that our overweight condition is a result of a large number of snacks. Children with behavior problems may similarly be unaware of how little assigned work they do, how frequently they miss class or come late, how often they ridicule others or talk out of turn, and how their behavior makes others feel. A good discipline procedure, especially for difficult problems, must help the students come to grips with their own behavior and bring it under their own control. Such *self-control* is the purpose of the record keeping in point 4. For many problems therefore, it should be considered indispensible.

Most of us, after having been largely unaware of our own behaviors, make global resolutions when we finally realize the extent of our errors. Thus many an overweight person, to continue the analogy, resolves to stop snacking and to lose 20 lbs. in the next 20 days. Such grandiose plans for self-control hardly ever continue past the first few days, however, because we find that we only lost two lbs. the first week. So we give up. The problem is that the goals are too remote and difficult to reach.

It is apparently not at all uncommon for adolescents in trouble with the schools to be truly remorseful and willing to promise anything for "one more chance." But the teacher who lets the student agree to an impossible dream is not helping that student learn self-control of behavior; rather they are both contributing to the student's very likely next failure. These problems are addressed in rules 3 and 7.

Exactly what a contract should look like is difficult to prescribe, given the range of possible problems and our emphasis on students suggesting the wording. Hall and Hall (1982) suggest, however, that each contract should include a column headed "Behavior" and one headed "Consequence" with spaces for "Who," "What," "When" and "How Much" under each to specify who does what behavior under what conditions to what standard (e.g., 4 out of 5 days next week). This is probably good advice for most situations.

OTHER ISSUES

WHO "OWNS" THE PROBLEM?

Alschuler (1980) described the heart of the discipline problem to be the battle for the students' attention. In observational studies of the proportion of time students are attentive in class, he found it was rare to be over 50% and often much less in typical "orderly" classes. The reason for this, he says, is that students and teachers have different agenda. The teachers want students to master subject matter objectives, while students focus on more immediate matters of concern to the peer group—friends, records, movies, clothes, sex, and so forth. It's not that students will not pay attention; they will, when asked, for as long as necessary. Then they will go back to attending to what matters to them. Meanwhile, the games (Alschuler calls them war games) go on. For example, at the beginning of most classes, including college and graduate level classes, there is the "milling game," where students individually approach the teacher with their questions and comments to which the teacher pays attention, if only by asking the student to sit down and raise the question later. The purpose of the game from the students' standpoint is to delay the beginning of class and thereby decrease the amount of attention to the task.

Part of the difficulty is the rescuer role that many teachers assume: they take on students' problems and become involved in them. If two students are having a dispute, the problem is "owned" by them, not by the teacher. The teacher can maintain order in the rest of the class by *having the two involved students write out their complaints along with some suggestions for improving the situation.* This serves at least the following functions: (1) it allows the disputants a cooling-off period while they are writing; (2) it may provide useful ways of solving the problem; and (3) it does not bring others, including the teacher, into the problem.

One of the important discriminations we must all learn is which problems are ours and which are not.[8] An obstetrician reported (in Madsen and Madsen,

1981) that one of his major tasks was to have his pregnant clients stop talking about the "we who were having the baby," when it was only the she who had to eat properly, stop smoking and drinking, and so on. Most students have a ready excuse for their unfinished homework—a test in another subject, band practice, parents had a fight, and so on. It is natural to want to blame one's failings on situational constraints or someone else. But since we do not want to attribute our successes to those same external causes, preferring instead to take personal credit for them, we are being a bit hypocritical. This is where Glasser's policy of "accepting no excuses" can be quite helpful. Students need to learn that it is their effort which solves their problems and that they cannot give their own problems away by letting others (e.g., teachers) solve them or by blaming others.

It follows that teachers may not allow students' games to induce them to accept ownership of the problem. To stop the "milling game," for example, a set routine at the beginning of class could be established and followed. Blinking the lights, for example, can serve the same function as the command to stand and bow in oriental schools. The teacher is refusing to be party to the problem why Johnny forgot a pencil, Mary lost her homework and Jimmy hit me. If those student-owned problems are serious, they can be discussed between classes, before or after school, or at other specified times.

LABELING AS DISABLING

The approach throughout this book has been to show that it is situations that often create conflicts or certainly to maintain them. This is not to say that some individuals do not stir up more trouble than others; there are such individuals. Therefore it will always be possible to find the "troublemakers" and then keep our eyes out for them in the future. Teachers who do that are being affected by labels.

A former teacher went on a school outing as a parental chaperone and observed first-hand the following incident on the school bus. One of the fourth-grade girls was teasing the boys in the row behind her by swinging her anklets (which she had removed from her feet) in front of them. One of the boys predictably grabbed the anklets and, as he pulled his arm back, the anklets fell out of the open bus window. The girl, now incensed, rushed to the teacher in front of the bus and complained. The teacher stormed to the back and confronted the boys. The guilty party blamed another boy, Danny, at which point the teacher shouted, "How dare you take another person's property? What are you, an animal?" The teacher then sat next to Danny the rest of the trip. Danny, who was innocent, told the girl he would pay her the $2.00 he had with him for her socks. At this point, the parent spoke up and told the teacher the whole story, including the fact that Danny was not guilty. That calmed things down somewhat, but no apologies were made to Danny and nothing further was said about the incident.

169

PIGEONS, PECKING ORDERS
AND PUBLIC EDUCATION

For years certain psychologists have been lecturing the schools that it doesn't matter how students are classified; they will not learn until we treat them as individuals as is done in the experimental psychological laboratory. In those studies all pigeons and rats—regardless of race, creed or color—were able to learn all that the experimenter wanted them to learn. School personnel have been singularly unimpressed by that point of view because psychologists study individual pigeons in well-controlled Skinner boxes. Thus, they retort that psychological laboratory studies are irrelevant to the schools, which do not have the leisure to teach individuals in the ways prescribed.

To test the irrelevance hypothesis, Gentile (1972) conducted a study in which he arranged the conditions to be like those of the schools. First, he selected pigeons to parallel the heterogeneous population of the schools by randomly selecting 14 male and 14 female pigeons from a breeding company called Pigeonholers, Inc. Half were of genetically bright parentage—the Well-Bred Group—and half of duller stock—the Poor-Bred Group. The author further describes the selection procedures as follows (pp. 105–106).

> Pigeonholers . . . uses the well-known Suburban-Innercity Classification Kit (SICK) to classify pigeons on an ordinal scale on the basis of the neighborhood in which they were reared. The SICK kit provides a pecking order of pigeons from those who were reared in dentist's office buildings or science laboratories (the highest classification) to those reared in the slum dwellings of unemployed persons (the lowest classification). To assure further that the strains were drawn from different populations, each subject was individually administered the Shock Pigeon Intelligence Test (SPIT), which yields scores on the rate at which pigeons learn to avoid shock. When the strains were compared, the mean SPIT I.Q. of the Well-Bred Group was 108.7 (S.D. = 14.23), while that of the Poor-Bred Group was 91.2 (S.D. = 15.02). These scores are in close agreement to the kinds of differences found in the population as a whole, and validate the selection procedure.

Danny, it turns out, was by reputation the class trouble-maker. Whenever anything went wrong, everyone knew whom to blame it on. Interestingly, Danny accepted this role not only when he was guilty, but when he was innocent.

When we label people—Johnny Bright, Sammy Slow (from the previous chapter), Tommy Trouble or Billy Buzzard—we tend to stereotype them and no longer to observe their behavior. Then we treat them as we expect them to be and, more often than not, they behave appropriately for that role. Labels can therefore lead to self-fulfilling prophecy (Good and Brophy, 1978).

Are there no labels that are real, you might ask? What about hyperactivity? What about dyslexia or specific learning disabilities?[9] Our answer is that a label tells more about the labeler than the person labeled—since as we've said, "There are two kinds of people: those who divide the world into

Because the Experimenter was assumed to be from a socio-cultural group more like the Well-Bred subjects, an assistant Experimenter of low socioeconomic status was hired . . . No attempt was made to control for experimenter effect along the sex-role dimension . . . since neither experimenter was able to identify sex of any of the pigeons.

The behavior to be learned was a complicated chain of responses in which the pigeons had to learn to climb a perch, ring a bell, hop on one foot, roll over, turn and peck to appropriate written stimuli. The teaching was done in a large Skinner box with 28 Key panels spaced in such a way as to simulate desks in a classroom. The Well-Bred and Poor-Bred groups were separated by a center aisle to simulate ability grouping. Food reinforcement could be delivered electronically from the teacher's console to individuals or the whole group at once. But (p. 106),

> As in the classroom setting, it was difficult to reinforce all appropriate behaviors and it was impossible to establish a strict reinforcement schedule. In addition, there were several hyperactive pigeons whose strutting around the room was a continual interference to the serious pigeons and occupied a considerable portion of the Experimenters' attention. A few severe discipline problems occurred, but these were handled by removing the deviants to a special penalty box, on the wall of which hung a picture of an authoritative-looking pigeon.

To make a short story shorter, none of the pigeons learned very well, though the Well-Bred ones did better than the Poor-Bred. The author recommended that the latter group, in particular, needed early intervention efforts perhaps by a federally funded program. It is difficult to get pigeons early enough in childhood to give them a "head start" or "early push" program, however, so a program aimed at adolescent pigeons—the "late yank" program—was suggested.

The final conclusion was that pigeon studies are indeed relevant to the schools: *when we treat pigeons like we do people, they have trouble learning, too.*

two kinds of people and those who don't." Wisecracks aside, however children are labeled, the teacher still has to deal with them all. We have seen that Japanese and Chinese children are given many opportunities to be active between classes; it would seem unfair to disallow such behaviors in an American school and then label a nonconforming child hyperactive.

The procedures described in this chapter emphasize present behavior and natural consequences; there is no reason to label people slow, clumsy, lazy, hyperactive, buzzard, or anything else. Instead, if there is a real problem behavior, it can be described and attempts made to commit to more successful behavior. Fay (1978, pp. 7–8) makes a similar point. A patient came into his office and announced pessimistically, "I am a voyeur." The therapist asked whether that meant he liked looking at nude women through windows. When the patient agreed, he said, "Who wouldn't enjoy that?" The therapist then went on to explore the patient's concern that he had no social skills to interact with women in ways that would be more rewarding. Their contract was that the therapist would teach him such social skills.

Belligerent students are also often deficient in social skills that would help them get along better with teachers and other students. Sensitive teachers will see this as part of the problem and try to teach them some of those skills, possibly through a contract. Then instead of seeing a label, the teacher will see a person who is trying some new behaviors and a whole new interaction becomes possible.

One study (reported by Gray et al., 1974) gave students with a long history of belligerent behaviors formal behavior modification instruction. The purpose was to teach the students how to modify their teachers' behaviors by positively reinforcing appropriate behaviors or by ignoring or mildly rebuking inappropriate behaviors by asserting their rights and expressing their feelings (e.g., by saying, "It's hard for me to do my best when you're angry at me.") The results of this training were quite positive: the teachers' behaviors changed, which reinforced the students' behaviors, so each continued with their new improved pro-social interactions. And each thought the other had changed to make the atmosphere improve. Of course, both had changed—reciprocal determinism was at work.

Educators and psychologists often use variations of this technique on their own children when they are having trouble dealing with teachers. They teach their children to say "Good morning" with a nice smile and some other ways to win the teacher over. It usually works, but in one case close to home the eleven-year-old said, "Sure it's a good idea. But I shouldn't have to be the one to be nice to the teacher first. She's the adult." He did have a point.

SPENDING TIME OR INVESTING TIME

Time, like money, can be used so that it is gone with little or nothing to show for it, or it can be used so that it returns a dividend in the future. For instance, a person can spend many hours and much money learning to play a video game, the long term effect of which is essentially nil. In a few months there will be a new game to replace it. If a person spent the same amount of time and money interacting with a computer the long term effect would be a skill that is either marketable or useful in many ways at home. Similarly, a person can spend time watching television or investing it in learning to play a musical instrument or a sport. The latter two skills open up possibilities for careers or hobbies later in life, while TV-watching has little, if any, long-term value.

School teachers, wittingly or unwittingly, often reinforce behavior which both they and the students know is "busy-work." Endless dittoes, given both to students who need the drill and those who do not, as well as assignments

Aw, Teach, do we hav'ta do what we wanna do again?

which are neither graded nor handed back for the students to correct, are two examples of time spent. It is possible to modify people's behavior so that they do such tasks, but probably only by establishing a workable behavior modification program with an adequate payoff or by threatening sufficient punishment.

On the other hand, time invested in mastering valuable tasks—such as learning to read, do mathematics, program a computer, and understand our own behavior—will eventually, if not immediately, become valued by students. Even if you have to use tangible reinforcers in the beginning to motivate such skill development, this can be phased out without losing the behavior, since the behavior is becoming an integral part of the person's self-concept. The non-reader is now a reader; the musically non-talented person is becoming a guitarist, the math-anxious person can now do algebra (e.g., Gentile, Frazier and Morris, 1973, pp. 45–46). The person's self-image changes when important competencies are developed. As Friedenberg (1959) put it, people's self-esteem is tied directly to their competencies: people know who they are by what they can do.

Time, then, is like money in another way. If it is used wisely it can create opportunities for the owner. If used unwisely, the owner will have only its memory as another example of "Why I'm a loser."

TEACHING AND DISCIPLINE

Third Grade School Teacher to parents at the first PTA open house of the year:

> We have a problem. For the first time at this school we have a number of students who are reading below grade level. Thus they are having trouble with the books. As a result, they get frustrated and cause discipline problems. Then I'm forced to take their free time and other privileges away from them and we work on the reading more. So, if your children come home tired and frustrated at the end of the day, I hope you'll understand, because I'm the same.
>
> Parent: If the reading level is so different this year, why don't you just use other books?
>
> Teacher: We'd like to, but the committee on new text books won't meet until next year to order books for two years after that.

The above interchange actually took place some years ago in what is considered a "good school district." Almost everyone accepts that there is a causal relationship between teaching/curriculum and discipline, but still we accept less than adequate teaching or curricula which do not match the students' entering knowledges or skills.

If students enter a particular class without the proper prerequisites (e.g., knowledge of facts and skills that will be built upon, a level of anxiety that is not too high, etc.), then *it is the teacher's responsibility either to teach them the prerequisites or have the student placed in a class in which the prerequisites will be learned. This is a problem the teacher owns!* Teachers are the professionals society trusts to make educational diagnoses and prescriptions. If teachers do not take this responsibility or carry it out improperly, then students will quickly feel frustrated, have difficulty understanding what is going on, pay less and less attention to the task, and sooner or later become a discipline problem. They will have known, in John Rassias' apt phrase,[10] "the agony of boredom and the triumph of recess."

Student success is central to a well-controlled classroom because it is central to the development of self-control, to competence vs. helplessness, to emotional development, to social power games—to everything in the individual's growth. The curriculum must be built around the students' needs and abilities, both collectively and individually. Teaching methods must be flexible, varied and perceived as directly related to important instructional outcomes. Students must know what those outcomes are. And students' work must be assessed and graded noncompetively against a high standard of achievement. That is, each student must be required to master these objectives to a high level of achievement with no excuses, but with additional attempts and instructional assistance as needed (e.g., Gentile and Stevens-Haslinger, 1983).

Ensuring student success is the most difficult aspect of teaching. On the other hand, seeing your students succeed is also the most joyful part of being a teacher.

EVER THE TWAIN SHALL MEET

Life is hard, as our common lament goes, and teaching is perhaps the most difficult activity in life. We tend to preach too much and model too little in practice; we tend to blame others for our failings and credit ourselves for our successes; we tend to catch people doing wrong instead of "catching them being good"; and we want to change the world by changing others, not by changing ourselves. The truth is we are a humorous lot, we humans, and if we can retain a sense of humor regarding our own frailties, perhaps our students' frailties may not appear as serious.

No one was better at self-deprecating humor than Samuel L. Clemens, better known as Mark Twain. He described his own self-control in an article introducing himself to the readers of the Buffalo Express on August 21, 1869. After assuring his readers that he would not cause any trouble or introduce any "startling reforms," he got to the heart of the self-discipline matter with the following promise:

I am simply going to do my plain, unpretending duty, when I cannot get out of it; I shall work diligently and honestly and faithfully at all times and upon all occasions, when privation and want, shall compel me to do it; in writing, I shall always confine myself strictly to the truth, except when it is attended with

175

inconvenience; I shall witheringly rebuke all forms of crime and misconduct, except when committed by the party inhabiting my own vest; I shall not make use of slang or vulgarity upon any occasion or under any circumstances, and shall never use profanity except in discussing house rent and taxes.

There was an honest man whom we can model!

NOTES

1. The author had the good fortune to spend his last two sabbatical leaves in Japan from January to April of 1976 and China from April to June 1983 observing classrooms, among other things. Whenever possible he visited a school for as much as a week and stayed with a class from a full day to three days. This allowed him to see their entire schedule as well as to have the students and teachers become accustomed to him. The observations in this section are based on these experiences.
2. Sensei (pronounced sen-say) is the Japanese word for teacher, which is used with great respect. For example, to show honor to a physician, you call him or her "Sensei."
3. Based on the psychiatric techniques of Milton Erickson (see Haley, 1973).
4. Compare this conceptualization with Bandura's reciprocal determinism in Chapter I.
5. Notice we did not say "never."
6. Berkowitz (1962) and Feshbach (1964) also stress the importance of intent in inciting aggression. The latter gives the following example (p. 265). "A student may be annoyed and disappointed at receiving a failing grade. But if he should discover that the instructor is pleased by his failure, he is likely to become furious."
7. Ginott also pointed out that people who refused his advice would often insist, "Haim ginott gonna do it!"
8. Ownership of the problem is a central concern of Teacher Effectiveness Training, T.E.T. (Gordon, 1974).
9. Labels also offer the opportunity for much satire, which some people just cannot resist. For example, if you take the point of view that "every psychological problem of insufficiency has its complementary problem of excess" (Gentile, 1978, p. 111), then *dyslexia* (a disability to learn to read) has its counterpart in *hyperlexia* (the ability to read too well). Likewise, *dyscalculia*, a disability in learning mathematics, is complemented by *hypercalculia* (Gentile, 1984), a disability of mathematical excesses. And who can forget rapanoia (Gentile, 1974; 1982) the complement of paranoia? See also the "Pigeons, Pecking Orders" anecdote.
10. From a lecture "The Classroom as Theater," State University of New York at Buffalo, October 7, 1983.

Appendix A

RAPANOIA

J. Ronald Gentile

Fm
1. IF YOU KNOW YOUR TROUBLES ARE REAL AND THEY AN- NOY YA', YOU CAN
2. THE PROB-LEM IS THE THINGS THAT CAN DE-STROY YA' ARE

C7

Fm
1. CALL THE COPS OR ELSE JUST CALL A LAW - YA'. IF YOUR
2. DONE CO-VERT- LY SO THEY WON'T AN - NOY YA'. YOU DON'T

C7

B♭m
1. FEARS ARE NOT REAL, DON'T A - POL - O - GIZE, YOU'RE TOO
2. KNOW THAT E - VEN THE PAR A - NOID'S PER - SE

A♭

G♭
1. JUNG AND A - FREUD TO PSY - CHOL - O - GIZE, AND
2. CUT - ING YOU, THERE - FORE I'VE GOINED THE WOIDS. THIS

F

I
Fm
1. WHAT GOOD IS THE LA - BEL PAR - A - NOI - A? THE

C7

II
F
2. NON - FEARED THREAT I'VE LA - BELED RAP - A - NOI - A. WHEN YOU

6m
C7   F7

177

J. RONALD GENTILE

Appendix B

Chapter I

A Psychology of Behavior

1. What is the author's position on the "nature-nurture" issue?
2. What is meant by each of the following terms?
   a. respondent
   b. operant
   c. cognition
3. Which of the following terms is associated with operants and which with respondents? Give examples.
   a. motions
   b. emotions
   c. instrumental conditioning
   d. Pavlovian conditioning
   e. Skinnerian conditioning
   f. voluntary response
   g. reflexes
4. What is meant by each of the following symbols?
   a. S^{RF}
   b. S^{AV}
   c. R
   d. US
   e. UR
   f. CS
   g. CR
5. The author claims that cognitive processes such as learning to read can never be accomplished in the absence of respondent and operant conditioning. For example, a child is ridiculed while trying to read a word. What effect does this have on his:
   a. learning to read?
   b. willingness to try again?
   c. emotional response to reading?
6. What is meant by reciprocal determinism? How does this explain the relationship between behavior and environment according to Social Learning Theory?

Chapter II

Respondent Behavior: Emotions

1. Diagram the classical conditioning procedure using the symbols US, CS, UR and CR. Why can the learning that occurs here be considered stimulus substitution?
2. What is the procedure and the effect of *extinction?*

3. What is the relationship of each of the following to the rate or strength of formation of a CR?
   a. number of CS-US pairings
   b. interval between CS and US
   c. intensity of US
   d. "belongingness" of CS and US

4. What is the difference between *phobias* and *conditioned fears?*

5. What is meant by each of the following?
   a. generalization
   b. discrimination
   Give examples.

6. What is meant by *higher-order conditioning?* Describe a procedure for producing it. How might higher-order conditioning be involved in attaching emotion to words?

7. What is meant by learned helplessness?
   a. under what conditions does it occur?
   b. how can it be cured?
   c. how can it be prevented?

8. Give examples of the interdependence of motions, emotions and cognitions.

9. Describe the complexities in knowing what you are feeling in terms of the internal state of your body and the information provided by the environment (e.g., interpret the Schachter-Singer experiments).

10. What is meant by obtaining *voluntary control* over involuntary processes?

11. Define biofeedback. Give some examples of how it is being used to solve human problems.

12. Describe some benefits and limitations of biofeedback.

13. What is meant by each of the following techniques?
    a. relaxation (progressive relaxation)
    b. systematic desensitization and counter-conditioning
    c. flooding and implosion
    d. massed performance of unwanted behaviors
    e. self-control

Chapter III

Operant Behavior: Motions

1. Describe operant behavior in terms of its means and ends, purpose and consequence.

2. It is now commonly accepted that reinforcement does not directly "strengthen" behavior; rather, it "regulates" behavior. What is meant by that?

3. Define each of the following types of reinforcement:
   a. Positive reinforcement
   b. Negative reinforcement
   Diagram the procedure and effects of each using the following symbols, where appropriate, (R, S^{RF}, S^{AV}, No S^{RF}, No S^{AV}). Give examples.

4. Distinguish between the common use of the word *reward* and the technical meaning of *positive reinforcement.*

5. Describe negative reinforcement as *escape* or *avoidance* of a noxious event. Give examples (e.g., drug-taking, peer pressure, etc.)

6. Describe the *extinction* procedure for an operant behavior. What is meant by each of the following during the extinction process?
   a. the frustration effect
   b. spontaneous recovery

7. Define punishment and diagram it using the following symbols: R, S^{AV}. Give examples.

8. Distinguish between punishment and negative reinforcement in terms of:
   a. the procedure used
   b. the effects on behavior

9. What is *discrimination learning?* Give examples of it using the following symbols ($S^D = S^+$ = discriminative stimulus; $S^\Delta = S^-$ = other stimuli; R; S^{RF}).

10. What is *generalization?* How does it relate to discrimination learning? Draw a *generalization gradient* for a typical learning situation?
    a. before discrimination training
    b. after a few trials of discrimination training
    c. after many trials of discrimination training

11. What is meant by each of the following types of reinforcement?
    a. primary
    b. secondary
       (1) social
       (2) tokens
       (3) activities

12. What is the Premack Principle?

13. What is meant by *resistance to extinction?*

14. What is the effect of each of the following on *learning* and on *persistence* (i.e., resistance to extinction)?
    a. Type of reinforcement
    b. Quantity of reinforcement
    c. Delay of reinforcement
    d. Reinforcement contingencies
    e. Schedules of reinforcement
       (1) Continuous
       (2) Intermittent

15. What is *shaping?*

16. Describe each of the following schedules of reinforcement:
    a. Ratio Schedules
       (1) Fixed (FR)
       (2) Variable (VR)
    b. Interval Schedules
       (2) Fixed (FI)
       (2) Variable (VI)

17. Describe practical applications of the above (i.e., items 14–16) in terms of such topics as the following:
    a. Student attention spans
    b. student/teacher ratios
    c. patterned sequences of reinforcement

18. What is a *token economy?* What is the author's opinion on its use in "ordinary" classrooms?

19. Describe how each of the following "amazing effects" of punishment can be learned:
    a. masochistic behaviors
    b. punishment as a cue for reinforcement (e.g., battered child)
20. How do each of the following contribute to the effects of punishment?
    a. severity of punishment
    b. delay of punishment
    c. punishment contingencies

Chapter IV

Modeling and Social Learning

1. Analyze the following components of a modeling episode:
    a. the model (M)
    b. the observer (0)
    c. direct consequences (reinforcement or punishment)
    d. vicarious consequences (reinforcement or punishment)
2. What is the distinction between *learning* and *performance?* Upon which do reinforcement and punishment have their effects?
3. Describe each of the following three effects of modeling:
    a. the learning effect
    b. the inhibitory or disinhibitory effect
    c. the response facilitation effect
    Give examples.
4. What are some of the characteristics of people whom we are most likely to model?
5. What is the authors' opinion on the relationship between TV violence and subsequent aggression by viewers?
6. Compare the effects of TV-modeled pro-social and anti-social behaviors.
7. Describe some of the ways that advertisers attempt to manipulate our behaviors as consumers.
8. Why is logical persuasion an inefficient means of changing attitudes and behaviors? Include the concept of cognitive dissonance in your answer.
9. What is meant by vicarious emotional learning? How is it learned?
10. What is meant by self-control? Describe the typical developmental sequence for the learning of
    (a) self-control.
    (b) standards.
11. What does the research evidence cited have to say on the following aspects of conformity?
    a. the individual vs. the group
    b. assuming the behaviors of the role you play (e.g., guards vs. prisoners)
    c. obedience to an authority
    d. norms
12. What is meant by sociometric wealth (the sociodynamic law)?
    a. How is it related to friendships in classes?
    b. How is it related to intergroup rivalries in classes?
    c. How does it apply to ability grouping or tracking?

13. What is meant by goal structures? Define the following kinds of goal structures and describe their likely classroom effects:
    a. cooperative goal structures
    b. competitive goal structures
    c. individualistic goal structures

14. Review each of the eight recommendations provided as a summary from this chapter. Describe ways to apply them to real classroom situations.

Chapter V

Discipline: Motions, Emotions and Commotions

1. What is the book's definition of misbehavior?

2. Analyze a discipline problem in terms of the interaction between student and teacher. Whose behavior is being
    a. positively reinforced?
    b. negatively reinforced?
    c. extinguished?
    d. punished?

3. Contrast the amount of unstructured free time for physical activity in Japanese, Chinese and American schools. What are the natural consequences of littering or vandalism in these schools?

4. What is meant by each of the following (reality therapy) concepts? Give examples.
    a. natural consequences
    b. accepting no excuses
    c. reality therapy needs
       (1) for love
       (2) for self-worth
    d. asking "what?" instead of "why?"
    e. ignoring past failures
    f. committing to a new behavior

5. What is meant by each of the following concerning rules?
    a. How many rules should there be?
    b. What are "reasonable rules"?
    c. How should teachers express their emotions when rules are broken?
    Give examples.

6. What are the effects of punishment in discipline situations?

7. Distinguish between each of the following in purpose, procedure and likely effects. Give examples.
    a. retribution and restitution
    b. physical restraint and corporal punishment
    c. time out and solitary confinement

8. What are characteristics of a good *contract?*

9. What is meant by "owning" a problem?

10. Why can labeling become disabling?

11. What is meant by
    a. the relationship between curriculum decisions/teaching quality and discipline?
    b. the distinction between *spending* time and *investing* time?

Appendix C

THE ISSUE OF HEREDITY VS. ENVIRONMENT:
A REINTERPRETATION
OF JOHN B. WATSON'S
FAMOUS QUOTATION

The most important difference to separate behaviorists from other theorists is usually considered to be the relative influence of heredity and environment in determining behavior. The point is usually made that behaviorists believe in Locke's "tabula rasa", that infants are born with a "blank tablet" as a mind upon which the environment writes. Thus genetic and maturational factors are assumed to be minimal, if they exist at all, and experience is everything. The following remark of Watson's (1930, p. 104) is widely cited as evidence of this belief:

> Give me a dozen healthy infants, well-formed, and my own specified world to bring them up in and I'll guarantee to take any one at random and train him to become any type of specialist I might select—doctor, lawyer, artist, merchant-chief and, yes, even beggar-man and thief, regardless of his talents, penchants, tendencies, abilities, vocations, and race of his ancestors.

What is overlooked by those who cite this statement is the context in which it occurs. The next two sentences, less frequently quoted, finish the paragraph:

> I am going beyond my facts and I admit it, but so have the advocates of the contrary and they have been doing it for many thousands of years. Please note then when this experiment is made I am to be allowed to specify the way the children are to be brought up and the world they have to live in.

More important than these qualifications, however, is the total context in which these statements were made. Watson's book, as was his research program, was an attempt to organize the evidence on what is inborn and what is learned, to understand where heredity ends and experience begins. Thus on page 138 he presented "The Activity Stream", which was a chronology of a long list of behaviors ranging from blinking to love, indicating whether they were conditionable and at what ages. Of this activity stream he said the following (1930, p. 139):

> This chart gives quickly in graphic form the whole scope of psychology. Every problem the behaviorist works upon has some kind of setting in this stream of definite, tangible, actually observable happenings. It presents, too, the fundamental point of view of the behaviorist—viz. that in order to understand man we have to understand the life history of his activities. It shows too most convincingly that psychology is a natural science—a definite part of biology.

Watson, considered to be the most extreme environmentalist, can be seen to believe in ". . . heritable differences in form, in structure" (p. 97), in shape and delicacy of throat structures, etc. But then he goes on to be an interactionist—that is, to state his belief in the interaction of heredity and environment. He points out that heritable structures tell us little about function because that depends upon the environment in which the organism lives. He gives examples of obvious cultural differences in life styles among men and women despite the structural similarities of all people. He then drives home his interactionist point of view with the following hypothetical instructional example. The older of two boys is shaped like the father with long flexible fingers. The father, a pianist, loves him dearly. The second has short fingers and is loved more by the mother, a distinguished artist. With their differential attachments, the time each parent spends with each child leads the older child to become "a wonderful pianist, the younger an indifferent artist." Assuming that the younger boy could not have become a pianist under normal circumstances, perhaps because of his short fingers and the musculature of his hands, does that make him genetically unfit for the piano? Watson points out that the piano is an arbitrary, but standardized instrument and then draws the following conclusion to this scenario (1930, p. 103):

> But suppose the father had been fond of the younger child and said, "I want him to be a pianist and I am going to try an experiment—his fingers are short—he'll never have a flexible hand, so I'll build him a piano. I'll make the keys so narrow that even with his short fingers his span will be sufficient, and I'll make leverage for the keys so that no particular strength or even flexibility will be needed." Who knowns—the younger son under these conditions might have become the world's greatest pianist.

We bring this up to point out that even the so-called most extreme environmentalist position is really an interactionists view (see also Skinner's neo-Darwinist view; 1971, 1974). Most theorists, whether empiricist like Watson and Skinner or rationalist like Piaget and Erikson, are interactionists on this issue. This is not to say that there are no differences among positions; rather it is to say that all major theorists believe that *learning occurs on top of development; environment interacts with heredity and maturational structures to produce the behavior and cognition that we call human.*

Glossary

Aversive stimulus. An unpleasant stimulus, such as a slap, blow, loud noise, or electric shock.

Avoidance. Removing an aversive situation before the noxious event begins as a result of learning to respond to a cue which predicts the onset of the aversive stimulus; avoidance is therefore discriminated escape learning and is based on negative reinforcement.

Baseline data. Same as *Base rate.*

Base rate. A measure of the naturally occurring frequency of a response before any attempt has been made to change it.

Behavioral self-control. See *Self-control.*

Belongingness. The relationship between US and CS that exists along a natural dimension—e.g., between taste and food or between a sudden loud noise and a startle behavior.

Biofeedback. A process whereby physiological functions not ordinarily under voluntary control are mirrored back to us, usually by instrumentation, to allow these functions to be brought under voluntary control.

Classroom goal structures. The types of interactions occurring among students striving to fulfill educational objectives.

Cognitions. A general term for all of the so-called "higher-order" functions, including verbal behavior; the learning, retention and transfer of facts, concepts and principles; thinking; creativity; analysis and synthesis.

Cognitive dissonance. The situation that exists in a person when two contradictory beliefs are held concurrently or when facts are not consistent with the beliefs.

Competence. The capability to control one's own environment and, therefore, the consequences of one's own behavior; mastery over the situation.

Competitive goal structures. The situation that exists when individual students succeed at the expense of others in achieving educational objectives.

Conditioned reinforcer. Same as *Secondary reinforcer.*

Conditioned response (conditioned reflex; C.R). A reflex that has been transferred from an unconditioned stimulus to a neutral stimulus, now called the conditioned stimulus.

Conditioned stimulus (CS) A stimulus that was neutral before conditioning began but became capable of eliciting the response after being paired with an unconditioned stimulus.

Conditioning. A procedure in which an increase in the frequency of response occurs because a stimulus is paired with the response.

Conformity. Behavior that is in agreement with a reference group.

Consequence. The event that follows a behavior; e.g., a reinforcing or punishing stimulus.

Contingent reinforcement. The presentation of a reinforcing stimulus only if the correct response has been made.

Continuous reinforcement. The procedure of reinforcing every correct response.

Contracts. Written agreements (e.g., between teachers and students) specifying acceptable behavior and the consequences of fulfilling or not fulfilling the agreement.

Contrast (or Context) Effect. Comparing the magnitude of a reinforcer with previous reinforcements; it usually produces larger effects than if no previous experience occurred with such reinforcers.

Cooperative goal structures. The situation that exists when individual students' efforts are coordinated in order to achieve instructional objectives.

Counter-conditioning. The process of replacing an emotional response (e.g., fear and tension) with an opposite emotional response (e.g., relaxation).

Criterion-referenced assessment. The interpretation of a person's score (e.g., test score) compared with an established and more-or-less absolute standard of performance on a given set of objectives.

Deviancy. See *misbehavior.*

Discrimination training. The procedure of increasing the rate of responding in the presence of one stimulus and decreasing it in the presence of another.

Discriminative stimulus (S^D or S^+). The particular stimulus in the presence of which a correct response is likely to be reinforced.

Entering behavior. The specific behaviors the student can perform in relation to the hierarchy of skills required by the task. Knowing the student's entering behavior allows the teacher to start the student at the point in the curriculum at which the material will be neither too easy nor too difficult.

Escape. Removing an aversive situation (e.g., leaving), the consequence of which is favorable and, therefore, likely to be repeated. Escape is based on negative reinforcement.

Extinction. In operant conditioning, the process of withholding reinforcement following performance of an operant; in respondent conditioning, the process of withholding the unconditioned stimulus following the presentation of the conditioned stimulus. Its usual effect is to reduce the strength or frequency of the response.

Fixed-interval (FI) schedule. An interval schedule in which reinforcement is given for the next correct response after a fixed amount of time since the last reinforcement.

Fixed-ratio (FR) schedule. A ratio schedule in which a fixed number of responses must be emitted before reinforcement is given.

Flooding. A counter-conditioning technique like bronco-busting: the CS is presented for a long time so that the person becomes more weary than fearful and eventually relaxes.

Frustration Effect. In extinction, an increase in the rate of a behavior shortly after non-reinforcement has begun.

Generalization. Same as *Stimulus generalization.*

Generalization gradient. The curve of response frequencies which shows that the more similar a stimulus is to the original S^D, the more likely the response will be performed in its presence.

Higher-order conditioning. The process of attaching a CR (e.g., fear) learned to one stimulus (CS_1) to another neutral stimulus (CS_2) by following CS_2 by CS_1. In this case CS_1 acts as a US to transfer the CR to the new stimulus (CS_2).

Imitation. The procedure whereby an observer performs the behavior that he has seen some other person (the model) perform.

Imitative behavior. The behavior performed by an observer as a result of witnessing the behavior of some other person (a model).

Implosion. A counter-conditioning technique, like flooding, which uses bizarre images to extinguish fears.

Incompatible behavior. Behavior that is opposed to the behavior of interest. Examples of incompatible behavior are competing and cooperating, hoarding and sharing, paying attention and being inattentive.

Indiscipline. See *misbehavior.*

Individualistic goal structures. The situation that exists when students achieve instructional objectives without interaction with other students.

Inhibitory or disinhibitory effect of modeling. The suppression or facilitation of a performance as a result of witnessing the consequences of a model's similar behavior.

Instructional objectives. Specific performances stated in terms of observable behaviors that students are expected to acquire through instructional procedures.

Intermittent reinforcement. Same as *Partial reinforcement.*

Interval schedule. A reinforcement schedule in which reinforcement is contingent on a correct response following a specified amount of time that has passed since the last reinforcement.

Involuntary behaviors. Environmentally controlled behaviors; reflexes; respondents.

Learned helplessness. An emotional, motivational and cognitive disability that results from exposure to noncontingent, unavoidable punishing consequences.

Learning effect of modeling. New behaviors that are acquired as a result of observing a model perform them.

Locus of control. In attribution theory the belief that people attribute their successes or failures to their own efforts (internal locus of control) or to outside forces (external locus of control).

Mastery learning. An instructional system based on mastery testing.

Mastery testing. Requiring that a student achieve above a minimum standard of performance on a specified set of educational objectives (criterion-referenced assessment), even if several attempts must be made to achieve that standard.

Misbehavior. Any action taken where it is not wanted.

Model. In imitation, the person whose behavior is imitated.

Negative reinforcement. The removal of an aversive stimulus as a consequence of the performance of an operant response (e.g., escape). Its effect is to increase or maintain the rate of the response.

Noncontingent reinforcement. The presentation of a reinforcing stimulus whether or not the correct response has been made.

Norm-referenced assessment. The interpretation of a person's score (e.g., test score) compared with the distribution of others' scores (the norm) on the same exercise.

Norms. Shared expectations or attitudes about what are appropriate and inappropriate behaviors.

Observer. In imitation, the person who witnesses the behavior of a model.

Operant. A response for which no eliciting stimulus can be found but whose rate is determined by its consequences (the stimuli that follow). Such a response is usually called "purposeful," or "voluntary."

Partial reinforcement. A reinforcement schedule in which reinforcement is provided only after some, not all, of the correct responses.

Persistence. The ability to continue to respond despite non-reinforcement; frustration tolerance; resistance to extinction.

Phobia. An extreme fear which is out of proportion to the situation, cannot be reduced by reasoning, is usually beyond voluntary control, leads to avoidance of the feared object, and for which we may have some biological preparation.

Physical restraint. "Holding back" a person from aggressive behavior until the person calms down and assumes self-control (an alternative to punishment).

Positive reinforcement. The use of a (reinforcing) stimulus to increase or maintain the rate or frequency of an operant response.

Preferred activity. A type of secondary or conditioned reinforcer that consists of activities or behaviors people engage in frequently (given no external constraints).

Premack principle. A behavioral principle which states that of two activities, if the more preferred (more probable) behavior is a consequence of the less preferred, it will act to reinforce the latter (and therefore increase its probability).

Primary reinforcement. (a) A reinforcer that satisfies a biological need (e.g., food); (b) The process of rewarding an operant response with a primary reinforcer.

Primary reinforcer. A stimulus that is rewarding because it fulfills some basic biological need (for example, food, water, or sleep).

Progressive relaxation. A systematic procedure for relaxing the whole body by tensing and then relaxing each major muscle group in turn.

Pro-social behavior. Behaviors such as cooperation, sharing and showing empathy; opposite of aggressive or hostile behavior.

Punishment. The procedure of applying an aversive stimulus to the subject as a consequence of his behavior. Its usual effect is to decrease temporarily the rate of responding.

Rapanoia. The (pathological?) non-fear of real threats that should be feared.

Rate of response. Same as *Response frequency.*

Ratio schedule. A reinforcement schedule in which reinforcement is contingent on the number of responses performed, no matter how long it takes to emit the response.

Reality therapy. An approach to learning self-discipline that makes people accept the natural consequences of their own behavior, accepts no excuses for inappropriate behavior, and requires people to recommit to new, more appropriate behavior if their behavior is unsuccessful.

Reciprocal determinism. The interdependence of organism with organism or organism with environment in which each affects, causes or in some way controls the other.

Reinforcement. A consequence of a behavior that has the effect of increasing or maintaining the frequency of that behavior; the procedure of regulating behavior in the above way.

Reinforcement contingency. The operative rule governing which responses are to be reinforced.

Reinforcement schedule. A statement or rule that specifies how many or what proportion of the correct responses will be reinforced.

Reinforcer. A *reinforcing stimulus.*

Reinforcing stimulus. (a) A stimulus that comes after a response has been made and that increases the rate or frequency of that response; (b) A reward.

Resistance to extinction. The ability of a response to maintain its previous frequency when it is no longer reinforced; persistence; frustration tolerance.

Respondent. A response that follows a stimulus and is elicited by it as a reflex; involuntary behavior.

Response. An act that can be described as a single operation. The act can be as simple as a reflex or as complicated as the operation of walking or talking.

Response facilitation effect of modeling. A behavior of an observer that occurs because a model's behavior serves as a cue (e.g., applauding when others do).

Response frequency. A description of how often a response occurs in some period of time.

Restitution. Correcting for misbehavior, making right what went wrong; using natural consequences of a misbehavior to correct the behavior (an alternative to punishment).

Retribution. Punishment based on retaliation or revenge: "an eye for an eye."

Satiation. The process of making a stimulus excessively available so that it is no longer reinforcing.

S-delta (S^Δ or S^-). The particular stimulus that represents an occasion on which a response is not reinforced, in contrast to S^D, which represents the occasion on which the response will likely be reinforced.

Second-order conditioning. See *higher-order conditioning.*

Secondary reinforcer. A stimulus, such as money or praise, that is reinforcing because it has been paired with (or is exchangeable for) a primary reinforcer.

Self-control. Behavior that occurs in the relative absence of external constraints that is less likely than some alternative available behavior (e.g., not eating instead of eating when at a buffet).

Self-evaluation. Comparing one's own behavior to some standard of acceptable performance; part of the self-control process.

Self-monitoring. Observing and recording one's own behavior (usually for the purpose of developing self-control).

Self-reward. Reinforcing oneself with praise or a favorite activity as a result of a favorable self-evaluation; part of the self-control process.

Shaping. The procedure of reinforcing successively closer approximations of the desired behavior in order to teach a new response.

Social reinforcer. A type of secondary or conditioned reinforcer that is provided by interaction with another person. Examples are smiles and praise.

Socialization. The developmental process whereby children adopt the behavioral patterns within the range of what is acceptable to the culture in which they grow up.

Sociodynamic law. In any group of people a few will have many friends and admirers and the majority will have few friends and admirers.

Sociometric wealth. See the *sociodynamic law.*

Sociometry. A procedure for assessing the friendship patterns (liking and disliking) within a group.

Spontaneous recovery. In extinction, an increase in the rate of behavior after the rate of behavior has been reduced to nearly zero; the cause is seldom known, but it is a well-known effect during long sequences of non-reinforced behavior.

Stimulus. An environmental event to which an animal or person is sensitive.

Stimulus generalization. The finding that a response originally reinforced in the presence of one stimulus (S^D) will also occur in the presence of other similar stimuli.

Successively closer approximations. Responses that are getting closer and closer to the desired behavior. These responses are reinforced in order to shape more complex responses out of simple responses.

Systematic desensitization and counter-conditioning. A procedure for establishing a hierarchy of anxiety-producing stimuli or events and learning to relax instead of feel tense in their presence; used to reduce fears and phobias.

Target behavior. The particular behavior, defined very specifically, that is of concern and is therefore to be observed and perhaps changed.

Time out (from reinforcement). A technique for reducing the frequency of undesirable behaviors by moving the subject from the situation in which reinforcements are available to a situation in which they are not available.

Time sampling. An observational technique in which selected aspects of behavior are observed and counted within short time intervals sampled throughout days or weeks.

Token. A type of secondary or conditioned reinforcer that is a physical or countable item, such as money or course grades.

Token economy. A small social system in which reinforcement in the form of some kind of token is provided immediately following the performance of desired responses by its members.

Unconditioned response (UR). A response that is automatically elicited by a stimulus; a reflex. Also called a *Respondent.*

Unconditioned stimulus (US). A stimulus that comes before and elicits or causes a reflexive response (the response is called a respondent or unconditioned response).

Variable-interval (VI) schedule. An interval schedule in which reinforcement is contingent on performance of the next correct response following passage of the average of some predetermined amount of time.

Variable-ratio (VR) schedule. A ratio schedule in which reinforcement is contingent on performance of the average of some predetermined number of responses.

Vicarious consequences. Witnessing the consequences of a model's behavior (e.g., reinforcement or punishment) which has a parallel effect on the observer's behavior.

Vicarious emotional learning. The situation that exists when an observer imitates the emotional response of a model, despite not directly being influenced by the cause of the model's behavior (e.g., fearing a spider because a model fears spiders).

Vicarious reinforcement. In imitation, the procedure of an observer witnessing a model's behavior reinforced, with the usual result that the probability of that behavior by the observer is increased.

Voluntary behavior. Purposeful behavior; operants.

References

Abramson, L. Y., Seligman, M. E. P. and Teasdale, J. D. "Learned Helplessness in Humans: Critique and Reformulation," *Journal of Abnormal Psychology,* 1978, *87,* 49–74.

Alexander, R. N. and Apfel, C. H. "Altering Schedules of Reinforcement for Improved Classroom Behavior," *Exceptional Children,* 1976, *43,* No. 10, 97–99.

Alschuler, A. S. *School Discipline: A Socially Literate Solution.* New York: McGraw-Hill, 1980.

Amsel, A. "The Role of Frustrative Nonreward in Noncontinuous Reward Situations." *Psychological Bulletin,* 1958, *55,* 102–119.

Amsel, A. "Frustrative Nonreward in Partial Reinforcement and Discrimination Learning: Some Recent History and a Theoretical Extension." *Psychological Review,* 1962, *69,* 306–328.

Amsel, A. "Positive Induction, Behavioral Contrast, and Generalization of Inhibition in Discrimination Learning." in H. H. Kendler and J. T. Spence (Eds.) *Essays in Neo-Behaviorism: A Memorial Volume to Kenneth W. Spence,* New York: Appleton-Century-Crofts, 1971.

Asch, S. E. "Studies of Independence and Conformity: A Minority of One Against a Unanimous Majority," *Psychological Monographs,* 1956, *70* (No. 9), Whole No. 416.

Azrin, N. H. and Holz, W. C. "Punishment" in W. K. Honig (Ed.) *Operant Behavior: Areas of Research and Application.* New York: Appleton-Century-Crofts, 1966, pp. 380–447.

Bair, J. H. "Development of Voluntary Control," *Psychological Review,* 1901, *8,* 474–510.

Balsam, P. D. and Bondy, A. S. "The Negative Side Effects of Reward, " *Journal of Applied Behavior Analysis,* 1983, *16,* 283–296.

Bandura, A. "Social Learning Through Imitation," in M. R. Jones (Ed.) *Nebraska Symposium on Motivation,* Lincoln: University of Nebraska Press, 1962, pp. 211–269.

Bandura, A. "Vicarious Processes: A Case of No-Trial Learning," in L. Berkowitz (Ed.) *Advances in Experimental Social Psychology,* Vol. II, New York: Academic Press, 1965, pp. 1–55. (a)

Bandura, A. "Influence of Models' Reinforcement Contingencies on the Acquisition of Imitative Responses," *Journal of Personality and Social Psychology,* 1965, *1,* 589–595. (b)

Bandura, A. *Principles of Behavior Modification,* New York: Holt, Rinehart and Winston, 1969.

Bandura, A. "Vicarious and Self-Reinforcement Processes," in R. Glaser (Ed.) *The Nature of Reinforcement,* New York: Academic Press, 1971.

Bandura, A. *Social Learning Theory,* Englewood Cliffs, NJ: Prentice-Hall, 1977.

Bandura, A., Grusec, J. E. and Menlove, F. L. "Some Social Determinants of Self-Monitoring Reinforcement Systems," *Journal of Personality and Social Psychology,* 1967, *5,* 449–455.

Bandura, A. and Huston, A. C. "Identification as a Process of Incidental Learning," *Journal of Abnormal and Social Psychology,* 1961, *63,* 311-318.

Bandura, A. and Kupers, C. J. "The Transmission of Patterns of Self-Reinforcement Through Modeling." *Journal of Abnormal and Social Psychology,* 1964, *69,* 1–9.

Bandura, A., Ross, D. and Ross, S. A. "Imitation of Film-Mediated Aggressive Models," *Journal of Abnormal and Social Psychology,* 1963, *66,* 3–11. (a)

Bandura, A., Ross, D. and Ross, S. A. "A Comparative Test of the Status Envy, Social Power, and the Secondary Reinforcement Theories of Identificatory Learning," *Journal of Abnormal and Social Psychology,* 1963, *67,* 527–534. (b)

Bandura, A., Ross, D. and Ross, S. A. " 'Vicarious' Reinforcement and Imitative Learning," *Journal of Abnormal and Social Psychology,* 1963, *67,* 601–607. (c)

Bandura, A. and Walters, R. H. *Social Learning and Personality Development,* New York: Holt, Rinehart and Winston, 1963.

Bandura, A. and Whalen, C. K. "The Influence of Antecedent Reinforcement and Divergent Modeling Cues on Patterns of Self-Reward," *Journal of Personality and Social Psychology,* 1966, *3,* 373–382.

Barabasz, A. "Group Desensitization of Text Anxiety in Elementary School," *Journal of Psychology,* 1973, *83,* 295–301.

Barkley, R. A. *Hyperactive Children: A Handbook for Diagnosis and Treatment,* New York: Guilford, 1981.

Becker, W. C., Madsen, C. H., Arnold, C. R. and Thomas, D. R. "The Contingent Use of Teacher Attention and Praise in Reducing Classroom Behavior Problems," *Journal of Special Education,* 1967, *1,* 287–307.

Bem, D. J. *Beliefs, Attitudes and Human Affairs,* Belmont, CA: Brooks/Cole, 1970.

Berger, S. M. "Conditioning Through Vicarious Instigation," *Psychological Review,* 1962, *69,* 450–466.

Berkowitz, L. *Aggression: A Social Psychological Analysis.* New York: McGraw-Hill, 1962.

Berkowitz, L. "The Effects of Observing Violence," *Scientific American,* 1964, *210,* 2–8.

Berkowitz, L. "The Contagion of Violence: An S-R Mediational Analysis of Some Effects of Observed Aggression," in W. J. Arnold and M. M. Page (Eds.) *Nebraska Symposium on Motivation,* Lincoln: University of Nebraska Press, 1970, *18,* 95–136.

Blanchard, E. B. and Epstein, L. H. *A Biofeedback Primer,* Reading, MA: Addison-Wesley, 1978.

Blanchard, E. B. and Young, L. D. "Self-Control of Cardiac Functioning: A Promise as Yet Unfulfilled," *Psychological Bulletin,* 1973, *79,* 145–163.

Bloch, A. *Murphy's Law and Other Reasons Why Things Go Wrong.* Los Angeles: Price/Stern/Sloan, 1980.

Bloom, B. S. (Ed.) *Taxonomy of Educational Objectives: The Classification of Educational Goals. Handbook 1. Cognitive Domain,* New York: McKay, 1956.

Bloom, B. S., Hastings, J. T. and Madaus, G. F. *Handbook on formative and Summative Evaluation of Student Learning,* New York: McGraw-Hill, 1971.

Boe, E. E. "Bibliography on Punishment," in B. A. Campbell and R. M. Church (Eds.) *Punishment and Aversive Behavior,* New York: Appleton-Century-Crofts, 1969, pp. 531–587.

Bolles, R. C. *Theory of Motivation,* New York: Harper, 1975.

Boulle, P. *Planet of the Apes,* (translation by X. Fielding), New York: Vanguard Press, 1963.

Bower, G. H. "A Contrast Effect in Differential Conditioning," *Journal of Experimental Psychology,* 1961, *62,* 196–199.

Bower, G. H. and Hilgard, E. R. *Theories of Learning* (Fifth Edition), Englewood Cliffs, NJ: Prentice-Hall, 1981.

Brady, J. V. "Ulcers in 'Executive' Monkeys," *Scientific American,* 1958, *199,* 95–100.

Brady, J. V., Porter, R. W. Conrad, D. G. and Mason, J. W. "Avoidance Behavior and the Development of Gastroduodenal Ulcers," *Journal of the Experimental Analysis of Behavior,* 1958, *1,* 69–72.

Braud, L. W. "The Effects of Frontal EMG Biofeedback and Progressive Relaxation Upon Hyperactivity and Its Behavioral Concomitants," *Biofeedback and Self-Regulation,* 1978, *3,* 69–89.

Braud, L. W., Lupin, M. N. and Braud, W. B. "The Case of Electromyographic Biofeedback in the Control of Hyperactivity," *Journal of Learning Disabilities,* 1975, *8,* 420–425.

Bregman, E. "An Attempt to Modify the Emotional Attitude of Infants by the Conditioned Response Technique," *Journal of Genetic Psychology,* 1934, *45,* 169–198.

Brim. O. G. "Family Structure and Sex Role Learning by Children: A Further Analysis of Helen Koch's Data," *Sociometry,* 1958, *21,* 1–16.

Brown, B. B. *New Mind, New Body: Biofeedback: New Directions for the Mind,* New York: Harper and Row, 1974.

Brown, G. D. and Tyler, V. O., Jr. "The Use of Swift, Brief Isolation as a Group Control Device for Institutionalized Delinquents," *Behavior Research and Therapy,* 1967, *5,* 1–9.

Brown, R. *Social Psychology,* New York: Free Press, 1965.

Burgess, A. *A Clockwork Orange,* New York: W. W. Norton, 1963.

Butkowski, I. S. and Willows, P. M. "Cognitive-Motivational Characteristics of Children Varying in Reading Ability: Evidence for Learned Helplessness in Poor Readers," *Journal of Educational Psychology,* 1980, *72,* 408–422.

Canter, L. and Canter, M. *Assertive Discipline: A Take-Charge Approach for Today's Educator.* Seal Beach, CA: Canter and Associates, 1976.

Chaffee, S. H. "Television and Adolescent Aggressiveness (an Overview)," in G. A. Comstock and E. A. Rubinstein (Eds.) *Television and Social Behavior.* Technical Report (Vol. III) To The Surgeon General's Scientific Advisory Committee on Television and Social Behavior, Washington, D.C., U.S. Government Printing Office, 1972.

Charles, C. M. *Building Classroom Discipline: From Models to Practice,* New York: Longman, 1981.

Child, I. L. "Socialization," in G. Lindzey (Ed.) *Handbook of Social Psychology,* (Vol. 2), Cambridge, MA: Addison-Wesley, 1954, pp. 655–692.

Church, R. M. "The Varied Effects of Punishment on Behavior." *Psychological Review,* 1963, *70,* 369–402.

Church, R. M. "Response Suppression," in Campbell, B. A. and Church, R. M. (Eds.) *Punishment and Aversive Behavior,* New York: Appleton-Century-Crofts, 1969.

Cobb, D. E. and Evans, J. R. "The Use of Biofeedback Techniques with School-Aged Children Exhibiting Behavioral and/or Learning Problems," *Journal of Abnormal Child Psychology,* 1981, *9,* 251–281.

Combs, A. W. *Myths in Education,* Boston: Allyn and Bacon, 1979.

Cooper, J. O. *Measuring Behavior,* Columbus, Ohio: Charles E. Merrill, 1981.

Crespi, L. "Quantitative Variation of Incentive and Performance in the White Rat," *American Journal of Psychology,* 1942, *15,* 467–517.

Crider, A., Schwartz, G. E. and Shnidman, S. "On the Criteria for Instrumental Autonomic Conditioning: A Reply to Katkin and Murray," *Psychological Bulletin,* 1969, *71,* 455–461.

Davenport, J. W. Higher-order Conditioning of Fear," *Psychonomic Science,* 1966, *4,* 27–28.

Davis, M., Eshelman, E. R. and McKay, M. *The Relaxation and Stress Reduction Workbook,* Richmond, CA: New Harbinger Publications, 1980.

Davison, G. C. "Systematic Desensitization as a Counter-Conditioning Process," *Journal of Abnormal Psychology,* 1968, *73,* 91–99.

DeCecco, J. P. and Richards, A. K. "Civil War in the High Schools," *Psychology Today,* 1975, *9* (November), 51–56; 120.

De Roo, C. "Changing Chronic Pain Behavior: A Case Study of a Traumatic Industrial Amputee," paper presented at the National Pain Symposium, Indianapolis, IN: September 11–15, 1982.

de Saint Exupery, A. *The Little Prince,* New York: Harbrace Paperbound Library, 1971.

Diener, C. I. and Dweck, C. S. "An Analysis of Learned Helplessness: Continuous Changes in Performance, Strategy, and Achievement Cognitions Following Failure," *Journal of Personality and Social Psychology,* 1978, *36,* 451–462.

Dilendik, J. R. "A Sociometric Analysis of Two Sixth Grade Integrated Classrooms," State University of New York at Buffalo, unpublished manuscript, 1972.

Dollard, J., Miller, N. E., Doob, L. W., Mowrer, O. H. and Sears, R. R. *Frustration and Aggression.* New Haven: Yale University Press, 1939.

Doyle, W. "Are Students Behaving Worse Than They Used To Behave?" *Journal of Research and Development in Education,* 1978, *11,* 3–16.

Dreikurs, R. *Psychology in the Classroom,* New York: Harper & Row, 1968.

Dreikurs, R., Grunwald, B. and Pepper, F. *Maintaining Sanity in the Classroom,* New York: Harper and Row, 1971.

Dweck, C. S. "The Role of Expectations and Attributions in the Alleviation of Learned Helplessness," *Journal of Personality and Social Psychology,* 1975, *31,* 674–685.

Dweck, C. S. and Licht, B. G. "Learned Helplessness and Intellectual Achievement," in J. Garber and M. E. P. Seligman (Eds.) *Human Helplessness: Theory and Applications,* New York: Academic Press, 1980.

Dweck, C. S. and Reppucci, N. D. "Learned Helplessness and Reinforcement Responsibility in Children." *Journal of Personality and Social Psychology,* 1973, *25,* 109–116.

Early, C. J. "Attitude Learning in Children," *Journal of Educational Psychology,* 1968, *59,* 176–180.

Englehart, L. "Awareness and Relaxation Through Biofeedback in Public Schools," Proceedings of the Biofeedback Society of America, Ninth Annual Meeting, Albuquerque, NM, March 3–7, 1978.

English, H. B. "Three Cases of the 'Conditioned Fear Response'," *Journal of Abnormal and Social Psychology,* 1929, *24,* 221–225.

Fay, A. *Making Things Better by Making Them Worse,* New York: Hawthorn Books, 1978.

Feldhusen, J. F. "Behavior Problems in Secondary Schools," *Journal of Research and Development in Education,* 1978, *11,* 17–28.

Ferritor, D. E., Buckholdt, D., Hamblin, R. L. and Smith, L. "The Noneffects of Contingent Reinforcement for Attending Behavior on Work Accomplished," *Journal of Applied Behavior Analysis,* 1972, *5,* 7–17.

Ferster, C. B. and Appel, J. B. "Punishment of S Responding in Matched-To-Sample By Timeout from Positive Reinforcement," *Journal of the Experimental Analysis of Behavior,* 1961, *4,* 45–56.

Ferster, C. B. and Skinner, B. F. *Schedules of Reinforcement,* New York: Appleton-Century-Crofts, 1957.

Feshbach, S. "The Drive-Reducing Function of Fantasy Behavior." *Journal of Abnormal and Social Psychology,* 1955, *50,* 3–11.

Feshbach, S. "The Function of Aggression and the Regulation of Aggressive Drive," *Psychological Review,* 1964, *71,* 257–272.

Feshbach, S. "Aggression," in P. H. Mussen (Ed.) *Carmichael's Manual of Child Psychology* (3rd Ed.), Vol. 2, New York: Wiley, 1970, pp. 159–260.

Festinger, L. *A Theory of Cognitive Dissonance.* Evanston, IL: Row, Peterson, 1957.

Festinger, L., Riecken, H. W., Jr., & Schachter, S. *When Prophecy Fails,* Minneapolis: University of Minnesota Press, 1956.

Flanders, J. P. "A Review of Research on Imitative Behavior," *Psychological Bulletin,* 1968, *69,* 316–337.

Foster, H. L. *Ribbin', Jivin', and Playin' the Dozens: The Unrecognized Dilemma of Inner City Schools,* Cambridge, MA: Ballinger, 1974.

Fowler, S. and Baer, D. M. " 'Do I Have To Be Good All Day?' The Timing of Delayed Reinforcement as a Factor in Generalization," *Journal of Applied Behavior Analysis,* 1981, *14,* 13–24.

Franklin, B. In B. F. Skinner, "Operant reinforcement of prayer." *Journal of Applied Behavior Analysis,* 1969, *2,* 247.

Frazier, T. W. "Avoidance Conditioning of Heart Rate in Humans," *Psychophysiology,* 1966, *3,* 188–202.

Friar, L. R. and Beatty, J. "Migraine: Management by Trained Control of Vasoconstriction," *Journal of Consulting and Clinical Psychology,* 1976, *44,* 46–53.

Friedenberg, E. Z. *The Vanishing Adolescent,* New York: Dell, 1959.

Friedrich, L. K. and Stein, A. H. "Aggressive and Prosocial Television Programs and the Natural Behavior of Preschool Children," *Monographs of the Society for Research in Child Development,* 1973, *38,* (4, Serial No. 151).

Friedrich, L. K. and Stein, A. H. "Prosocial Television and Young Children: The Effects of Verbal Labeling and Role Playing on Learning and Behavior," *Child Development,* 1975, *46,* 27–38.

Fuller, G. D. *Biofeedback: Methods and Procedures in Clinical Practice,* San Francisco: Biofeedback Press, 1977.

Garber, J. and Seligman, M. E. P. *Human Helplessness: Theory and Applications.* New York: Academic Press, 1980.

Garcia, J. and Koelling, R. "Relation of Cue to Consequence in Avoidance Learning," *Psychonomic Science,* 1966, *4,* 123–124.

Gardner, R. A. and Gardner, B. T. "Teaching Sign Language to a Chimpanzee," *Science,* 1969, *165,* 664–672.

Gebhart, R. H. (Ed.) *A Standard Guide to Cat Breeds,* New York: McGraw-Hill, 1979.

Gentile, J. R. "Pigeons, Pecking Orders and Public Education," *The Worm-Runner's Digest,* 1972, *14,* 105–108.

Gentile, J. R. "Rapanoia: A New Psychiatric Syndrome," *The Worm-Runner's Digest,* 1974, *16,* 140–142; Also recorded on the double-album set *Randy and Ron,* Clarence, NY: Mark Records, 1977.

Gentile, J. R. "Help Me Find the Rest I Need," a song on the double-album set *Randy and Ron,* Clarence, NY: Mark Records, 1977.

Gentile, J. R. "Hyperlexia: A New Psychoeducational Syndrome," *The Worm-Runner's Digest,* 1978, *20*(2), 111–112.

Gentile, J. R. "Education and Other Social Diseases: Rapanoia Revisited," *Newsletter for Educational Psychologists,* 1981, *5*(1), 11.

Gentile, J. R. "Hypercalculia—A New Psycho-educational Syndrome," *Newsletter for Educational Psychologists,* 1984, in press.

Gentile, J. R., Frazier, T. W. and Morris, M. C. *Instructional Applications of Behavior Principles,* Monterey, CA: Brooks/Cole, 1973.

Gentile, J. R. and Stevens-Haslinger, C. "A Comprehensive Grading Scheme," *Nursing Outlook,* 1983, *31*(No. 1), 49–54.

Gibson, W. *The Miracle Worker,* New York: Bantam Books, 1960.

Ginott, H. *Teacher and Child,* New York: Macmillan, 1972.

Glasser, W. *Reality Therapy.* New York: Harper and Row, 1965.

Glasser, W. *Schools Without Failure,* New York: Harper and Row, 1968.

Glasser, W. "10 Steps to Good Discipline," *Today's Education,* 1977, *66*(4), 61–63.

Gnagey, W. J. *The Psychology of Discipline in the Classroom,* Toronto: Macmillan, 1968.

Good, T. L. and Brophy, J. E. *Looking in Classrooms,* New York: Harper and Row, 1978.

Gordon, T. *T.E.T.: Teacher Effectiveness Training,* New York: David McKay, 1974.

Gormezano, I. and Moore, J. W. "Classical Conditioning," in M. H. Marx (Ed.) *Learning: Processes,* London: Macmillan, 1969, pp. 119–203.

Gray, F., Graubard, P. S. and Rosenberg, H. "Little Brother Is Changing You," *Psychology Today,* 1974, *7* (March), 42–46.

Graziano, A. M., De Giovanni, I. S. and Garcia, K. A. "Behavioral Treatment of Children's Fears: A Review," *Psychological Bulletin,* 1979, *86,* 804–830.

Graziano, A. M. and Mooney, K. C. "Family Self-Control Instruction for Children's Nighttime Fear Reduction," *Journal of Consulting and Clincial Psychology,* 1980, *48,* 206–213.

Green, E. and Green, A. *Beyond Biofeedback,* New York: Delta, 1977.

Gross, A. M. and Drabman, R. S. "Teaching Self-Recording, Self-Evaluation, and Self-Reward to Nonclinic Children and Adolescents," in P. Karoly and F. H. Kanfer (Eds.) *Self-Management and Behavior Change: From Theory to Practice,* New York: Pergamon, 1982, pp. 285–314.

Grusec, J. E. and Mischel, W. "The Model's Characteristics as Determinants of Social Learning," *Journal of Personality and Social Psychology,* 1966, *4,* 211–215.

Guthrie, E. R. *The Psychology of Learning,* New York: Harper, 1935.

Guttman, N. and Kalish, H. I. "Discriminability and Stimulus Generalization," *Journal of Experimental Psychology,* 1956, *51,* 79–88.

Haley, J. *Uncommon Therapy. The Psychiatric Technique of Milton H. Erickson, M.D.,* New York: W. W. Norton, 1973.

Hall, E. "The Sufi Tradition: 'Some Gurus Are Frankly Phonies, and They Don't Try To Hide It From Me. They Think I Am One, Too." Conversation with Idries Shah, *Psychology Today,* 1975, *9*(No. 2), 53–61.

Hall, R. V. and Hall, M. C. *How to Use Time Out,* Lawrence, KS: H & H Enterprises, 1980.

Hall, R. V. and Hall, M. C. *How to Negotiate a Behavioral Contract.* Lawrence, KS: H & H Enterprises, 1982.

Hall, R. V., Lund, D., and Jackson, D. "The Effects of Teacher Attention on Study Behavior," *Journal of Applied Behavior Analysis,* 1968, *1,* 1–12.

Haney, C. and Zimbardo, P. G. "The Socialization into Criminality: On Becoming a Prisoner and a Guard," In J. L. Tapp and F. L. Levine (Eds.) *Law, Justice and the Individual in Society: Psychological and Legal Issues,* New York: Holt, Rinehart & Winston, 1977, pp. 198–223.

Harris, F. A. "Inapproprioception: A Possibly Sensory Base for Athetoid Movements," *Physical Therapy,* 1971, *51,* 761–770.

Harris, F. A., Spelman, F. A. and Hymer, J. W. "Electronic Sensory Aids as Treatment for Cerebral-Palsied Children: Inapproprioception. Part II." *Physical Therapy,* 1974, *54,* 354–365.

Harter, S. "A Developmental Perspective on Some Parameters of Self-Regulation in Children," in P. Karoly and F. H. Kanfer (Eds.) *Self-Management and Behavior Change: From Theory to Practice,* New York: Pergamon, 1982, pp. 165–204.

Heider, F. *The Psychology of Interpersonal Relations,* New York: Wiley, 1958.

Hiroto, D. S. "Locus of Control and Learned Helplessness," *Journal of Experimental Psychology,* 1974, *102,* 187–193.

Holt, J. *How Children Fail,* New York: Dell, 1964.

Hosie, T. W., Gentile, J. R. and Carroll, J. D. "Pupil Preferences and the Premack Principle," *American Educational Research Journal,* 1974, *11,* 241–247.

Hovland, C. I. "The Generalization of Conditioned Responses: I. The Sensory Generalization of Conditioned Responses with Varying Frequencies of Tone," *Journal of General Psychology,* 1937, *17,* 125–148.

Huesmann, L. R. (Ed.) "Special Issue: Learned Helplessness as a Model of Depression," *Journal of Abnormal Psychology,* 1978, *87* (Whole No. 1), 1–198.

Hulse, S. H. "Amount and Percentage of Reinforcement and Duration of Goal Confinement in Conditioning and Extinction," *Journal of Experimental Psychology,* 1958, *56,* 48–57.

Hulse, S. H. "Patterned Reinforcement." in G. Bower (Ed.) *The Psychology of Learning and Motivation* (Vol. 7) New York: Academic Press, 1973.

Hulse, S. H., Egeth H., and Deese, J. *The Psychology of Learning,* New York: McGraw-Hill, 1980.

Huston-Stein, A. "Televised Aggression and Prosocial Behavior," in H. L. Pick, Jr., H. W. Liebowitz, J. E. Singer, A. Steinschneider, and H. W. Stevenson (Eds.) *Psychology From Research To Practice,* New York: Plenum, 1978, pp. 75–94.

Jackson, P. W. *Life in Classrooms,* New York: Holt, Rinehart and Winston, 1968.

Jacobsen, E. *Progressive Relaxation,* Chicago: University of Chicago Press, 1938.

James, W. *Talks to Teachers,* New York: W. W. Norton, 1958 (first published, 1904).

Jenkins, H. M. "Resistance To Extinction When Partial Reinforcement Is Followed By Regular Reinforcement," *Journal of Experimental Psychology,* 1962, *64,* 441–450.

Jenkins, H. M. and Harrison, R. H. "Effect of Discrimination Training on Auditory Generalizations," *Journal of Experimental Psychology,* 1960, *59,* 246–253.

Jenson, W. R. "Behavior Modification in Secondary Schools: A Review," *Journal of Research and Development in Education,* 1978, *11*(4), 53–63.

Johnson, D. W. and Johnson, R. T. *Learning Together and Alone: Cooperation, Competition and Individualization,* Englewood Cliffs, NJ: Prentice-Hall, 1975.

Johnson, K. "Do As You Would Be Done By," a song on the album, "Faith, Hope, Love." Williamsville, NY: Median Enterprises, 1978.

Johnston, J. M. "Punishment of Human Behavior," *American Psychologist,* 1972, *27,* 1033–1054.

Jones, H. E. "The Retention of Conditioned Emotional Reactions in Infancy," *Journal of Genetic Psychology,* 1930, *37,* 485–498.

Jones, H. E. "The Conditioning of Overt Emotional Responses," *Journal of Educational Psychology,* 1931, *22,* 127–130.

Jones, H. E. and Jones, M. C. "Genetic Studies of Emotions," *Psychological Bulletin,* 1930, *27,* 40–64.

Jones, M. C. "The Elimination of Children's Fears," *Journal of Experimental Psychology,* 1924, *7,* 382–390.

Jones, V. F. and Jones, L. S. *Responsible Classroom Discipline,* Boston: Allyn & Bacon, 1981.

Juliano, D. B. and Gentile, J. R. "Will the Real Hyperactive Child Please Sit Down? Problems of Diagnosis and Remediation." *Child Study Journal Monographs,* No. 1, 1974, 1–38.

Kalish, H. I. "Stimulus Generalization," in M. H. Marx (Ed.) *Learning: Processes,* London: Macmillan, 1969, pp. 205–297.

Kanfer, F. H. "Self-Regulation: Research, Issues and Speculations," in C. Neuringer and J. L. Michael (Eds.) *Behavior Modification in Clinical Psychology,* New York: Appleton, 1970, pp. 178–220.

Kanfer, F. H., Karoly, P. and Newman, A. "Reduction of Children's Fear of the Dark by Competence-Related and Situational Threat-Related Verbal Cues," *Journal of Consulting and Clinical Psychology,* 1975, *43,* 251–258.

Kater, D. and Spires, J. "Biofeedback: The Beat Goes On," *School Counselor*, 1975, *23*(1), 16–21.

Katkin, E. S., Fitzgerald, C. R. and Shapiro, D. "Clinical Applications of Biofeedback: Current Status and Future Prospects," In H. L. Pick, Jr., H. W. Liebowitz, J. E. Singer, A. Steinschneider, and H. W. Stevenson (Eds.) *Psychology From Research to Practice*, New York: Plenum, 1978, pp. 267–292.

Katkin, E. S. and Murray, E. N. "Instrumental Conditioning of Autonomically Mediated Behavior: Theoretical and Methodological Issues," *Psychological Bulletin*, 1968, *70*, 52–68.

Katkin, E. S., Murray, E. N. and Lachman, R. "Concerning Instrumental Autonomic Conditioning: A Rejoinder," *Psychological Bulletin*, 1969, *71*, 462–466.

Kazdin, A. E. "Methodological and Assessment Considerations in Evaluating Reinforcement Programs in Applied Settings," *Journal of Applied Behavior Analysis*, Monograph No. 3, 1973, *6*, 1–23.

Kazdin, A. E. "The Token Economy: A Decade Later," *Journal of Applied Behavior Analysis*, 1982, *15*, 431–445.

Kazdin, A. E. and Bootzin, R. R. "The Token Economy: An Evaluative Review." *Journal of Applied Behavior Analysis*, 1972, *5* (Whole Monograph #1), 1–30.

Kazdin, A. E. and Mascitelli, S. "The Opportunity to Earn Oneself Off a Token System as a Reinforcer for Attentive Behavior." *Behavior Therapy*, 1980, *11*, 68–78.

Keller, H. *The Story of My Life*, New York: Doubleday, 1954.

Kelley, M. L. and Stokes, T. F. "Contingency Contracting with Disadvantaged Youths: Improving Classroom Performance," *Journal of Applied Behavior Analysis*, 1982, *15*, 447–454.

Kelly, E. W. "School Phobia: A Review of Theory and Treatment," *Psychology in the Schools*, 1973, *10*, 33–42.

Key, W. B. *Media Sexploitation*, New York: Signet New American Library, 1976.

Kimble, G. A. *Hilgard and Marquis' Conditioning and Learning*, New York: Appleton-Century-Crofts, 1961.

Kondas, O. "Reduction of Examination Anxiety and 'Stage Fright' By Group Desensitization and Relaxation," *Behavior Research and Therapy*, 1967, *5*, 275–281.

Kounin, J. S. and Gump, P. V. "The Ripple Effect on Discipline," *Elementary School Journal*, 1958, *59*, 158–162.

Kozol, J. *Death at an Early Age*, Boston: Houghton-Mifflin, 1967.

Krasner, L. "Behavior Therapy," in P. H. Mussen and M. R. Rosenzweig (Eds.) *Annual Review of Psychology*, 1971, *22*, 483–532.

Krathwohl, D. R., Bloom, B. S. and Masia, B. B. *Taxonomy of Educational Objectives: The Classification of Educational Goals. Handbook 2. Affective Domain*, New York: McKay, 1964.

Kravetz, R. J. and Forness, S. R. "The Special Classroom as a Desensitization Setting," *Exceptional Children*, 1971, *37*, 389–391.

Krech, D., Crutchfield, R. S. and Ballachey, E. L. *Individual in Society*, New York: McGraw-Hill, 1962.

Kreschevsky, I. " 'Hypotheses' in Rats," *Psychological Review*, 1932, *38*, 516–532.

Krumboltz, J. D. and Krumboltz, H. B. *Changing Children's Behavior*, Englewood Cliffs, NJ: Prentice-Hall, 1972.

Kuhn, T. S. *The Structure of Scientific Revolutions*, Chicago: University of Chicago Press, 1962.

Kuypers, D. S., Becker, W. C. and O'Leary, K. D. "How to Make a Token System Fail," *Exceptional Education*, 1968, *35*, 101–109.

Lang, P. J. "Autonomic Control or Learning to Play the Internal Organs," *Psychology Today*, 1970, *4* (No. 5); 37–41, 86.

Lazarus, R. S. "Thoughts on the Relations Between Emotion and Cognition," *American Psychologist*, 1982, *37*, 1019–1024.

Leeper, R. W. "Cognitive Learning Theory," in M. H. Marx (Ed.) *Learning: Theories*, New York: MacMillan, 1970, 235–331.

Lepper, M. R. and Greene, D. *The Hidden Costs of Reward: New Perspectives on the Psychology of Human Motivation*, Hillsdale, NJ: Lawrence Erlbaum, 1978.

Lewis, R. and St. John, N. "Contribution of Cross-Racial Friendship To Minority Group Achievement in Desegregated Classrooms," *Sociometry*, 1974, *37*, 79–91.

Liebeskind, J. C. and Paul, L. A. "Psychological and Physiological Mechanisms of Pain," in M. R. Rosenzweig and L. W. Porter (Eds.) *Annual Review of Psychology*, 1977, *28*, 41–60.

Lipsitt, L. P. "Assessment of Sensory and Behavioral Functions in Infancy," In H. L. Pick, Jr., H. W. Leibowitz, J. E. Singer, A. Steinschneider and H. W. Stevenson (Eds.) *Psychology From Research to Practice*, New York: Plenum, 1978, 9–27.

Logan, F. A. "Experimental Psychology of Animal Learning and Now," *American Psychologist*, 1972, *27*, 1055–1062.

London, P. "The End of Ideology in Behavior Modification," *American Psychologist*, 1972, *27*, 913–920.

Loughry-Machado, G. and Suter, S. "Skin Temperature Biofeedback in Children and Their Parents," Proceedings of the Biofeedback Society of America, Tenth Annual Meeting, San Diego, CA: February 23–27, 1979.

Luthe, W. (Ed.) *Autogenic Therapy* (six volumes) New York: Grune and Stratton, 1969.

Lykken, D. T. "Uses and Abuses of the Polygraph," in H. L. Pick, Jr., H. W. Leibowitz, J. E. Singer, A. Steinschneider, and H. W. Stevenson (Eds.) *Psychology From Research to Practice*, New York: Plenum Press, 1978, pp. 171–191.

Madsen, C. H., Becker, W. C. and Thomas, D. R. "Rules, Praise and Ignoring: Elements of Elementary Classroom Control," *Journal of Applied Behavior Analysis*, 1968, *1*, 139–150.

Madsen, C. H., Jr. and Madsen, C. K. *Teaching/Discipline: A Positive Approach for Educational Development*, Boston; Allyn and Bacon, 1981.

Marks, I. M. *Fears and Phobias*, New York: Academic Press, 1969.

Maslow, A. H. *Motivation and Personality*, New York: Harper, 1954.

Mazrui, A. A. *The Trial of Christopher Okigbo*, London: Heinemann, 1971.

McIntire, R. W. *For Love of Children: Behavioral Psychology for Parents*, Del Mar, CA: CRM Publishers, 1970.

McNamara, J. R. "Behavior Therapy in the Classroom," *Journal of School Psychology*, 1968, *1*, 48–51.

McNamara, J. R. "Teacher and Students as Sources for Behavior Modification in the Classroom." *Behavior Therapy*, 1971, *2*, 205–213.

Meehl, P. E. "On the Circularity of the Law of Effect," *Psychological Bulletin*, 1950, *47*, 52–75.

Melzack, R. "The Promise of Biofeedback: Don't Hold the Party Yet," *Psychology Today*, 1975, *9*(No. 2) 18–22; 80–81.

Mikulas, W. L. "Buddhism and Behavior Modification," *Psychological Record*, 1981, *31*, 331–342.

Milgram, S. "Behavioral Study of Obedience," *Journal of Abnormal and Social Psychology*, 1963, *67*, 371–378.

Miller, I. W. and Norman, W. H. "Learned Helplessness in Humans: A Review and Attribution Theory Model," *Psychological Bulletin*, 1979, *86*, 93–118.

Miller, N. E. "Learning of Visceral and Glandular Responses," *Science*, 1969, *163*, 434–445.

Miller, N. E. "Biofeedback and Visceral Learning," In M. R. Rosenzweig and L. W. Porter (Eds.) *Annual Review of Psychology*, 1978, *29*, 373–404.

Miller, N. E. and Dworkin, B. R. "Visceral Learning: Recent Difficulties with Curarized Rats and Significant Problems for Human Research," in P. A. Obrist, A. H. Black, J. Brener, L. J. DiCara (Eds.) *Cardiovascular Psychophysiology,* Chicago: Aldine, 1974, pp. 312–331.

Miller, R. E. "Experimental Approaches to the Physiological and Behavioral Concomitants of Affective Communication in Rhesus Monkeys," in S. A. Altman (Ed.) *Social Communication Among Primates,* Chicago: University of Chicago Press, 1967, pp. 125–134.

Mischel, W. and Liebert, R. M. "Effects of Discrepancies Between Observed and Imposed Reward Criteria on Their Acquisition and Transmission," *Journal of Personality and Social Psychology,* 1966, *3,* 45–53.

Moreno, J. L. *Who Shall Survive? Foundations of Sociometry, Group Psychotherapy and Sociodrama,* Beacon, NY: Beacon House, 1953.

Morris, R. J. and Kratochwill, T. R. *Treating Children's Fears and Phobias: A Behavioral Approach,* New York: Pergamon Press, 1983.

Mowrer, O. H. *Learning Theory and Behavior,* New York: John Wiley & Sons, 1960.

Mowrer, O. H. "The Psychologist Looks at Language," *American Psychologist,* 1954, *9,* 660–694.

Mowrer, O. H. and Viek, P. "An Experimental Analogue of Fear from a Sense of Helplessness," *Journal of Abnormal and Social Psychology,* 1948, *43,* 193–200.

Murphy, G. and Murphy, L. B. *Asian Psychology,* New York: Basic Books, 1968.

Nisbett, R. E. and Schachter, S. "Cognitive Manipulation of Pain," *Journal of Experimental Social Psychology,* 1966, *2,* 227–236.

O'Leary, K. D. and Drabman, R. "Token Reinforcement Programs in the Classroom: A Review," *Psychological Bulletin,* 1971, *75,* 379–398.

O'Leary, K. D. and O'Leary, S. G. (Eds.) *Classroom Management: The Successful Use of Behavior Modification,* New York: Pergamon Press, 1972.

Osborne, J. G. "Free-time as a Reinforcer in the Management of Classroom Behavior," *Journal of Applied Behavior Analysis,* 1969, *2,* 113—118.

Papp, K. K. "A Test of Premack's Relational Theory." State University of New York at Buffalo, unpublished Ph.D. dissertation, 1980.

Parke, R. D., Berkowitz, L., Leyens, J. P., West, S. G. and Sebastian, R. J. "Some Effects of Violent and Nonviolent Movies on the Behavior of Juvenile Delinquents." in L. Berkowitz (Ed.) *Advances in Experimental Social Psychology,* New York: Academic Press, 1977, *10,* pp. 136–172.

Pavlov, I. P. *Conditioned Reflexes,* (Trans. Anrep, G. V.), London: Oxford, 1927.

Polin, A. T. "The Effects of Flooding and Physical Suppression as Extinction Techniques on an Anxiety Motivated Avoidance Locomotor Response," *Journal of Psychology,* 1959, *47,* 235–245.

Porter, R. W., Brady, J. V., Conrad, D., Mason, J. W. Galambos, R. and Rioch, D. McK. "Some Experimental Observations on Gastrointestinal Lesions in Behaviorally Conditioned Monkeys," *Psychosomatic Medicine,* 1958, *20,* 379–394.

Premack, D. "Toward Empirical Behavior Laws: 1. Positive Reinforcement," *Psychological Review,* 1959, *66,* 219–233.

Premack, D. "Reversibility of the Reinforcement Relation," *Science,* 1962, *136,* 255–257.

Premack, D. "Reinforcement Theory." in Levine, D. (Ed.) *Nebraska Symposium on Motivation (Vol. 13),* Lincoln: University of Nebraska Press, 1965.

Premack, D. "Catching Up With Common Sense or Two Sides of a Generalization: Reinforcement and Punishment," in R. Glaser (Ed.) *The Nature of Reinforcement,* New York: Academic Press, 1971, pp. 121–150. (a)

Premack, D. "Language in Chimpanzee?" *Science,* 1971, *172,* 808–822. (b)

Ray, W. J., Raczynski, J. M., Rogers, T. and Kimball, W. H. *Evaluation of Clinical Biofeedback,* New York: Plenum, 1979.

Reese, E. P., *The Analysis of Human Operant Behavior,* Dubuque, Iowa: Wm. C. Brown Company Publishers, 1966.

Renner, K. E. "Delay of Reinforcement: A Historical Review," *Psychological Bulletin,* 1964, *61,* 341–361.

Rescorla, R. A. *Pavlovian Second-Order Conditioning: Studies in Associative Learning,* Hillsdale, N.J.: Lawrence Erlbaum, 1980.

Rescorla, R. A. and Holland, P. C. "Behavioral Studies of Associative Learning in Animals," in M. R. Rosenzweig and L. W. Porter (Eds.) *Annual Review of Psychology,* 1982, *33,* 265–308.

Resnick, L. B. "Applying Applied Reinforcement," in R. Glaser (Ed.) *The Nature of Reinforcement,* New York: Academic Press, 1971, pp. 326–333.

Reynolds, G. S. "Behavioral Contrast," *Journal of the Experimental Analysis of Behavior,* 1961, *4,* 57–71.

Roden, A. H. and Hapkiewicz, W. G. "Respondent Learning and Classroom Practice," in R. D. Klein, W. G. Hapkiewicz, and A. H. Roden (Eds.) *Behavior Modification in Educational Settings,* Springfield, IL: Thomas, 1973, pp. 421–437.

Ross, D. M. and Ross, S. A. *Hyperactivity: Current Issues, Research and Theory.* New York: Wiley, 1982.

Rotter, J. B. "Generalized Expectancies for Internal versus External Control of Reinforcement," *Psychological Monographs: General and Applied,* 1966, *80,* 1–28.

Rounds, J. B. Jr. and Hendel, D. D. "Measurement and Dimensionality of Mathematics Anxiety," *Journal of Counseling Psychology,* 1980, *27,* 138–149.

Ryan, B. A. "A Case Against Behavior Modification in the 'Ordinary' Classroom," *Journal of School Psychology,* 1979, *17,* 131–136.

Sandler, J. and Quagliano, J. "Punishment in a Signal Avoidance Situation," Southeastern Psychological Association Meetings, Gatlinburg, TN, 1964. In A. Bandura *Principles of Behavior Modification,* New York: Holt, Rinehart & Winston, 1969, p. 297.

Sargent, J. D., Green, E. E. and Walters, E. D. "Preliminary Report on the Use of Autogenic Feedback Training in the Treatment of Migraine and Tension Headaches," *Psychosomatic Medicine,* 1973, *35,* 129–135.

Schachter, S. "Deviation, Rejection and Communication," *Journal of Abnormal and Social Psychology,* 1951, *46,* 190–207.

Schachter, S. and Singer, J. "Cognitive, Social and Physiological Determinants of Emotional State," *Psychological Review,* 1962, *69,* 379–399.

Schmuck, R. A. and Schmuck, P. A. *Group Processes in the Classroom,* Dubuque, Iowa: Wm. C. Brown Company Publishers, 1983.

Seligman, M. E. P. "Phobias and Preparedness," *Behavior Therapy,* 1971, *2,* 307–320.

Seligman, M. E. P. *Helplessness.* San Francisco: Freeman, 1975.

Sherif, M. "Group Influences Upon the Formation of Norms and Attitudes," In T. M. Newcomb and E. L. Harley (Eds.) *Readings in Social Psychology,* New York: Holt, 1947.

Shirley, K. W. The Prosocial Effects of Publicly Broadcast Children's Television. Unpublished Doctoral Dissertation. University of Kansas, 1974.

Sidman, M. "Two Temporal Parameters of the Maintenance of Avoidance Behavior By the White Rat." *Journal of Comparative and Physiological Psychology,* 1953, *46,* 253–261.

Sidman, M. "Normal Sources of Pathological Behavior," *Science,* 1960, *132,* 61–68.

Skinner, B. F. *The Behavior of Organisms,* New York: Appleton-Century-Crofts, 1938.

Skinner, B. F. "Superstition in the Pigeon," *Journal of Experimental Psychology,* 1948, *38,* 168–172.

Skinner, B. F. *Science and Human Behavior,* New York: Free Press, 1953.

Skinner, B. F. *Beyond Freedom and Dignity,* New York: Alfred A. Knopf, 1971.

Skinner, B. F. *About Behaviorism,* New York: Knopf, 1974.

Slavin, R. E. "Cooperative Learning," *Review of Educational Research,* 1980, *50,* 315–342.

Solomon, R. L., Kamin, L. J. and Wynne, L. C. "Traumatic Avoidance Learning: The Outcomes of Several Extinction Procedures withDogs," *Journal of Abnormal and Social Psychology,* 1953, *48,* 291–302.

Spence, K. W. "The Differential Response in Animals to Stimuli Varying within a Single Dimension." *Psychological Review,* 1937, *44,* 430–444.

Spence, K. W. "Continuous vs. Non-continuous Interpretations of Discrimination Learning," *Psychological Review,* 1940, *47,* 271–288.

Staats, A. W. and Staats, C. K. "Attitudes Established by Classical Conditioning," *Journal of Abnormal and Social Psychology,* 1958, *57,* 37–40.

Stainback, W. C., Payne, J. S., Stainback, S. B., and Payne, R. A. *Establishing a Token Economy in the Classroom,* Columbus, Ohio: Merrill, 1973.

Stampfl, T. G. and Levis, D. J. "Essentials of Implosive Therapy: A Learning-Theory Based Psychodynamic Behavioral Therapy," *Journal of Abnormal Psychology,* 1967, *72,* 496–503.

Stein, A. H. and Friedrich, L. K. "Television Content and Young Children's Behavior." In J. P. Murray, E. A. Rubenstein, And G. A. Comstock (Eds.) *Television and Social Behavior, Vol. 2. Television and Social Learning.* Washington, D.C.: U.S. Government Printing Office: 1972, pp. 202–317.

Stokes, T. F. and Baer, D. M. "An Implicit Technology of Generalization," *Journal of Applied Behavior Analysis,* 1977, *10,* 349–367.

Suinn, R. M. and Richardson, F. "Anxiety Management Training: A Nonspecific Behavior Therapy Program for Anxiety Control," *Behavior Therapy,* 1971, *2,* 498–510.

Sulzer-Azaroff, B. and Reese, E. P. *Applying Behavioral Analysis: A Program for Developing Professional Competence,* New York: CBS College Publishing Co., 1982.

Taffel, S. J. and O'Leary, K. D. "Reinforcing Math with More Math: Choosing Special Activities as a Reward for Academic Performance."; *Journal of Educational Psychology,* 1976, *68,* 579–587.

Terhune, J. and Premack, D. "On the Proportionality Between the Probability of Not-Running and the Punishment Effect of Being Forced to Run," *Learning and Motivation,* 1970, *1,* 141–147.

Theios, J. "The Partial Reinforcement Effect Sustained Through Blocks of Continuous Reinforcement." *Journal of Experimental Psychology,* 1962, *64,* 1–6.

Thoresen, C. E. and Mahoney, M. J. *Behavioral Self-Control,* New York: Holt, Rinehart & Winston, 1974.

Thorndike, E. L. *Animal Intelligence,* New York: Macmillan, 1911.

Tolman, E. C. *Purposive Behavior in Animals and Men,* New York: Appleton-Century-Crofts, 1932.

Tolman, E. C. "Principles of Purposive Behavior," In S. Koch (Ed.) *Psychology: A Study of a Science* (Vol. 2), New York: McGraw-Hill, 1959, pp. 92–157.

Varela, J. A. "Attitude Change," in H. L. Pick, Jr., H. W. Liebowitz, J. E. Singer, A. Steinschneider, and H. W. Stevenson (Eds.) *Psychology From Research To Practice,* New York: Plenum, 1978, pp. 121–144.

Watson, J. B. "Psychology as the Behaviorist Views It," *Psychological Review,* 1913, *20,* 158–177.

Watson, J. B. *Psychology from the Standpoint of a Behaviorist,* Philadelphia: J. B. Lippincott, 1919.

Watson, J. B. *Behaviorism.* Chicago: Phoenix Books, 1930 (reprinted, 1963).

Watson, J. B. and Rayner, R. "Conditioned Emotional Reactions," *Journal of Experimental Psychology,* 1920, *3,* 1–14.

Weisberg, P. and Waldrop, P. B. "Fixed-Interval Work Habits of Congress," *Journal of Applied Behavior Analysis,* 1972, *5,* 93–97.

Weiss, J. M. "Effects of Coping Response on Stress," *Journal of Comparative and Physiological Psychology,* 1968, *65,* 251–260.

Weiss, J. M. "Somatic Effects of Predictable and Unpredictable Shock," *Psychosomatic Medicine,* 1970, *32,* 397–409.

Weiss, J. M. "Effects of Coping Behavior in Different Warning Signal Conditions on Stress Pathology in Rats," *Journal of Comparative and Physiological Psychology,* 1971, *77,* 1–13.

Werder, D. S. "An Exploratory Study of Childhood Migraine Using Thermal Biofeedback as a Treatment Alternative," Proceedings of the Biofeedback Society of America, Ninth Annual Meeting, Albuquerque, NM: March 3–7, 1978.

White, R. W. "Motivation Reconsidered: The Concept of Competence," *Psychological Review,* 1959, *66,* 297–333.

Wolf, M. M., Hanley, E. L., King, L. A., Lachowicz, J. and Giles, K. "The Timer-Game: A Variable Interval Contingency for the Management of Out-of-Seat Behavior," *Exceptional Children,* 1970, *37*(No. 2), 113–117.

Wolpe, J. *The Practice of Behavior Therapy,* New York: Pergamon Press, 1969.

Woodworth, R. S. "On the Voluntary Control of the Force of Movement," *Psychological Review,* 1901, *8,* 350–359.

Yates, A. J. *Biofeedback and the Modification of Behavior,* New York: Plenum, 1980.

Zajonc, R. B. "Feeling and Thinking: Preferences Need No Inferences," *American Psychologist,* 1980, *35,* 151–175.

Zimmerman, E. H. and Zimmerman, J. "The Alteration of Behavior in a Special Classroom Situation," *Journal of the Experimental Analysis of Behavior,* 1962, *5,* 59–60.

Author Index

Subject Index